Vicious Modernism: Black Harlem and the Literary Imagination

Vicious Modernism
Black Harlem and the Literary Imagination

JAMES DE JONGH

The City College and The Graduate School and University
Center of The City University of New York

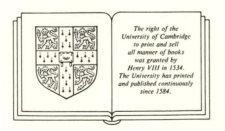

The right of the
University of Cambridge
to print and sell
all manner of books
was granted by
Henry VIII in 1534.
The University has printed
and published continuously
since 1584.

CAMBRIDGE UNIVERSITY PRESS

Cambridge

New York   Port Chester   Melbourne   Sydney

Published by the Press Syndicate of the University of Cambridge
The Pitt Building, Trumpington Street, Cambridge CB2 1RP
40 West 20th Street, New York, NY 10011, USA
10 Stamford Road, Oakleigh, Melbourne 3166, Australia

© Cambridge University Press 1990

First published 1990

Printed in the United States of America

Library of Congress Cataloging-in-Publication Data
de Jongh, James.
Vicious modernism : Black Harlem and the literary imagination / by
James de Jongh.
    p.   cm.
Includes bibliographical references.
ISBN 0-521-32620-6
1. American literature – Afro-American authors – History and
criticism.   2. American literature – New York (N.Y.) – History and
criticism.   3. American literature – 20th century – History and
criticism.   4. Afro-Americans – New York (N.Y.) – Intellectual life.
5. Harlem (New York, N.Y.) in literature.   6. Modernism
(Literature) – United States.   7. New York (N.Y.) in literature.
8. Afro-Americans in literature.   9. Harlem Renaissance.   I. Title.
PS153.N5D4   1990
810.9′327471–dc20   90–31333
                                                                              CIP

British Library Cataloguing in Publication Data
de Jongh, James
Vicious modernism : black Harlem and the literary
imagination.
1. Literature. Special subjects. (City) New York. Harlem.
Critical studies
808.93327471

ISBN 0-521-32620-6 hardback

Harlem is vicious
modernism. BangClash.
Vicious the way it's made.
Can you stand such beauty.
So violent and transforming.

"Return of the Native"
Amiri Baraka / LeRoi Jones

Contents

Acknowledgments

This study would not have been completed without the generous support of the National Endowment for the Humanities; the Center for Black Studies of the University of California at Santa Barbara; the Simon H. Rifkind Center for the Humanities of the City College of the City University of New York; and the Professional Staff Congress and City University of New York Research Grants of the Research Foundation of the City University of New York; or the encouragement, constructive criticism, and other interventions of colleagues and friends too numerous to name individually.

Introduction: Vicious Modernism

What writers have made of Harlem is a fascinating question, for in literature, as in other fields, black Harlem quickly became a familiar feature of the landscape of the modern imagination. In Harlem, black New Yorkers had performed an epic deed by seizing a desired territory in the face of extraordinary obstacles and creating a black city that, in the years following World War I, promised to be the cultural capital of the race. Ever since, the idea of Harlem has inspired a great many writers, black and non-black alike, in a remarkably large number of works. After each of the race riots of 1919, 1943, and 1964 in American cities with large black populations, a new international generation of Africana writers – authors of African descent and heritage but writing in modern European languages (usually English, French, Spanish or Portuguese) – emerged throughout the black world, employing the Harlem motif as the emblem of an ethos of racial renewal. Many non-black authors also celebrated the city-within-a-city north of Central Park, for the idea of Harlem has come to be part of the figurative geography of modern writers of all races.

Why does the idea of Harlem so pique and intrigue the literary imagination? Harlem has been a singular icon of the twentieth-century confrontation with inherited but unacceptable understandings of race predicted by W. E. B. Du Bois in *The Souls of Black Folks* (1903): "The problem of the twentieth century is the problem of the color line, – the relation of the darker to the lighter races of men in Asia, Africa and the islands of the sea." When Alain Locke reformulated Du Bois's dictum two decades later in the classic manifesto of the New Negro movement, Locke cited Harlem as the locus classicus of the new psychology that was transforming the status of the darker races in the modern world. In a century marked by the vicious dynamics of the color line, Harlem has remained modernity's preeminent popular image of black racial being and interracial contact. "Vicious," in the sense of being of an intense, extreme, even cruel degree, with roots in the Latin words for vital force (*vis*) as well as vice (*vitium*), is a provocative but fair modifier of Harlem's modernism, if not necessarily of Harlem itself, in "Return of the Native" by Amiri Baraka/Le Roi Jones, the poem from which this book takes its title.

The "BangClash" of Harlem's modernism – the violent, transforming beauty in "the way it is made" – is a reminder of the fusion of what is literal and figurative, observational and imaginative, in cultural imagery and literary creation. The motif of black Harlem, like other literary figures, has been shaped and inflected by processes of literary imagining; views of Harlem in literature are transformations of concrete details of description (sound, sight, feeling, smell, and taste), made over into imagery. Yet for too long the forms black Harlem has taken in creative literature have been regarded as if they could not be otherwise, as if a writer's conception of black Harlem were simply a "given" of inevitable racial forces or ineluctable societal influences, not wrought in the specific medium of language by the deliberate exercise of individual perception and artistic choice. Several fine works have explored the social and cultural dimensions of black Harlem's emergence and development over the decades, but literary critics have too often taken the form of the modern literary commonplace of black Harlem for granted, as a dimension of the sociology of Negro life.[1] This is doubly misleading, for American popular culture began reading black Harlem as a trope even before writers began using the motif in creative literature.

Harlem became a symbolic figure in the cultural syntax of the United States as soon as this former community of gentlemen farmers, developed in the late nineteenth century as a comfortable suburb for a new class of prosperous white homeowners, was popularly perceived to have become black. The question of what writers have made of black Harlem ever since offers a novel vantage from which to view modern cultural as well as literary history.

I

The Legendary Capital:
The 1920s and 1930s

UNIA Convention Parade, Harlem, August, 1920.

1

The Legendary Capital

Harlem was not identified with African-American life in the city of New York until the early decades of the twentieth century. Although blacks had lived on Manhattan Island since the earliest days of Dutch New Amsterdam, and some had lived in Harlem for nearly as long, for most of the nineteenth century Harlem was just a formerly prosperous farming community with no particular connection to black life. The transformation of Harlem into a black community was swift and unexpected – a by-product of the phenomenal northward growth of New York City, which reached Harlem's borders in the 1880s, when most of the houses standing in Harlem today began to be built.[1]

During the centuries before Harlem was black, Manhattan's small and relatively stable Negro population had lived in dispersed clusters surrounded by white residential areas, first in the Five Points district, where City Hall stands today; later in Greenwich Village, in Little Africa (what is now called Little Italy); and finally in a number of blocks between Twentieth Street and Sixtieth Street, on the West Side, known as the Tenderloin and San Juan Hill districts. Between 1890 and 1910, however, the black population of New York City almost tripled, as the first generation of blacks born after Emancipation moved steadily away from the South, fleeing racial violence and seeking a different and better way of life. In this same period, the real-estate market in Harlem, which had been expanding for just over two decades, collapsed during the depression of 1904–5. The need of a burgeoning black population for a place to live conspired with the overextended finances of some Harlem developers to create an opportunity for black realtors like Phillip A. Payton, Jr., the so-called Father of Colored Harlem. Around 1904, Payton's Afro-American Realty Company won control of a few buildings on 134th and 135th Streets, between Lenox Avenue and Fifth Avenue, by a combination of subterfuge and highly publicized block-busting exploits, setting in motion a process that would transform Harlem's racial character and make it New York City's first self-contained Negro community.

No population was less expected – and less welcome – than blacks in the Harlem housing market. The idea of Negroes occupying the new, upscale area seemed bizarre and outlandish to many residents and property owners. Resistance was swift and vigorous, but ineffective in the end. Real-estate values, battered by economic recession, were forced even lower by panic selling. "The opponents of Negro settlement faced the dilemma of maintaining a 'White Only' policy and probably losing everything, or renting to Negroes at higher prices and surviving."[2] Harlem housing, in increasing numbers and improving categories, became available to blacks. By the end of the decade, Harlem was the neighborhood of choice in New York, for blacks who could afford it. In 1911, following the lead of St. Philip's, the major black churches in New York began buying property and moving to Harlem. Social clubs, fraternal organizations, newspapers, and the black Democratic and Republican clubhouses soon followed, bringing with them the infrastructure of New York City's black population. By 1914, the blocks from 130th Street to 140th Street between Seventh Avenue and the Harlem River had been occupied by an expanding black enclave. By 1919, the year of the triumphal homecoming of the black 369th Infantry Regiment to Harlem, after the Great War in Europe, Harlem was a firmly established, stylish black community, in an attractive, well-built section of Manhattan.

The typical Harlemite of that period was a black Southerner, who had spent time in some smaller town or city along the way, as part of a major migration to the northern industrial centers. Employment opportunity and the freedom to live a better life also made Harlem a haven for many foreign-born blacks, especially from the Caribbean, for the building of the Panama Canal, which had made Panama an earlier migratory focus for black West Indians, had been completed in 1914 and no longer relieved the pressures of poverty and population growth on the limited economies of the islands. Life in New York may have been harsh, but the migrants themselves often came from backgrounds of such extreme poverty and oppression that Harlem, in contrast, seemed to be the Promised Land. The migrants sent home glowing letters, often written by storefront amanuenses, and traveled back and forth themselves, sporting ready money, stylish clothes, and tales of all kinds, evidence encouraging others back home to believe in the good life of Harlem, and many of the others followed.

The development of black Harlem was typical of the emergence of large, segregated black communities in America's northern industrial centers in the early decades of the twentieth century, but it seemed unique in other respects. First, in Harlem black New Yorkers possessed an area that had been envisioned as "a district . . . distinctly devoted to the mansions of the wealthy, the homes of the well-to-do, and the places of business of the trades that minister to their wants,"[3] and in the opening of such housing to blacks in Harlem a fundamental racial threshold seemed to have been crossed. James Weldon Johnson's *Black Manhattan* returned repeatedly to the point that "the Negro's situation in Harlem is without precedent in all his history in New York; never before has he been so securely anchored, never before has he owned the land, never before has he had so well established a community life."[4]

Second, the relative safety and security of blacks in Harlem stood in stark contrast to their evident oppression in the rest of the black world. In Africa, colonial policy was beginning to be executed with an ever more ruthless logic in the new colonial hegemony established by the victorious European powers as part of the spoils of World War I. In the Caribbean, navy administrators – white Southerners who thought they best knew how to deal with Negroes – were applying the principles of Jim Crow to the occupied territories of Haiti, Puerto Rico, and Cuba, as well as to the recently purchased Virgin Islands. In the United States, an extralegal policy of anti-black violence – ritual lynchings of individuals in the South, and race riots against blacks as a group in northern cities – still enjoyed wide acceptance as popular methods of defining and controlling interracial conduct. Black New Yorkers had suffered racial violence in the neighborhoods of Hell's Kitchen and the Tenderloin as recently as the summer of 1900, and before that in the notorious draft riots of 1863. Yet in the bloody "Red Summer" of 1919 – when, according to Johnson, "even the stoutest-hearted Negroes felt terror and dismay"[5] at the orgy of anti-black violence scarring other African-American communities – blacks walked the streets of Harlem in relative safety from attacks of that sort.

Harlem also offered something else that was virtually unprecedented in the African diaspora: a place for blacks to be themselves, as they saw fit. Harlem was host to a pantheon of colorful and freewheeling individualists and eccentrics, more akin to the vivid and self-expressive characters of African-American folklore than to the severe personages of black history in America, who, in too many cases, had to be self-effacing in order to be acceptable to white mentors. One such Harlemite – Lillian Harris Dean (known as "Pig Foot Mary") – had built a real-estate empire on pigs' feet. She started, around the turn of the century, by selling pork trotters in a saloon in the San Juan Hill section. Later, when blacks shifted to Harlem, she sold her wares from a stall next to John Dean's newspaper and shoeshine stand on Lenox Avenue at 135th Street. "Madam" C. J. Walker, once an impoverished St. Louis washerwoman, made millions with a hair-straightening process revealed to her in a dream and built a mansion in Harlem in 1913. A'Lelia Walker, Madam Walker's daughter and principal heir, became the foremost salon hostess of the Harlem Renaissance, giving legendary parties at which sophisticates of all colors, classes, philosophies, and predilections mingled and mixed. Hubert Fauntleroy Julian ("the Black Eagle"), after living off his good looks and related charms, set off a riotous celebration by parachuting into a vacant lot in Harlem; he next proposed a solo flight to Ethiopia, taking off with grand fanfare only to crash in Flushing Bay. And "Father Divine," born George Baker, claiming to be none other than God Himself, demonstrated His omnipotence when a judge, who had blasphemed by sentencing Him to a maximum jail term as a public nuisance, dropped dead shortly thereafter, in spite of apparent good health.

More than anything else, the time and the circumstances of Harlem's creation signified the African-American's "spiritual Coming of Age."[6] By the end of World War I, the influence of Booker T. Washington's philosophy of dependence, which had dominated black leadership since the death of Frederick Douglass a generation earlier, was waning, and Harlem was becoming the center of black opinion in America. By the time of Washington's death, in 1916, two principal policies proclaimed figuratively in his Atlanta Exposition Address had both been contradicted by the very existence of Harlem. Washington's call to blacks to "put down your buckets where you are" and remain in the rural South had been rejected implicitly by the great migration that had brought Harlem into existence, and the political acquiescence to white dominance, promised by Washington's other parable of "the fingers and the hand," was ignored by the "fierce journalism of defiance"[7] of a crusading Harlem press. The number of black newspapers in New York City had doubled between 1912 and 1921, and they conveyed black nationalist, communist, and socialist ideologies (as well as more conservative philosophies) across a wide political spectrum to a mass readership, from the *Age* and the *Amsterdam News* to A. Phillip Randolph and Chandler Owen's socialist *Messenger,* William Bridges's black-nationalist *Challenge,* Cyrill V. Briggs's revolutionary *Crusader,* and George Padmore's communist *Negro Worker.* The Associated Negro Press, founded in 1919 in Harlem, along with the active Negro press in the media capital of America, magnified Harlem's very real importance as a central source of information and thought about Negro life. The presence in Harlem of the rival successors to Booker T. Washington's mantle of national leadership of black America – Marcus Garvey, founder of the Universal Negro

Improvement Association (UNIA); James Weldon Johnson and W. E. B. Du Bois, leaders of the National Association for the Advancement of Colored People (NAACP); and Charles S. Johnson, director of the Urban League – and their respective house journals – *Negro World, Crisis,* and *Opportunity* – made Harlem, rather than Tuskegee, the center of black political ferment.

Harlem's promise and sense of liberation made it possible to overlook a widening range of social evils the community was already suffering even in the early 1920s. Although Harlemites earned less ($1,300 a year, compared to $1,570) than other New Yorkers, they paid far more for housing ($9.50 a month per room, compared to $6.67). In Harlem's five-, six-, and seven-room apartments – originally built for large families, with large incomes, rather than for Harlem's growing population of young, unmarried migrants with relatively few children – taking lodgers became a familiar practice, accelerating deterioration. In spite of a youthful adult population, the death rate was 42 percent higher for Harlemites than for the rest of the city. In specific categories (such as infant mortality, death from tuberculosis, and violent death), the rates doubled or tripled, and venereal disease and malnutrition were commonplace. In spite of fewer numbers of teenagers, the incidence of juvenile crime was higher. Working mothers had little time to care for children. Schools were overcrowded, with as much as a 100 percent turnover each year, in some instances, as students followed their rootless families from one residence to another. Quacks, healers, confidence men, loan sharks, and religious charlatans, exploiting the crisis of the community, only made the situation worse. In addition, Harlem was a "wide-open city," where the sale of alcohol flourished with few restrictions during Prohibition, along with vice, gambling, and narcotics.[8]

If Harlem shared some of the worst aspects of black life in America, that was only to be expected. The raw side of Harlem was simply taken for granted. What figured in popular culture were the ways in which it was different, and better. Affirmation of the wonder of it seems to have been the characteristic attitude about black Harlem in the 1920s. Harlem was taken to be a harbinger of change in who blacks were and their position among the races of the world. Although they sensed tensions and even contradictions in their optimism, blacks seemed to regard Harlem as a liberated black community, freed from the worst oppressions of racism. In Harlem, at least, a black had a chance to succeed and fulfill his selfhood, and new kinds of Negroes, with new ways of thinking, could flourish. An optimistic sense of progress and opportunity remained the dominant mood, for in many respects Harlem was undeniably a breakthrough for blacks.

The symbolism of Harlem, in this period, was embodied in the image of the cabaret. The legendary Harlem cabarets of the 1920s had their roots in the Negro bohemia (the so-called Satan's Circus) of the old Tenderloin district, described by Paul Laurence Dunbar's *Sport of the Gods* (1902) and James Weldon Johnson's *Autobiography of an Ex-Colored Man* (1912). The music and sporting culture of the Tenderloin had moved to Harlem, along with the churches, newspapers, and other institutions of black New York, but the Harlem migrants added the variety of the folk forms that they had brought with them from different parts of African America and the diaspora. As the saloons vied for customers in their new locations by featuring musical performers who worked mostly for tips, the different cultural styles of ragtime, blues, stride piano, and dixieland mixed and cross-fertilized one another. Vivid dance steps, improvised at "tango teas" and "rent parties," found themselves depicted in uptown productions like *Darktown Follies* (1913) at Harlem's Lafayette Theatre. Slang and musical folk forms began to cross over into restricted precincts of white popular entertainment and sanctuaries of high culture. Florenz Zeigfeld bought the rights to a portion of *Darktown Follies* and moved it downtown to the Zeigfeld Follies. "Purified" ballroom versions of Negro dance steps were popularized by Irene and Vernon Castle to the music of James Europe's band, and "going to Harlem" became a stylish thing for whites to do. By the end of World War I, the Harlem saloons had begun to evolve into cabarets, with central stages and slick productions, designed to please the whites who came uptown to see the latest craze. The Harlem "high style" of Florence Mills, in *Shuffle Along* (by Eubie Blake, Noble Sissle, and Flournoy Miller), moved downtown to Broadway in 1921 with great success, creating a seemingly insatiable market for similar Harlem musicals in the early 1920s. And with Prohibition, the trend toward cabarets featuring increasingly elaborate floor shows culminated in spots like the Cotton Club (1922), tailor-made, by the bosses of organized crime, to suit the passions and prejudices of an influential and high-spending white clientele. The image of Harlem of the cabarets was confirmed in the public imagination by years of broadcasts, via the new medium of radio, from the stage of the Cotton Club and reinforced over the decades by a vast catalog of songs about Harlem by legendary figures from Duke Ellington and Cab Calloway to the Rolling Stones.[9]

The fascination of whites with Harlem was a revisionist rendering of the traditional romantic conception of blacks as cultural primitives and exotics. In *New York,* Paul Morand described Harlem as "a place of exotic gaiety, of picturesque human confusion," where blacks "shatter the mechanical rhythm of America." "Standing erect at the street crossing

symbolic of white civilization, the policeman keeps his eye on this minia-
ture Africa; if that policeman happened to disappear, Harlem would
quickly revert to Haiti, given over to voodoo and the rhetorical despo-
tism of a plumed Soulouque."[10] Harlem's atavistic primitive forces
seemed scarcely altered by a few centuries of contact with civilized Europe. The uninhibited gaiety and childlike sexuality could be reinter-
preted to seem almost providential, in the light of the circumstances of
the new century, although the old stereotype remained the same. The
exposure of Europe's high culture as a "grand illusion" by the barbarism
of World War I seemed to discredit the traditional ideals of manliness,
privilege, and personal honor of the aristocratic and hereditary warrior
class. The collapse of many of the royal houses that had ruled Europe
for centuries, and the validation of disconcerting scientific ideas (such as
the existence of subatomic particles and of hitherto unknown planets, or
of the relativity of time to velocity and of matter to energy), put com-
monly accepted wisdom in doubt. The popularization of Freudian ideas
about the personal consequences and psychic discontents of civilization
undermined the foundation of inhibitions and self-denial on which civilized culture was assumed to be built. At the same time, a growing
awareness of German ethnographic studies of Africa, and an extensive
literature about the Negro in French, along with the acknowledgment
of the influence of African sculpture on ground-breaking experiments of
Picasso, Matisse, and many other artists, was beginning to demonstrate
that the West had underestimated the sophistication of the Negro's despised "primitive" aesthetic. Such developments peculiar to the period,
Nathan Huggins explains, intensified the traditional use of the black image by whites to fulfill their own deep psychic needs, and "Jazz Age"
Harlem became the unique focus of this attention. "Men who sensed that
they were slaves to moral codes . . . found Harlem a tonic and
release. . . . Harlem seemed a cultural enclave that had magically survived the psychic fetters of Puritanism. . . . So viewed, Harlem was a
means of soft rebellion for those who rejected the Babbittry and sterility
of their lives, yet could not find within their familiar culture the genius
to redefine themselves in more human and vital terms."[11] Nancy Cunard
put it more bluntly: "Notice how whites are unreal in America: they are
dim. But the negro is very real. He is there. And the ofays know it.
That's why they come to Harlem – out of curiosity and jealousy and
don't know why."[12] Although the reading of Harlem that was luring the
white after-hours trade uptown was so patently not their own, some
black opinion makers wondered whether the voguish interest in the high
style of Harlem's cabaret life might be one more ameliorating – albeit
problematic – sign of change in their place in American life. "Willingly

would I be an outsider in this if I could know that I read it aright – that out of this change in the old familiar ways some finer thing may come. . . . Is it significant of basic human responses, the effect of which, once admitted, will extend far beyond cabarets? Maybe these Nordics at last have tuned in on our wavelength. Maybe they are at last learning to speak our language."[13]

By 1925, the allure of Harlem was a compelling influence on the consciousness of a vanguard of young black painters and writers waiting in the wings to be proclaimed as the New Negroes of the Harlem Renaissance. Few of them were native Harlemites or had discovered their artistic gifts in Harlem. Claude McKay was from Jamaica; Jessie Redmon Fauset from Philadelphia; Rudolph Fisher and Sterling Brown from Washington; Helene Johnson from Boston; Langston Hughes from Joplin, Missouri, Lawrence, Kansas, and Cleveland, Ohio; Nella Larsen from St. Croix, in the Virgin Islands; George Schulyer from Providence; Wallace Thurman from Boise and Los Angeles; and Walter White from Atlanta. Not even Countee Cullen, it appears, was a native son of Harlem, but Harlem had become their nexus. Its creation corresponded, in dramatic ways, to historical alterations in the lives of black and white Americans in the early decades of this century; its mystique was intoxicating; it symbolized the very quality of black life. "[T]here can be no doubt," Arna Bontemps recalled, that "there was a happening in America in those days and that suddenly stars started falling on a part of Manhattan that white residents had begun abandoning to black newcomers."[14]

The presence of this vanguard in Harlem, and its spectacular debut before the arbiters of American culture at a pair of superbly stage-managed dinners, were in large part the successful outcome of a deliberate policy pursued by a handful of Harlem's cultural "midwives." Langston Hughes cites three. Jessie Fauset, as literary editor of *Crisis,* discovered and first published several of the major voices of the Renaissance, including Langston Hughes himself. Charles Johnson kept dossiers on talented young African-Americans, tempted them to come to Harlem, and manipulated their career moves thereafter from behind the scenes. Alain Locke, the first black Rhodes scholar, acted as "chamberlain" in the Park Avenue court of Charlotte Osgood Mason, the fabled "godmother" and patron to young Langston Hughes, Zora Neale Hurston, and others. To these, David Levering Lewis adds three others. Walter White, the first black novelist since Paul Laurence Dunbar, exploited his celebrity to make his apartment at 90 Edgecombe Avenue "a stock exchange for cultural commodities." Caspar Holstein, the numbers banker, financed many of the awards and prizes. James Weldon Johnson, executive secretary of the NAACP, endorsed and supported Fauset and White's cultural program, sometimes over the objections of Du Bois.[15] At a dinner at the Civic Club, held on March 24, 1924, ostensibly to celebrate the publication of Fauset's first novel, Johnson and White assembled a literary and intellectual who's who of the 1920s to meet their young black protégés. Afterward, Paul Kellogg, the editor of *Survey Graphic,* proposed to devote an entire issue to the young Harlem writers and artists he had met that evening. The March 1925 issue of *Survey Graphic,* edited by Alain Locke, enjoyed an astonishing success and was reissued later in the year, in expanded book form, as *The New Negro,* introducing to a national audience the most promising of the young painters and writers, many of whom were already well known to readers of black periodicals.

The Harlem number of *Survey Graphic,* and *The New Negro,* were the cultural manifestos of a new generation that expected to complete the legal emancipation of African Americans in 1863 by effecting their spiritual emancipation in Harlem a half-century later. James Weldon Johnson declared Harlem to be "the greatest Negro City in the world."[16] Arthur A. Schomburg, whose personal collection would form the core of the renowned collections of Harlem's Schomburg Center for Research in Black Culture, stated that "the American Negro must remake his past in order to make his future."[17] W. E. B. Du Bois reaffirmed the famous prophecy he had made a quarter of a century earlier, in *The Souls of Black Folk:* "The problem of the twentieth century is the problem of the color line." Now, he asserted, "led by American Negroes, the Negroes of the world are reaching out hands towards each other to know, to sympathize, to inquire."[18] Locke, in his editorial essay in *The New Negro,* identified the implicit ethos of these related ideas by associating the existence of a new spirit and psychology abroad among Negroes with its most characteristic instance in Harlem. "In Harlem, Negro life is seizing its first chances for group expression and self determination,"[19] Locke proclaimed, as he defined the fundamental tenets of the New Negro movement:

> One is the consciousness of acting as the advance-guard of the African peoples in their contact with Twentieth Century civilization; the other, the sense of a mission of rehabilitating the race in world esteem from that loss of prestige for which the fate and conditions of slavery have so largely been responsible. Harlem . . . is the center of both these movements; she is the home of the Negro's Zionism. The pulse of the Negro world has begun to beat in Harlem.[20]

Two months after the well-received Harlem issue of *Survey Graphic* came another consequence of the Civic Club dinner: a banquet at the Fifth Avenue Hotel, to fete the winners of a literary competition sponsored by *Opportunity Magazine*. The judges included Carl Van Doren, Fannie Hurst, Witter Byrne, Clement Wood, Eugene O'Neill, Alexander Woollcott, Robert Benchley, and Van Wyck Brooks. Among the prizewinners were Langston Hughes, Countee Cullen, Sterling Brown, E. Franklin Frazier, and Zora Neale Hurston. A few days later, on May 7, 1925, the *New York Herald Tribune* announced that America was on the edge of "what might not improperly be called a Negro renaissance." And so the New Negro cultural movements, gestating in the communities of African-America and the Caribbean for nearly a decade, reached critical mass in the national consciousness of America as a "Harlem Renaissance" – a misleading but not inappropriate term, since popular readings molded the generation's imaging of black Harlem, just as the Renaissance writers' literary acts of imagination were to shape the evolving form and use of the motif.

2

City of Refuge

In its racial transformation, Harlem had become the embodiment of an idea, for by its very existence Harlem posed a challenge to contemporary limits and cultural terms within which personal being for both blacks and whites were imagined and defined. Whether one was a Park Avenue "swell," exploring the heart of darkness in the comfort of a cabaret, or a black migrant looking for the Promised Land, by the mid-1920s "going to Harlem" was an act fraught with connotations and implications. Not surprisingly, writers of all races were attracted to the theme of Harlem. Yet the physical Harlem of the 1920s was not markedly unlike other sections of New York City. "Physically, Harlem is little more than a note of sharper color in the kaleidoscope of New York," Alain Locke had observed.[1] Harlem's appeal to writers lay not in its distinctive details of setting but in its power as a sign; consequently, the impulse of the first literary generations employing the motif was to regard black Harlem as a trope, a received cultural artifact for a writer's imaginative re-making, as if only through figurative elaboration could the novel idea of a great black city in the very heart of America's premier metropolis begin to be comprehended and conveyed.

Even the very earliest rendering of black Harlem in creative literature – "Harlem: The Black City," by Fenton Johnson, in *Songs of the Soil* (1916) – imagined Harlem in figurative terms. Only the boon from Johnson's deific Harlem remains in question in the poem's final apostrophe:

> O, Harlem, weary are thy sons
> Of living that they never chose;
> Give not to them the lotus leaf,
> But Mary's wreath and England's rose.[2]

Similarly, the early Harlem poems collected in *Harlem Shadows* (1922),[3] the first volume of poetry that Claude McKay published in the United States, exhibit a manifold sensibility to the Harlem setting that reaches beyond mere observation of setting. In "Harlem Dancer," published in 1917 under the pseudonym Eli Edwards, McKay's speaker also directs us to a vision of an inner reality. The world may observe a pandering Harlem exotic, dancing for prostitutes and "wine-flushed boys," but the speaker focuses on her contrasting essential and ineluctable self. This consummate selfhood is sensed in the innocence of her voice – "like the sound of blended flutes / Blown by black players on a picnic day" – and is rendered principally by allusion to its absence, but in the end it remains ineffable. In "Harlem Shadows,"[4] the sensibility of the speaker penetrates the Harlem prostitutes' erotic facade, emphasizing the

> halting footsteps . . . slippered feet
> . . . prowling through the night from street to street. . . .
> Through the night until the silver break
> Of day the little gray feet know no rest . . . tired feet . . .
> . . . the timid little feet of clay,
>   The sacred brown feet of my fallen race!
> Ah, heart of me, the weary, weary feet
> In Harlem wandering from street to street.   (p. 60)

It directs us to perceive the prostitutes as victims, rather than seductresses, by emphasizing the "weary, weary feet" that belie the stereotype of facile, exuberant black sexuality in Harlem. McKay's manifold sensibility pervades all of his city poems, some of which may be understood implicitly as Harlem scenes. In "Tropics in New York" (p. 31), the mangoes, ginger roots, alligator pears, and cocoa pods set on a windowsill (presumably in Harlem) bring memories that obscure the scene ("my eyes grow dim") and cause the speaker to turn away and weep, but in other poems without the stimulus of association, McKay's speakers perceive visions, memories, or dreams completely at odds with the scene observed.

Harlem is also a landscape of visions and memory in Helene Johnson's two poems about Harlem. "Sonnet to a Negro in Harlem," anthologized in James Weldon Johnson's ground-breaking *Book of American Negro Poetry* (1922), celebrates a Negro, "too splendid for this city street," who overwhelms the urban reality with the authority of his interior visions:

> Your shoulders towering high above the throng,
> Your head thrown back in rich, barbaric song,
> Palm trees and mangoes stretched before your eyes.[5]

And "Bottled: New York" expresses the same theme in a different idiom. A bottle of sand in a library, which "some bozo's been all the way
to Africa to get," recalls to a precocious Harlem child the image of "a
Negro dressed to kill / In yellow gloves and swallow tail coat / And
swirling a cane" on Seventh Avenue the day before. At first the child
had laughed at the man making a spectacle of himself on the streets of
Harlem. Then he had imagined the man in "a real honest-to-goodness
jungle," "black and naked, / and gleaming," with "rings in his ears and
on his nose / And bracelets and necklaces of elephants' teeth," and his
cane become a spear, "dipped in some kind of hoodoo poison." With a
fine irony, Helene Johnson's childish speaker is made to visualize Africa
in terms of *Tarzan of the Jungle* and *She Who Must be Obeyed,* but, even
at this unsophisticated level, the child glimpses the duality perceived by
McKay's speaker in "Harlem Dancer."

> Gee, I bet he'd be beautiful all right.
> No one would laugh at him then I bet.
> . . . .
> Say! That man that took that sand from the Sahara desert
> And put it in a little bottle on the shelf in the library,
> That's what they done to this dancer, ain't it? Bottled him.
> Trick shoes, trick coat, trick cane, trick everything – all
> > glass –
> But inside –
> Gee, that poor guy![6]

Rudolph Fisher's short story "City of Refuge," whose ironic title became a byword for Harlem in the parlance of the Renaissance, is among
three creative works about Harlem that were included in *The New Negro*
and in the Harlem issue of *Survey Graphic*. "City of Refuge" begins with
the arrival of King Solomon Gillis – dazed, bewildered, and fresh from
the South – at the mouth of the 135th Street subway, like "Jonah emerging from the whale" (p. 57)[7] – and again Harlem is interpreted rather
than described. Gillis's flight from his native North Carolina, to escape
lynching, is a traditional motif, with roots in the archetypal flight north
of the slave narratives of abolitionist literature. The choice of Harlem as
the "refuge" was still a relatively novel one in fiction, even though Fisher's narrator says that Harlem already has received the sanction of community consensus as a safe place in the tales of a traveling preacher, the
letters of a local boy gone off to war who never got past Harlem on his
return, and the occasional "colored" newspaper from New York "that
mentioned Negroes without comment, but always spoke of a white person as 'So and so, white.' That was the point. In Harlem, black was

white" (p. 58). But even the most exaggerated tales have not prepared Gillis for the sight of a black policeman intimidating a white driver. "It was beyond belief – impossible. Black might be white, but it couldn't be that white" (p. 59).

Harlem proves to be a dubious refuge, however. Unlike Hebron, and the other biblical cities of refuge of ancient Israel, which gave genuine sanctuary to accused murderers, Harlem shelters Gillis, only to sacrifice him later. On his first day in Harlem, Gillis runs into the very same former soldier from his hometown whose letters home had enticed him to Harlem in the first place. To his "homeboy" Gillis is "a baby jess in from the land o' cotton . . . an' ripe f' the pluckin." He gets Gillis a job in a grocery store and convinces him to pass out packets of "French medicine" to customers who slip him a "marker" when they make a small purchase. Gillis takes the bait and becomes the unwitting bagman for a cocaine ring. His homeboy reaps the profits, while Gillis runs the risk. When white detectives eventually turn up to arrest him, Gillis realizes how he has been conned, and he goes berserk. The crazed giant, betrayed by everyone who had seemed to befriend him in Harlem, boxes the detectives around viciously until he finds himself face to face with a black policeman.

> [Gillis] stopped as if stunned. For a moment he simply stared. Into his mind swept his own words like a forgotten song, suddenly recalled: –
> "Cullud policemans!"
> The officer stood ready, awaiting his rush.
> "Even – got – cullud – policemans – "
> Very slowly King Solomon's arms relaxed; very slowly he stood erect; the grin that came over his features had something exultant about it. (pp. 73–4)

Although he is neither clever nor perceptive, King Solomon Gillis seems to appreciate that Harlem, in spite of everything, has been true to its symbolic promise. If he is to be punished for his naïveté, at least Gillis can honor and accept the figure by whom justice will be served – one conceivable only in Harlem.

Like Rudolph Fisher's other Harlem vignettes, the elements are the same: the first sight of Harlem, the sure grasp of the migrants' language and turn of mind; the gradual revelation of an underlying ironic truth. "City of Refuge" is simply the most perfect of these vignettes, because of Fisher's economic texturing of the simple parable with the allusive vernacular of the black church ("Jonah emerging from the whale"; "the city of refuge"; "the land of plenty") and his telling identification of the migrant's Harlem as the new "Canada," "Northstar," or "North" – the

mysterious destinations of flight from slavery in the cryptic nomencla-
ture of freedom, and later from the peonage that replaced slavery in the
post-Reconstruction era. Tragically, by the early 1930s, this multital-
ented African-American roentgenologist, who could also write so
knowledgeably about Harlem's migrants, had fallen victim to the not yet
fully understood side effects of the medical technology he was helping to
pioneer.

"Harlem Life" – the rubric for the seven poems by Countee Cullen in
the Harlem number of *Survey Graphic* – introduced the laureate New
Negro poet to a wider audience. Six of these lyric sketches – a black boy
and a white boy playing together; two cautionary songs of love, to a
black girl and to a black boy respectively; a paean to a dancing girl; a
memorial to the then top-ranking African-American in the U.S. Army;
and a poem describing how a brown girl's funeral is paid for with her
mother's pawned wedding ring – could have been set in any black community in the United States. Nothing identifies them with Harlem, even
indirectly, and one wonders if the title "Harlem Life" was more than a
hook to the editorial premise of the Harlem issue of the magazine, since
it was dropped when the poems were reprinted in *The New Negro*. But
the seventh poem, "Harlem Wine," evokes Harlem in visionary and teleological terms:

> This is not water running here,
> These thick rebellious streams
> That hurtle flesh and bone past fear
> Down alleyways of dreams.
>
> This is wine that must flow on
> Not caring how or where,
> So it has ways to flow upon
> Where song is in the air.
>
> So it can woo an artful flute
> With loose elastic lips.
> Its measurements of joy compute
> With blithe, ecstatic hips.[8]

Cullen's evocation of Harlem, couched as a rebuttal to some unstated
postulation about Harlem life, transfigures implicit primitivist notions
about the intoxicating quality of Harlem life with sacramental echoes of
the Last Supper and the Wedding Feast at Cana, as well as with Diony-
sian narcosis. Thus, the image of Harlem wine illustrates an evolving
level of figurative complexity in the motif of black Harlem, for the liquid
flowing through Harlem's veins is transubstantiated into a metaphor

with overlapping and contradictory associations that illuminate a resonant, but ambiguous, sense of the vitality of Harlem.

Sterling Brown, who had won second prize in the *Opportunity Maga-*
zine competition (1925) with his essay on Roland Hayes, took a sly swipe
at Cullen's "Harlem Wine," McKay's "Harlem Shadows," and the
whole Harlem craze, in the three Harlem poems in *Southern Road* (1932).
In "Maumee Ruth," the lady in question is laid out in her best gown but
with none of her children to mourn her, because they are stupefied by
the narcosis of the Harlem wine:

> Boy that she suckled –
>   How should he know,
> Hiding in city holes,
>   Sniffing the "snow"?
>
> And how should the news
>   Pierce Harlem's din
> To reach her baby gal,
>   Sodden with gin?[9]

In "Harlem Street Walkers," Brown reconsiders the significance of the
weary footsteps pacing the Harlem shadows, with a metaphysical jibe:

> Why do they walk so tragical
> Oh, never mind. When they are in
> The grateful grave, each whitened skull
> Will grin. . . .[10]

And in "Mecca," he debunks the hyperbole of Harlem's reputation as
the celebrated Mecca of the New Negro:

> Maggie came up from Spartansburg,
>   Tom from Martinique,
> They met at a Harlem house-rent stomp,
>   And were steadies in a week.
>
> Tom bought him a derby and pearl gray spats,
>   When his first week's work was done,
> Mag bought herself a sealskin coat,
>   Hot in more ways than one.
>
> O milk and honey of the promised land!
>   When Sunday rolls round again,
> Lady Margaret, lord! . . . She tips for fair,
>   And Lord Thomas . . . twirls his cane.[11]

Black Harlem – an occasional and infrequent theme in the work of Cullen, McKay, Brown, and Johnson – would be a lifelong literary preoccupation of Langston Hughes. "Jazzonia," Hughes's only Harlem poem in *The New Negro,* speaks, if cryptically and indirectly, to the relevance of blues and its free-form derivative, jazz, in the riddling complexity of Harlem:

> Oh, silver tree!
> Oh, shining rivers of the soul!
>
> In a Harlem cabaret
> Six long-headed jazzers play.
> A dancing girl whose eyes are bold
> Lifts high a dress of silken gold.
>
> Oh, singing tree!
> Oh, shining rivers of the soul!

Here the physical scene of a Harlem cabaret is juxtaposed simply to its contrasting landscape of the spirit, and the resonating opposites are amplified in riddles.

> Were Eve's eyes
> In the first garden
> Just a bit too bold?
> Was Cleopatra gorgeous
> In a gown of gold?
>
> Oh, shining tree!
> Oh, silver rivers of the soul!
>
> In a whirling cabaret
> Six long-headed jazzers play.[12]
>
> (p. 25)

The title "Jazzonia" has usually been interpreted in the sense of "jazz-zone-ia," but the term also may be read as a contraction of "jazz" and "harmonia," understood to refer to the dynamic resonance between the abstracted landscape of shining, silver trees and rivers of the soul and the provocative eroticism of the cabaret show girls that is at once the essence of Harlem and the dualism of the blues. The term "jazzonia," therefore, may be interpreted more broadly to denominate the creative bridge between the observed actuality and perceived spirituality, in the manner of African-America, with the music of jazz and blues at the point of synapse in Harlem.

The Weary Blues (1926),[13] Hughes's first volume of poetry, named for the poem that had won him first prize in the *Opportunity Magazine* competition, contained more Harlem poems (including "Jazzonia") than the entire corpus of his New Negro coetanes combined. Its first section, also entitled "The Weary Blues," consists of a series of fifteen individual poems that, like blues, flow together to form a unified continuum for which Harlem is the stated or implied setting. These poems – as marked by irony, paradox, contradiction, and ambiguity as those of Hughes's African-American literary contemporaries just discussed – associate the dualism of Harlem with the quintessential patterns of twoness (that is, call and response; problem and resolution; being and becoming) that are the structure and spirit of the blues. The title poem "The Weary Blues," paired at the beginning of the sequence with "Jazzonia," captures the blues experience in process with a classic blues (sometimes attributed to Bessie Smith, among others) that biographer Arnold Rampersad says Hughes first heard as a child in Kansas:[14]

> Droning a drowsy syncopated tune,
> Rocking back and forth to a mellow croon,
>   I heard a Negro play.
> Down on Lenox Avenue the other night
> By the pale dull pallor of an old gas light
>   He did a lazy sway. . . .
>   He did a lazy sway. . . .
> To the tune o' those Weary Blues.
> With his ebony hands on each ivory key
> He made that poor piano moan with melody.
>   O Blues!
> Swaying to and fro on his rickety stool
> He played that sad raggy tune like a musical fool.
>   Sweet Blues!
> Coming from a black man's soul.   (p. 23)

A similar pair of poems concludes "The Weary Blues" sequence, on a similar note. "Blues Fantasy" emphasizes the aesthetic experience of the blues, which can musically transform trouble and pain into a kind of paradoxical laughter:

> Hey! Hey!
> That's what the
> Blues singers say.
> Singing minor melodies

They laugh,
Hey, Hey!   (p. 37)

And "Lenox Avenue: Midnight" returns us to the scene of the blues experience of the title poem, iterating what was implicit in "Jazzonia" and making the final statement of the collection:

> The rhythm of life
> Is a jazz rhythm,
> Honey.
> The gods are laughing at us.
>   (p. 29)

The intervening poems of "The Weary Blues" sequence are vignettes of Harlem, voices of the cabarets, which validate the truth of the two pairs of poems that frame the other eleven. Some imitate Harlem voices, with little or no authorial intrusion, like "Negro Dancers" (p. 26), composed almost entirely of the double-entendre boasts of the black dancers, with only a few verses sketching the envying presence of white onlookers, and "The Cat and the Saxophone" (p. 27), composed only of the intertwined voices of the cat's bluntly effective seduction and the saxophone's naive boast that "my baby don't love nobody but me." A few, like "Harlem Night Club" (p. 32), "Song for a Banjo Man" (p. 36), and "Midnight Nan at Leroy's" (p. 30), are Harlem variations on the *topos* of *carpe diem*. But others distance Harlem of the cabarets from the speaker with hauntingly reflective questions, such as "Cabaret" (p. 29), which asks, "Does a jazz-band ever sob?", and "Nude Young Dancer," which inquires:

> What jungle tree have you slept under,
> Midnight dancer of the jazzy hour?
> What great forest has hung its perfume
> Like a sweet veil about your bower?
>
> What jungle tree have you slept under,
> Night dark girl of the swaying hips?
> What star-white moon has been your mother?
> To what clean boy have you offered your lips?
>   (p. 33)

Three other poems about Harlem are included in subsequent sections of *The Weary Blues*. Two of these are nocturnes, in different modalities: "Harlem Night Song" is a romantic invitation: "Come / Let us roam the night together / singing" (p. 62); the other, "Summer Night," describes the sounds of the Harlem night drifting into stillness, as they are heard by a bone-weary Harlemite for whom the encroaching silence is as empty as his soul (p. 103). "Disillusion," the last Harlem poem in Hughes's first volume, expresses a wish to escape Harlem's tensions and contradictions (p. 104).

With these poems, Hughes initiated a commitment to the theme of Harlem as the landscape and dreamscape of the blues, a theme that for over half a century has been since the 1920s a principal force shaping the development of the Harlem motif among three generations of Africana poets. We may have to remind ourselves that Hughes's identification of Harlem with jazz and blues, which now seems so natural – perhaps even a bit trite – was severely criticized by black authority figures and rejected in its own time. The initial negative reaction to *The Weary Blues* objected as much to Hughes's using jazz and blues as literary material as to the flexible sexual morality of the cabarets. The spirituals had come to be accepted by the Negro elite as dignified and ennobling folk forms, but blues and jazz were embarrassing reminders of a status they were trying to escape. Hughes recalled being interrupted, during a reading of these poems in an Atlantic City church, by a note from the pastor demanding that he not read "any more blues in my pulpit."[15] In fact, it took a streak of daring and independence, as well as genius, for Hughes, in the 1920s, to invoke the cultural traditions of the Harlem folk and to vest his literary vision of Harlem with the authority of African-American musical and philosophical frames of reference. Few of the major African-American writers of Hughes's generation followed his lead in this respect.

Langston Hughes's identification of Harlem with jazz and blues was, nevertheless, characteristic of the genius that distinguished the consistent achievement of his long career from the frustrated promise of so many of his New Negro contemporaries. The choice of blues and jazz as the aesthetic for the Harlem motif reflected issues in African America that had preceded the existence of Harlem and the emergence of the New Negro and articulated the tendency of the new generation to comprehend Harlem in dualistic terms. After all, irony, paradox, and contradiction had not begun for blacks with Harlem. The opposition of black to white, North to South, master to slave; the paradox of Jim Crow's structuring of the daily intimacy of interracial contact into the procrustean categories of "separate but equal"; the problematic black rhetoric of silence, and the strategy of masks – all embraced by W. E. B. Du Bois's image of "twoness" and the "double self," in *The Souls of Black Folk* (1903)[16] – could be subsumed by the Harlem motif. The contradictions and resonances of the Harlem landscape postulated in figurative terms what Du Bois had called "this longing [of the black man] to achieve self-conscious manhood, to merge his double self into a better and truer self . . . [in which] neither of the older selves [is] to be lost."[17] Harlem's ambiguous quality crystallized the existential challenge of the duality of being black in America. By asserting the duality between the Harlem they observed and the Harlem they perceived, Langston Hughes, and his New Negro coetanes, took a significant evolutionary step in the elaboration and conception of a black identity delineated in the tensions and resonances in the trope of the Harlem landscape itself, and advanced beyond the kind of twoness characterized by Du Bois. These black authors, by measuring the spiritual actualities of Harlem against their own intimations of a potential racial selfhood, stepped irreversibly from behind the metaphoric veil that, in Du Bois's view, "yields [the black] no true self-consciousness, but only lets him see himself through the revelation of the other world . . . looking at one's self through the eyes of others . . . measuring one's soul by the tape of a world that looks on in amused contempt and pity."[18] Hughes succeeded in expressing the same sense of Harlem as other New Negro poets, but, because he associated the Harlem setting with jazz and blues (folk forms recognized to be black, and even African, in origin and values), his Harlem was placed squarely in an African-American, musical and philosophical frame of reference, in which the duality, paradox, and irony of jazz and blues could be embodied in culturally received forms – in the medium, as well as in the message. Thus, the ambivalence and ambiguity of Harlem – which may have seemed moot and problematic in Claude McKay's sensibility of an ineffable lost identity, in Helene Johnson's touching specters of Africa, in Countee Cullen's sacramental imagery of wine and water, even in Rudolph Fisher's ironic fictions and Sterling Brown's demystification of the Harlem vogue – could be more fully articulated by Langston Hughes with blues and jazz.

Hughes's synthesis of the black urban experience with the very forms the folk had chosen to bring with them to the city was a function of the role he played within his generation of writers as both receiver of a popular cultural legacy and as shaper of this tradition into literary form. By identifying the structure of the folk forms of blues and jazz of the New Negro writers' figuration of Harlem, Hughes conjoined the aspiration and the obstacles of African-American selfhood in a single motif, reflecting the terms of its subjectivity in the crucible of the urban environment where blacks, in the 1920s and 1930s, were transforming themselves from a rural to an urban people. In this respect, Hughes was a primary figure of the Harlem Renaissance: "a watershed marking the boundaries which bring together a black consciousness of self with its less sophisticated past, hence permitting the aural and written cultures to converge and proceed along a broader and more productive channel."[19] In Harlem of the blues, Hughes specified his transcendent apprehension of the expansiveness of human possibility within the confines of the actual world with the particular texture of the black condition perceived through the prism of the blues. One hesitates to apply the appropriate term, "universal," to this achievement only because the concept has been so abused by its employment against nonwhites as an instrument of cultural hegemony, in the name of outdated "universal" Western standards, and also because the negation of that abuse was a major objective of Hughes's generation. Yet Hughes's Harlem is a setting and symbol for universal human interplay, expressed in the fullest sense with a personal artistry shaped by the received but evolving art forms of his culture. Hughes himself ponders the transcendence and universality of his own work, in "Aesthete in Harlem," the only Harlem poem in *Dear Lovely Death* (1931):

> Strange,
> That in this nigger place,
> I should meet Life face to face
> When for years, I had been seeking
> Life in places gentler speaking
> Until I came to this near street
> And found Life – stepping on my feet.[20]

Langston Hughes's motif of Harlem as the landscape and dreamscape of blues and jazz carried with it the possibility of aesthetic, as well as thematic, revision. Hughes returned to the motif repeatedly over four decades, with a maturing and evolving vision. His reformulation and reinterpretation of the motif was able to respond to disheartening alterations in Harlem's circumstances as well as to its initial promise, and his practice pointed the way for Harlem's continued elaboration as an Africana motif in literature. Curiously, the influence of Hughes's Harlem was first felt neither among his New Negro cohorts nor in African-American literature, because for the remaining years of the Harlem Renaissance all previous interpretations of Harlem were overshadowed by two sensational, best-selling novels about Harlem. Carl Van Vechten's *Nigger Heaven* (1926) and Claude McKay's *Home to Harlem* (1928),[21] published at the height of the Harlem vogue, both explored the cabaret Harlem, of joyful, erotic, and musical exuberance, that exercised a dominant influence on the literary use of Harlem by black and non-black authors alike during the remaining years of the Harlem Renaissance and has resonated in the literary idea of Harlem ever since. This Harlem of exhilarating joy would eventually surrender, in the face of Harlem's evident decline, but never vanished entirely from later literary conceptions. In spite of this common ground, however, *Nigger Heaven* and *Home to Harlem* represent contrasting literary conceptions of Harlem in the 1920s.

In the opening chapter of *Home to Harlem*, black Harlem is evoked lyrically and figuratively rather than depicted by fictional technique:

It was two years since he had left Harlem. Fifth Avenue, Lenox Avenue, and One Hundred and Thirty-fifth Street, with their chocolate-brown and walnut-brown girls, were calling to him.

"Oh, them legs!" Jake thought. "Them tantalizing brown legs! . . . Barron's Cabaret! . . . Leroy's Cabaret! . . . Oh, boy!"

Brown girls rouged and painted like dark pansies. Brown flesh draped in soft colorful clothes. Brown lips full and pouted for sweet kissing. Brown breasts throbbing with love.

"Harlem for mine!" cried Jake. "I was crazy thinkin' I was happy over heah. I wasn't myself. I was a man charged up with dope everyday! That what it was. Oh, boy. Harlem for mine!

"Take me home to Harlem, Mister Ship! Take me home to the brown gals waiting for the brown boys that done show their mettle over there. Take me home, Mister Ship. Put your beak right into that water and jest move along." (pp. 8–9)

Here Jake rhapsodizes on the theme of Harlem; the elements of his lyric evocation are literary figures – metonymy, personification, apostrophe, synecdoche – rather than literal details of the landscape. When Jake dances with his "little brown girl" for the first time, he is again moved to apostrophize Harlem: "Harlem! Harlem! . . . Where else could I have all this life but Harlem? Good old Harlem! Chocolate Harlem! Sweet Harlem!" (p. 14). Later, when Jake experiences his first night of loving back in Harlem, the narrator echoes Robert Browning's "Home Thoughts from Abroad":

Oh, to be in Harlem again after two years away. The deep-dyed color, the thickness, the closeness of it. The noises of Harlem. The sugared laughter. The honey-talk on its streets. And all night long, ragtime and "blues" playing somewhere, dancing somewhere! Oh, the contagious fever of Harlem. Burning everywhere in dark-eyed Harlem. . . . Burning now in Jake's sweet blood. (p. 15)

And, after a night of loving, Jake evokes Harlem once again in lyrical terms:

Harlem! Harlem! Little thicker, little darker and noisier and smellier, but Harlem just the same. The niggers done plowed through Hundred and Thirtieth Street. Heading straight for One Hundred and Twenty-fifth. Spades beyond Eighth Avenue. Going, going, going Harlem! Going up! . . . Lawdy! Harlem bigger, Harlem better . . . and sweeter! (pp. 25–6)

Although this Harlem is evoked figuratively, rather than depicted with detail and description, we are given to understand that Jake has found the Harlem he came seeking: a Harlem that will allow him to be himself, within the liberating frame of an African-American community; a Harlem embodied in the joy of a little brown girl, who can match his open, steadfast nature. His cry of "Harlem for mine!" (p. 8), with its subjunctive and conditional modalities, has become a triumphant "Harlem is mine!" (p. 17), because Harlem responds to him in terms he can affirm and with which he can identify. After Jake's loss of Felice (still unnamed, at that point in the story), his search for her becomes the symbolic test of the spirit of Harlem evoked in the earlier chapters. Cabaret Harlem moves to the perceptual foreground of the novel, and the Harlem setting is particularized to a greater degree, but the narrator's tendency is still to set the scene by characterizing, rather than depicting, the setting. The affective attributes of the cabaret environment are conveyed, in lieu of pictorial description, and discriminations are made between the relative moral, cultural, and aesthetic orders of the various cabaret settings. Harlem reveals nuances, some of which are disorderly and animalistic, but Jake's Harlem, evoked in the opening chapters, remains the norm. Although he embraces it all, Jake remains essentially unchanged, and faithful to his first vision of Harlem. Even while making do with the available gratification of life with Congo Rose, Jake never acknowledges her as more than an inadequate substitute for Felice. Unlike his foil Zeddy, Jake refuses to be Rose's "sweet man," and, when Harlem threatens to overwhelm him with the force of its disorderly and compulsive aspects, Jake invokes the "room of the little lost brown [that] lived in his mind a highly magnified affair" (p. 114) and flees to a job on the railroad.

McKay's evocation of Jake's personal Harlem, which can be identified with the lyric approaches of his New Negro contemporaries, contrasts with the larger portion of *Nigger Heaven*. Most of Van Vechten's novel is guided by a didactic imperative, skillfully integrated with the fictional necessities of the story. The narrator, in his own phrase, is "a careful observer" (p. 151), who depicts Harlem dispassionately and varies setting systematically to convey a comprehensive and informed view of Negro life in America circa 1925. Mary Love's estrangement from so many elements of life in black Manhattan permits this "careful observer" to catalog and contemplate many facets of the Harlem landscape, without violating either the love story or his narrative point of view. With Mary, the reader tours a variety of Harlem environments: the Gatsby-like indulgence of the Long Island set, the Saint Nicholas Avenue pretensions of the Albrights, the Striver's Row luxury of Adora Boniface, and the refined comforts of the Sumners. All combine with glimpses of Craig's Restaurant, the 135th Street branch of the public library, and the

United Charities Ball to depict a variegated Harlem. Similarly, Byron
Kasson's need to earn a living while he tries to become a writer permits
a tour of working-class Harlem on the job, along with an informed con-
sideration of the status of black literature. In addition, the narrator explores the topology, as well as the topography, of Harlem. Mary's visit
to Adora Boniface's townhouse becomes the occasion for nostalgic remi-
niscences about the Tenderloin area of black Broadway at the turn of the
century, which anticipated and set the style of Harlem cabaret life, and
the family histories of the Sumners and the Loves hint at the roots of the
"talented tenth's" prosperity and urbanity. This careful observer is so
thorough that a careful reader should be able to dismiss a minor character's stereotyped view that Harlem is typified by the Black Venus cabaret: "Is all Harlem like this?" (p. 15). Byron, to whom the question is
directed, is characterized as an urbanized tragic mulatto: a person more
white than black, sensitive to the finer ways of life in the white world
but condemned to languish within the confines of the black because of
his share of Negro blood. Take, for example, Byron's apostrophe of
Harlem:

> Nigger Heaven! Byron moaned. Nigger Heaven! That's what
> Harlem is. We sit in our places in the gallery of this New York
> theatre and watch the white world sitting below in the good
> seats in the orchestra. Occasionally, they turn their faces up to-
> wards us, their hard, cruel faces, to laugh or sneer, but they
> never beckon. It never seems to occur to them that Nigger
> Heaven is crowded, that there isn't another seat, that something
> has to be done. It doesn't occur to them either, he went on
> fiercely, that we sit above them, that we can drop things down
> on them and crush them, that we can swoop down from this
> Nigger Heaven and take their seats. No they have no fear of
> that. Harlem! The Mecca of the New Negro! My God. (pp.
> 148–9)

The form and the figurative language invite comparison to Jake's evocations of Harlem, but the differences are more compelling. Jake's celebration is lyrical and enthusiastic. Byron's complaint is bitter and sardonic.
He is tortured by the proximity of the place from which he is excluded
and projects a defensive psychology and an abject aesthetic on the Harlem landscape that he has labeled "Nigger Heaven." Byron is depicted
as confused enough to defer to Baldwin's judgment of Harlem, after just
one jaunt to a Harlem cabaret:

> The question awakened a swarm of perverse, dancing images in
> Byron's brain. They crowded about each other, all the incon-

gruities, the savage inconsistencies, the peculiar discrepancies, of this cruel segregated life.

Yes, he replied, I suppose it is. (p. 215)

Once Byron begins his affair with Lasca Sartoris, the narrator discards the pose of a careful observer to immerse himself in the sensational side of Harlem. As Byron's middle-class persona is stripped away, the cabaret landscape of Harlem becomes an expression of a mental state which, the narrator implies, is racially characteristic of the primitive Negro psyche. When the urbane youth succumbs to the primitive forces within, the careful observer's precise pictorial descriptions give way to evocations of Harlem from Byron's feverish point of view. The pace of the language accelerates, until conventional syntax is lost in a concatenation of isolated words and phrases. Van Vechten's careful observer has become a voyeur, resonating with Byron's obsessions. The Harlem setting and Byron's deranged state of mind have merged and become one:

> It all became a jumble in Byron's mind, a jumble of meaningless phrases accompanied by the hard, insistent, regular beating of the drum, the groaning of the saxophone, the shrill squealing of the clarinet, the laughter of the customers and occasionally the echo of the refrain.
>
> If you hadn't gone away!
>
> A meaningless jumble. Like life. Like Negro life. Kicked from above. Pulled down from below. No cheer but dance, drink and happy dust . . . and golden browns. Wine, women, and song, and happy dust. Gin, shebas, Blues, and snow. However, you looked at it. . . . Whatever you called it. (p. 278)

The contrast with McKay's Harlem is seen even more clearly if one notes the congruence of McKay's use of other black settings in *Home to Harlem* with his employment of Harlem itself. For a time Jake abandons Harlem to work on the railroad, and the story takes up a new character and several colorful episodes unrelated to Harlem or Jake's quest for Felice. Yet a feeling for Afro–New World settings remains as a constant perceptual support through this erratic section of McKay's novel. Ray, the new character identified only with a first name, resembles Byron Kasson only to the degree that he is estranged from cruel and insensitive aspects of the Harlem landscape. Unlike Byron, who is drawn to the downtown world of the whites, beyond his reach, Ray is characterized by his identification with and nostalgia for his own Negro setting. Ray's equivalent to Jake's Harlem is the tropical landscape of Haiti:

> Home thoughts, if you can make them soft and sweet and misty-beautiful enough, can sometimes snare sleep. There was the quiet, chalky-dusty street and, jutting over it, the front of a house he had lived in. The high staircase built on the outside and pots of begonias and ferns on the landing. . . . All the flowering things he loved, red and white hibiscus, mimosas, rhododendrons, a thousand glowing creepers, climbing and spilling their vivid petals everywhere, and bright buzzing humming-birds and butter flies. All the tropic-warm lilies and roses. Giddy-high erect thatch palms, slender, tall, fur-fronded ferns, majestic cotton trees, stately bamboos creating a green grandeur in the heart of space. (pp. 152–3)

All that Harlem offers Jake, Haiti offers Ray, in "the green grandeur in the heart of space." Ray and Jake never discuss their respective landscapes with each other in the intense personal terms with which they evoke them privately, but their friendship is based on a common longing for heroic cultural and mythic ideals for which the landscapes of Harlem and Haiti are their respective personal analogs. Jake is drawn to the dreamscape of black myth and history, revealed to him by Ray. "A black man! A black man!", Jake exclaims, after Ray tells him about Toussaint L'Overture. "Oh, I wish I had been a soldier under sich [*sic*] a man" (p. 132). *Home to Harlem*'s consistent use of significant Afro–New World landscapes points to the spiritual kinship between Jake and Ray, rather than to the personality differences usually emphasized by scholars. *Home to Harlem* is powered by a lyrical, manifold perception of Harlem and other Afro–New World landscapes that transcends mere observation of the environs.

Yet *Home to Harlem* was denounced by important critics for what was taken to be meretricious mimicry of *Nigger Heaven*'s exploitation of the underside of Harlem life. "It looks," Du Bois accused, "as though McKay has set out to cater to that prurient demand on the part of white folk for a portrayal in Negroes of that utter licentiousness which convention holds white folk back from enjoying."[22] McKay seems to have anticipated the charge, because he took obviously deliberate steps in the text to set *Home to Harlem* apart from *Nigger Heaven* by threading unmistakable parodies of Van Vechten's novel through the Myrtle Street chapters of *Home to Harlem*. He defended himself, also, by insisting that early drafts of *Home to Harlem* antedated *Nigger Heaven*.[23] McKay needs no apology, however. McKay's fiction penetrated Harlem's surface to apprehend essential qualities, in the manner of his earlier Harlem poems and those of Langston Hughes and the other New Negro writers; Van Vechten had reduced his own carefully observed and varied depiction of black Harlem to the narrow scope of a stereotype by insisting, in the final chapters of *Nigger Heaven,* on Harlem's atavistic and bizarre primitivism. Unlike Van Vechten, McKay described figurative and imaginative perceptions of place in order to evoke a sense of Harlem's authentic inner life, frame black selfhood in positive terms, and elevate personal, cultural, and ethnic self-esteem, using the same narrow slice of Harlem cabaret life that Van Vechten had advanced as the epitome of the "meaningless jumble" of Negro life (p. 278). Nonetheless, the picturesque world of the cabarets, explored in their respective ways by the two authors, won such a degree of international acceptance that the literary use of the Harlem motif was redirected, for better or worse, in the decade following the publication of *Nigger Heaven* and *Home to Harlem;* the fundamental difference between McKay's and Van Vechten's visions of Harlem was overlooked.

3

Crossing the Color Line

In the decade before 1925, black writers had tackled the literary theme of Harlem in poetry and short fiction, with little visibility beyond the periodicals of the black community. Non-blacks, even those who specialized in writing popular fiction and poetry about blacks, had ignored Harlem as a literary theme, but the commercial success of the Harlem issue of *Survey Graphic* and *The New Negro,* followed almost immediately by the best-seller status of *Nigger Heaven,* and later of *Home to Harlem,* demonstrated the popular appetite for images of Harlem. Harlem's currency and sensational status as a cultural symbol made it an inviting target for writers of all races, and, for nearly a decade after 1926, imaginative literature about black Harlem became inescapable. Many of the poets and short-story writers published in *The New Negro* attempted longer works of fiction; several new black novelists began to cultivate the interest in Harlem; and in less than a decade some twenty novels by African-American writers were published, most of them set, in whole or in part, in Harlem. Harlem episodes became a not uncommon feature of works concerned neither with Harlem nor with black life by a series of white novelists, and a cosmopolitan array of non-black poets began interpreting the implications of Harlem's vitality.

The treatment of black Harlem by non-black authors with few exceptions depicted Harlem as being at one and the same time a fundamentally alien, and yet patently intelligible, environ. T. Bowyer Campbell's *Black Sadie* (1928), for example, imitates the worst aspects of Van Vechten's *Nigger Heaven,* depicting Negroes as amusing, quasi-human oddities, whose amoral lives drift in an endless present moment, with little structure or direction. Sadie, a domestic servant from the South, stumbles into wealth and celebrity when the notoriety of her nude portrait makes her the focus of a new, cultish interest in Negroes. A Harlem cabaret is

33

opened in her name; a Harlem dance step is dubbed the "Black Sadie"; and Broadway impresarios vie to put her in a Harlem revue. When a former lover is murdered by one of her numberless male relations, Sadie drifts, just as aimlessly, out of fame and fortune and departs for Chicago, with her nephew beside her and her defunct paramour in a trunk. Still, the Black Sadie Cabaret continues to prosper, for it is hawking a generic form of Harlem entertainment to a gullible clientele, and, as long as the cult of Harlem lasts, any substitute Sadie will do.[1] In *Ninth Avenue* (1926), Maxwell Bodenheim lampoons *Nigger Heaven*'s excesses, when the heroine, Blanche Palmer, finds herself at a mixed-raced soiree given by the author of *Black Paradise* and attended by recognizable parodies of Countee Cullen and other Harlem literati. In Bodenheim's *Naked on Roller Skates* (1931), however, a sensational Harlem episode (unrelated to rest of the novel) seems to have been inserted only to illustrate the range of hero Terry Barberlit's odyssey, through an instance of his understanding and effortless mastery of dangerous Negroes in the superlative Negro setting.[2] At least two novels, *Strange Brother* (1931) by Blair Niles and *The Young and the Evil* (1933) by Charles Henri Ford and Parker Tyler, include sorties to another kind of sensational Harlem venue: New Negro Harlem's gay scene.[3]

Non-black poets, like their New Negro counterparts, tended to characterize Harlem in symbolic, or even teleological, terms but seemed not to sense the tension and paradox in the idea that a place supposedly so alien could offer such transparent meanings. Sidney Alexander's "Lenox Avenue," for example, depicts the Harlem boulevard as a "strange forest," into which, "with hooves of a doe / my eye has wandered." "Cactuses of men" stand "weird against the sky." A black boy, with "eyes of a mountain pool suddenly freezing over," regards the speaker as "a lost stag in a lost valley." Questions of guilt and innocence whirl in the speaker's mind, and Lenox Avenue passes before him "like a dream half realized, / twisted by anger and fear." Yet in Alexander's visionary Harlem the cosmic consequence of contact between black and white is certain:

> Those who have cast you in the pit have fled.
> The caravan has come. Give me your hand!
> In that embrace stars shall explode,
> And brotherhood like a coat of many colors
> Cover the nakedness of man.[4]

The Harlem of Yvan Goll's *Jean Sans Terre* is, similarly, a primal and apocalyptic force. In "Harlem River," Harlem is apostrophized as

Harlem! Prêtresse noire
Saoûle du lait blanc de la rosée
· · · · · · · · · · · · · · · · · ·

Danse de toutes les mers dans le même allaitement
Massacre de toutes les mères dans le même haletement
· ·

Danseuse chaldéenne dans ce bouge d'Amérique.[5]

Harlem! Black priestess. Drunk on milk white dew
· ·

Dance of all the seas in one breast
Massacre of all mothers in one breath
· ·

Chaldean dancer in this dirty hole of America.[6]

And in "Jean Sans Terre a son frère noir" a clarion call is issued to the black brother to assert his blackness to save and vivify a pallid earth:

Bondis! Jaillis hors de ta solitude!
Hors de Harlem et de ton univers!
· ·

Toi qui caches le charbon millénaire
De la douleur dans la nuit de ton corps
C'est toi qu'il faut à cette faible terre
pour la guérir de sa pâleur de mort[7]

Leap! Burst out of your solitude!
Out of Harlem and of your universe!
· ·

You who hide the millennial coal
of sorrow in the nighttime of your body
It is you who are needed by the feeble earth
to cure her of her deathly pallor

Salvatore Quasimodo's "La chiesa dei negri ad Harlem" begins on a more quotidien note:

La chiesa dei negri ad Harlem
è al primo piano d'una casa e sembra
un *atelier*. Si entra come per comprare
un feticcio o un ricordo sacro.
Il luogo ha un altare decorato
come certi dolci del Sud, con rotonde
macchie rosse, azzurre, gialle.[8]

The Negro church in Harlem
is on the first floor of a house, and it resembles
a shop. You enter as if to buy
a fetish or holy relic.
The place has an altar decorated
like certain desserts from the South, with round
splotches of yellow, red, and blue.

But the mystic encounter between the Harlem devotees and the Christian god transforms the landscape. At the poem's end: "Le ossesse cantano, Dio le guarda / da nubi barocche nell' odore di candele umane / accese da speranza e da dolore"[9] (The obsessed are chanting, God watches over them / from the baroque clouds in the scent of human candles / lighted with hope and pain).

Even William Rose Benét's vividly, colorfully, rhythmically melodramatic "Harlem" imagines a kind of metaphysical landscape. In the poem "Harlem," from his *Harlem and Other Poems*, Benét presents an urban landscape animated, personified, and set to dancing by the jungle spirit of its denizens. The poem is rhapsodized on the repeated line "I want to sing Harlem," recalling the evocation of a muse by an epic poet undertaking a great theme, for Benét's Harlem has all the fantastic possibilities of the Mediterranean of Homer's *Odyssey* and Apollonius's *Argonautica*. In Harlem, though, the phantasmagoria has been generated by the atavistic influence of Africa:

> Those buildings lean, those buildings lean,
> they sway and shuffle to the streets between!
> Fly-drumming drones and drums make trouble
> (Crushed ruffs *[sic]*, long rolls, single and double)
> . . . .
> Fetish charm and exorcism
> Float like smoke from a black abysm
> Thicken like smoke from eastward rolled.
> Land of Ophir, land of Gold.
> . . . .
> Then fades, and flares, and fades once more
> That black volcano on a haunted shore
> Where writhing shadows wail and sob.
> Faint, more faint, the war-drums throb,
>
> Great Zulu Tshaka's war drums spent
> In the gloom of a lost dark continent.[10]

Alfred Kreymborg's "Crossing the Color Line" puts an ironic spin on these apocalyptic propensities:

> Harlem
> has a black belt
> where darkies dwell
> in a heaven
> where white men
> seek a little hell.[11]

But another poem by Kreymborg imagines Harlem as an enclave of Good Samaritan feeling, within a cityscape of numbing indifference, and, with the title, "Harlem," makes the vignette of an old colored man's feeling for a dead horse an epiphany of the Negro's place in a moral universe.[12] Finally, Max Eastman's "Jilted in Harlem" attributes a cosmic consequence to a rather ordinary event by characterizing unrequited love across the color line as

> The more than amorous desire,
>   The exile's yearning

> For earth's own children, whom the brooding sun
>   Has warmed with color,
> Who through life's drama dance and run
>   Immune to pallor.[13]

Maxwell Bodenheim, Sidney Alexander, Yvan Goll, Salvatore Quasimodo, William Rose Benét, Alfred Kreymborg, and Max Eastman presumed Harlem, however foreign, to be a landscape that would readily surrender its patent moral, cosmic, or teleological import. Any tensions in the Harlem environs of these writers derived from the sensational contrast with the civilized white world; the only duality informing their ideas of Harlem was the distinction of one's double, the alien other that puts one's self in stark relief. Other non-blacks avoided such interpretations by observing common humanity, rather than exoticism, in Harlem. Yonezo Hiroyama's "A Yellow Man Looks at a Black World within a White World" marvels at the Western habit of mind that reduces the evident variety of black Harlem to the sameness of a stereotype:

> In Harlem. . . . .
> Judges,
>   Army Captains,
>   Police Sergeants,
>   Composers of music,

Musicians,
Singers,
Actors,
Poets,
Authors:

Who are
black,
bronze,
brown,
yellow,
white, or
whiter than white men: –

All are the same –
common Negroes –
just plain Negroes –
negroes –
"niggers"!!¹⁴

Only Federico García Lorca seemed able to transcend the oblivious or simplistic approaches of most non-blacks writing about Harlem in this period. The authority and penetration of the Harlem landscape by the vision of this poet is extraordinary. The voice of *El poeta en Nueva York* resonates with the feelings of the king in "El rey de Harlem":

La sangre no tiene puertas en vuestra noche boca arriba.
No hay rubor. Sangre furiosa por debajo de las pieles
viva en la espina del puñal y en el pecho de los paisajes
bajo las pinzas y retamas de la celeste luna de cáncer.¹⁵

Blood has no doors in your mouth upward night.
Not even a blush. Furious blood under their skins
alive in the spine of a dagger and in the breast of the
landscapes,
under the claws and black furze of Cancer's heavenly moon.

Unlike those who regarded Harlem as alien and exotic, the poet of *El romancero gitano* may have felt, as Angel del Río suggested, that it was the least alien aspect of New York. "Lorca was also drawn by [the Negro theme] by the same temperamental reasons which made him the singer of gypsies: his feeling, as a poet and dramatist, for primitive, earthy passions; his feeling, as an artist, for rhythm and traditional music as well as movement, gesture and color."¹⁶ Before his travels to New York, García Lorca's poetry already reflected a feeling for African folk and musical forms in the Moorish and Gypsy traditions of Granada. Perhaps García Lorca could also identify with the inner life of Harlem because of conflicts and dualities of his own sexual nature, which recent studies have interpreted as the central theme of *El poeta en Nueva York*.[17] By extending patterns of diction and imagery that he had mastered earlier to a new context, to confront an aspect of himself rather than some postulation of a primal "other," Federico García Lorca may have achieved a more perceptive sense of Harlem than other non-black poets, who, unlike him, were predisposed to see only their alien opposite in Harlem.[18]

After the phenomenal commercial success of *Nigger Heaven* and *Home to Harlem,* many of the poets and short-story writers whose works were published in *The New Negro,* along with several new authors, began to cultivate the broader audience for novels from which they had previously been excluded. Only two novels by blacks – three, if one counts Jean Toomer's *Cane* (1923) – had been released by major American publishers in the decade prior to publication of *The New Negro,* but, although by that time the enclave had been black for some twenty years, these novels scarcely mentioned Harlem. In *Cane* (New York: Boni & Liveright, 1923), Harlem is merely a passing reference by the narrator to the incongruous idea of Fern sitting in a tenement window in Harlem. In Walter White's *The Fire in the Flint* (New York: Knopf, 1923), the black protagonist, Kenneth Harper, M.D., has completed his internship at New York's Bellevue Hospital and has just passed up the opportunity to practice in Harlem, in order to return to his native Central City, in the Black Belt of the South. In *There Is Confusion* (New York: Boni & Liveright, 1924), the prosperous professional lives and social activities of Jessie Fauset's characters take them into and out of New York City, but although they evidently live, shop, and socialize in the Negro neighborhood, Harlem goes unnamed, and largely undescribed. After 1926, though, Fauset and White both paid more attention to Harlem, employing it as a significant (although by no means central) narrative device, in novels about light-skinned mulatto protagonists who try to escape the challenges of Negro life by passing for white in New York City. In less than a decade, Negro writers published some twenty novels, many of them set in whole or in part in a Harlem defined largely in the terms of the joyful Negro erotic and musical exuberance so much in vogue in the mid-1920s.

Walter White's *Flight* (1926)[19] tells the story of Mimi Daquin, a native of New Orleans, who comes to Harlem after putting up for adoption a son born out of wedlock. In Harlem, Mimi "was thrilled by the new scene. Gone was the morbid, morose, worried air of the people encountered at the other end of the subway. Here was spontaneous laughter, shrewd observations which brought loud and free laughter from listeners. There was an exhilarating sense here that these people knew the secret of enjoying life" (p. 186). When Mimi is shamed by the exposure of her indiscretion in a Harlem gossip column, she flees across the color line, where her talents as a dress designer are quickly recognized. Mimi prospers, socially and professionally, but life in the white world leaves her restless and unfulfilled. Her initial fascination with Harlem, and a later visit to a Harlem cabaret, put the mechanistic materialism of the white world in perspective, and Mimi's yearning to return to her race takes a decisive turn when she undergoes a mystical experience of the panorama of black history, while hearing black spirituals sung at Carnegie Hall.

In Jessie Fauset's *Plum Bun* (1929),[20] Harlem is an impending – if often distant – presence, which Fauset employs to characterize her protagonist's shifting state of mind in the larger portion of the novel, the portion set in downtown New York City. The shifting ideas and changing attitudes toward Harlem of Angelé Mory (née Angela Murray) become a figurative expression of her confused but evolving relationship to her self, her somewhat darker sister, and her racial heritage. Initially, Harlem amazes and impresses Angela also, for she had "never seen coloured life so thick, so varied, so complete" (p. 96), but, unlike Mimi Daquin's attraction to Harlem, alienation is Angela's dominant reaction. The face of a professional man – "it might be of an artist" – etches itself on her memory, but she holds herself apart from Harlem, which she regards, like colored life generally, as defined by privation and want. "[H]e might of course be a musician, but it was unlikely that he was an artist like herself, for how could he exist. Ah, there lay the difference" (pp. 96–7). But, on a later visit, when she attends a lecture in Harlem, Angela senses her distance from the white friends who have brought her. "[L]ittle waves of feeling played out from groups within the audience and beat against her consciousness and against that of her friends, only the latter were without her secret powers of interpretation" (p. 216). And by the end of the novel, when she has come to identify with Miss Powell, a struggling black classmate who has won an art prize for a painting called *A Street in Harlem,* Angela announces her secret heritage to four newspaper reporters, thereby committing herself to the developing racial consciousness prefigured by her series of evolving responses to Harlem.

Nella Larsen follows the same narrative strategy with regard to Harlem in *Quicksand* (1928) and *Passing* (1929),[21] two novels about passing across the color line. Larsen's handling of the Harlem motif is richer in its particulars, and more accomplished in its approach, than either White's or Fauset's, for her novels are as much oblique and ambivalent treatments of black female sexuality as they are explorations of the mixed racial heritages of their mulatto protagonists. In *Passing,* the contrasting characterizations of Clare Kendry and Irene Redfield are expressed and dramatized most sharply in their distinct relationships to Harlem. For Clare, Harlem is the focus of "terrible wild desire," the missing element in her "pale life," and her increasingly reckless sexual flings in Harlem narcotize the torture of marriage to a rich white racist, who does not know his wife is black. Clare's interest in Harlem brings an unwelcome turbulence to the bourgeois order, elegance, and prosperity of Irene Redfield's Harlem, by tempting Irene's domesticated husband to jettison his medical practice and run off with Clare to pursue old dreams of adventure in South America.

In *Quicksand,* Harlem is the concrete expression of Helga Crane's conflicting desires for both sexual fulfillment and social respectability. Helga flees from the stultifying gentility of Naxos – a fictional black women's college whose name is an anagram for Saxon – to Harlem, and for a time she is satisfied. "For her this Harlem was enough. . . . Everything was there, vice and goodness, sadness and gayety [*sic*], ignorance and wisdom, ugliness and beauty, poverty and richness. And it seemed to her that somehow of goodness, gayety, wisdom and beauty always there was a little more than of vice, sadness, ignorance and ugliness" (pp. 45–6). But spring in Harlem, like spring at Naxos, brings the same restlessness, and Helga begins to feel "shut up, boxed up, with hundreds of her race" (p. 54), rejoicing that she does not, "in spite of her racial markings[,] belong to these dark segregated people" (p. 55). A night of reluctant after-dinner cabareting becomes a hellish descent into a vortex of contradictory forces, where she is totally seduced by the music and the atmosphere, and "a shameful certainty that not only had she been in the jungle, but that she had enjoyed it, began to taunt her." Helga flees to Copenhagen, to relatives who see her as a passionate exotic, quite different from their pale northern ways. There Helga is encouraged to emphasize her eroticism. What everyone else considers a brilliant match is arranged for her with Denmark's leading painter, but Helga rejects him. In the spring the restlessness returns once again, and an invitation to a friend's wedding gives Helga the excuse to return to Harlem, where she begins to acknowledge her conflicting desires: "physical freedom in Europe and spiritual freedom in America. . . . From the prejudiced restrictions of the New World to the easy formality of the Old, from the pale calm of Copenhagen to the colorful lure of Harlem" (p. 96). In Harlem, again "voluptuous visions haunt," and one evening, when she is walking aimlessly in the rain, Helga wanders into a religious service being held in a storefront church. Here, not unlike the earlier episode in the underworld of her emotions, in the cabaret, "she felt an echo of the weird orgy resound in her own heart; she felt herself possessed by madness; she too felt a brutal desire to shout and to sling herself about. Frightened at the strength of the obsession, she gathered herself for one last effort to escape, but vainly. . . . And in that moment she was lost – or saved" (p. 113). In the "confusion of seductive repentance," Helga is escorted home by the black country preacher who had led the service. He takes her home with him to the backwoods of a tiny Alabama town, where Helga sinks into a bog of "anaesthetic satisfaction for her senses" and five debilitating pregnancies.

Passing, of an extreme variety, is the subject of *Black No More* (1931),[22] George S. Schuyler's satire concerning the fetish of skin color, made by whites and blacks alike. *Black No More* is set in Harlem only as long as the protagonist, Max Disher, is black. The rest of the action of the novel takes place mostly in the South, after Disher's transformation. Schuyler's Harlem is a deliberate stereotype, the embodiment of the kind of disorienting context that, although seeming to celebrate blackness, panders in its own way to racism. The story opens on New Year's Eve in a Harlem cabaret. Max Disher, abandoned by his latest lady friend, is at the club with his Army buddy, Bunnie Brown. In the "smoky depths" of the Honky Tonk Club, Disher is enchanted by an extraordinary white beauty from Atlanta, who rejects his invitation to dance with a nasty racial insult. "Up here trying to get a thrill in the Black Belt," Disher sulks afterward, "but a thrill from observation instead of contact. Gee but white folks were funny. They didn't want black folks' game and yet they were always frequenting Negro resorts." But his desire for this lady has only been intensified perversely by the racist rejection. When a way to turn white comes along, Disher is the first in line. After having taken a regimen of "electrical treatment and glandular control" and become white, Disher hesitates, feeling a momentary pang for the joys of Harlem, which he recalls almost exclusively in the stereotyped forms of the cabaret scene: "the high yellow Minnie and her colorful apartment, the pleasant evenings at the Dahomey Casino doing the latest dances with the brown belles of Harlem, the prancing chorus of the Lafayette Theater, the hours he had whiled away at Boogies' and the Honky Tonk Club." The hesitation is just momentary. His need for the insulting white girl is so strong that he heads for Atlanta, where she is said to live, and so the satire of *Black No More* is launched, concluding finally, after many twists and turns, with the unattainable white lady – now his wife – confessing to her ersatz-white husband that her own hidden ancestry is to blame for the Negro characteristics of their baby.

The Blacker the Berry (1929)[23] is a penetrating character study of the psychology of Emma Lou Morgan, a dark-skinned woman whose sense of personal worth has been warped by the color prejudice of her light-skinned relatives. Harlem and other Negro locales are fundamentally the same for Emma Lou, because, in spite of all the other differences, Harlemites are just as color conscious as other African-Americans. Emma Lou, the only dark member of a "blue-veined" social circle in Boise, Idaho, has undergone psychological torture at the hands of her close relatives. Emma Lou's unfortunate experience has taught her, not to reject color prejudice, but rather to internalize her relatives' perverse values. Emma continues to make herself miserable long after she has escaped her family's direct abuse by looking for slights everywhere. She rejects the darker blacks who befriend her and, with her rouges, makeup, and skin lighteners, turns herself into a grotesque figure. After two years among color-conscious coeds at UCLA, Emma Lou flees to Harlem. For Emma, the fabled side of Harlem holds little initial interest. "Emma Lou should have read that Harlem number of *Survey Graphic* issued two or three years ago. But Harlem had not interested her then for she had had no idea at the time that she would ever come to Harlem" (p. 122). The cabaret terms of the Harlem vogue are both affirmed and repudiated in *The Blacker the Berry*. Emma Lou visits a cabaret only when she is practically forced to by her employer, a white actress playing a Harlem cabaret girl in a Broadway musical, who wants her brother from Chicago to see the real thing. But Emma is not impressed. She is struck by "the note of artificiality" of the cabaret. "This entire scene seemed staged, they were in a theater, only the proscenium arch had been obliterated" (p. 105). Nonetheless, at a low down rent party, evoked in the feverish and fragmented diction of the Black Venus section in *Nigger Heaven,* Emma Lou, like Byron Kasson before her, is caught up by powerful urges.

> The music augmented by the general atmosphere of the room and the liquor she had drunk had presumably created another person in her stead. She felt like flying into an emotional frenzy – felt like flinging her arms and legs in insane unison. She had become very fluid, very elastic, and all the while she was giving in more and more to the music and the liquor and the physical madness of the moment. (pp. 150–1)

Slights, both real and imagined, seem to await her at every turn in Harlem, and Emma begins to debase herself, in order to keep the attention of some rather patent scoundrels who know how to manipulate her obsession with skin color. At her nadir, Emma Lou manages to see how far she has sunk and resolves, not entirely believably, to take charge of her life.

Even Rudolph Fisher's *Walls of Jericho*[24] (1928), an entertaining tapestry of the characteristic genre elements of Harlem fiction of the 1920s, woven around an unexpected reversal of the standard blockbusting scenario, is focused largely on the issue of color consciousness in Harlem. The ironies of passing, of racist uplifters of the race, and of intraracial bigots stand out among the typical themes of Harlem fiction as the butt of Fisher's wit. His knack for inventing amusing ordinary black conversation is exercised expansively in the constant barrage of color-conscious bluster and aggression with which Jinx and Bubba deny to themselves, and everybody else, their powerful emotional bond. A Harlem ball (an obligatory scene in Harlem fiction), bringing together all of the elements of the story and levels of social distinction, momentarily, in an atavistic democracy of drums, is used to plant the unnoticed seed of the novel's trick ending. Nevertheless, *The Walls of Jericho* lacks the precise narrative center that drives the best of Fisher's short pieces and makes them so moving. The concealed plot reversal – that the light-skinned black, seemingly rising by moving into Harlem's most exclusive and all white Court Avenue, is really being hounded by black enemies – is withheld too long. Consequently, the reader tends to focus on the variety of brilliant effects of the Harlem episodes along the way and may not see that in *The Walls of Jericho,* as in his other short pieces, Rudolph Fisher is also exploring the ordinary black migrant's voyage of self-discovery and becoming in the new urban contexts of black Harlem.

Only Fisher's *The Conjure Man Dies*[25] (1932) and Countee Cullen's *One Way to Heaven*[26] (1932) manage, for the most part, to avoid entangling the literary use of Harlem with the theme of intraracial color consciousness, but both novels read like momentary divertisements from the broader literary concerns of their creators. *The Conjure Man Dies* places Jinx and Bubba at the center of a police procedural involving the apparent murder and resurrection of an African mystic practicing his bewitching craft in a Harlem of curious and compelling potentialities beyond the circle of the action that makes complicated and mysterious events possible. The story is at first tediously mundane, as the body is discovered and the suspects are interrogated, but when the corpus delicti vanishes for a time and reappears full of life, the novel becomes preposterous but entertaining. The exotic variety of Harlem life is taken for granted, since the unlikely social juxtaposition of such extreme varieties would seem to be possible only in Harlem, but Harlem itself seems excluded beyond the claustrophobic circle of the crime scene to which the various suspects and investigators are confined once the murder is discovered in the opening pages of the novel.

Countee Cullen's *One Way to Heaven* is a shambles of a novel but well written, nonetheless, and a lot of fun. The novel begins with a riveting episode: Sam Lucas, a one-armed confidence man, enters a Harlem watch-night service as the congregation is resisting the efforts of a famous preacher. At just the right moment, Sam pretends to receive the Lord, approaching the altar railing and discarding the classic implements of a sinful life – a straight-edged razor and a deck of cards. Sam's apparent gift of grace touches Mattie Johnson, a beautiful young lady, who until that moment had felt no great need for salvation. Mattie finds love and religion in the inspired faker, who, to his surprise, also falls in love with her and begins to live up to his drama of "conversion" and the obligations of monogamy. But having laid out this genial narrative foundation, Cullen ignores it altogether and turns his attention to Mrs. Constancia Brandon – a hilarious caricature of a Harlem socialite – for whom Mattie works as a domestic servant. First Constancia contrives, on a few hours notice, to make Sam and Mattie's nuptials the social event of the season. Then a job is found for Sam, getting him conveniently out of sight as *One Way to Heaven* concentrates on the winning adventures of our Mrs. Brandon and her set. At a literary soiree at the Brandon's, for example, Constancia invites one Professor Seth Calhoun to lecture on his chosen subject, "The Menace of the Negro to Our Civilization," without warning either the professor or her New Negro friends of what is about to ensue. In the final pages of the novel, Cullen returns perfunctorily to Sam Lucas, tracing his descent, via alcohol, adultery, and double pneumonia, to an implausibly beatific death in Mattie's arms.

The broader idea of Harlem as a cultural symbol is the theme of Wallace Thurman's *Infants of the Spring*[27] (1932). Major structural elements pose the question of the idea of Harlem. A communal artists' dwelling dubbed Niggerati Manor, the setting for most of of the novel, has been conceptualized as "a monument to the New Negro" (p. 57) by its owner, Euporia Blake, a Harlem entrepreneur who has accepted the optimistic vision of Harlem's cultural significance and has embodied that ideal in what she hopes will be both a vital cultural center and a going real-estate venture. Also, what passes for a plot revolves around the sensation of a white man who comes to live in Niggerati Manor. On a trip to Harlem on his first day in the United States, Stephen Jorgenson, a young Scandinavian, befriends Raymond, the novel's protagonist, and the friendship is cemented with the joy of conversation. "It is only when their talk veered to Harlem that they found themselves sitting on opposite poles"

(p. 36). Ray and Stephen agree that Harlem is both terrifying and fascinating, but Ray objects to people who romanticize Harlem and Harlem's Negroes. "Harlem is New York" he argues. "Please don't let the fact that it is black New York obscure your vision." When Stephen says that Ray is too close to Harlem to have perspective, Ray retorts that his friend "should live here for a while," to get past the novelty. Stephen takes up the challenge and moves into Niggerati Manor with Ray.

The question of Harlem posed by Raymond and Stephen is echoed and amplified in the chatter of other characters, for the ideals proclaimed for Harlem and its cultural vanguard in *The New Negro* are defined, discussed, evaluated, and satirized constantly by the various artists, thrill seekers, Negrotarians, and others who visit or reside at Niggerati Manor, and their views are illustrated or contravened by their often outrageous behavior. In one often-cited episode, the habitués of Niggerati Manor are joined by obvious caricatures of Langston Hughes, Rudolph Fisher, Zora Neale Hurston, Countee Cullen, and Eric Waldron, among others, for a literary salon presided over by Dr. A. L. [Alain Locke?] Parkes. At this gathering, many of the high-minded ambitions of the Harlem Renaissance are enunciated, along with more than a few cynical asides, but the session quickly degenerates almost to the level of a brawl. The fate of Dr. Parkes's literary salon anticipates the fate of the novel's questions about the idea of Harlem. No systematic idea of Harlem is elaborated finally, for the questions about Harlem posed by the setting and the plot are aborted by the flow of fictional events in a context of disillusionment and frustrated promise. The only work produced at the commune to reach any public whatsoever is some bad love poetry, turned against its creator as evidence in a rape trial. And when the manor is to be reconstituted as a "dormitory for working girls," one of the more self-dramatizing members of the commune stages his own suicide as a publicity stunt for his novel, but in doing so inadvertently destroys most of the manuscript he is trying to promote. The only scrap to survive intact is his drawing of "a distorted, inky black skyscraper, modeled after Niggerati Manor, and on which were focused blindingly white beams of light. The foundation of the building was composed of crumbling stone. At first glance it could be ascertained that the skyscraper would soon crumble and fall, leaving the dominating white lights in full possession of the sky" (p. 284).

In effect, Wallace Thurman wrote the epitaph of the Harlem school of his generation. The ability of a literary vanguard, whose abilities and reputations were forged in the writing of poetry and short fiction, suddenly to employ the extended narrative of the novel to advance a cultural agenda in the vortex of a commercial vogue was, as *Infants* suggests, problematic at best. More had been achieved previously, and would be achieved thereafter, with less support and encouragement. The works of the Harlem Renaissance that bear comparison with earlier and later monuments of African-American narrative are Jean Toomer's *Cane,* published before the Harlem vogue had taken hold, and the novels of Zora Neale Hurston,[28] published well after the craze had run its course. Too many of the New Negro novelists, influenced perhaps by the commercial demand for what was in effect a generic Harlem novel, focused thematically on disspiriting topics of passing, intraracial color prejudice, and class divisions, concentrated stylistically on the atavistic and exotic local color of the Harlem cabarets, and turned away from the manifold approach many of them had defined earlier, in poetry and short fiction, that perceived the potential of an immanent selfhood in Harlem but also faced the ironies and actualities of black life. The literary promise of New Negro Harlem would not be realized next within the borders of either American or African-American literature but among the other literary generations of the Black Awakening outside of the United States.

4

Me revoici, Harlem

Black Harlem's meteoric rise to prominence coincided with the emerging racial self-awareness of parallel international generations of young black writers, particularly poets, born around the turn of the century, at roughly the same time as the New Negro generation, in different parts of the black diaspora. These authors, coming to adulthood like their New Negro contemporaries in the United States in the 1920s and 1930s, had grown up in decades when racism carried the authority of wide popular and scientific acceptance, but they were not disposed to endure the status quo ante as the permanent condition of the Negro race. Guided by somewhat older luminaries, such as Jean Price-Mars in Haiti and Fernando Ortiz in Cuba, these racial cohorts undertook the elaboration of a Negro identity in literature. Corresponding to the New Negro movement in the United States, their parallel movements – indigenism, in Haiti; *negrismo,* in Cuba and Puerto Rico; and negritude, in French West Africa and the Caribbean – laid the cultural framework of a philosophy of racial selfhood that shaped and directed the evolution of Africana literatures in this century. The literary use of Harlem by the New Negro poets, particularly Claude McKay and Langston Hughes, was available to these artists as a historically unique portent of their own impulse to assert the primacy of their experience and the authority of their blackness against the supposedly universal values of European culture, and, according to the respective views of their distinct cultures, they repeated and revised the motif of black Harlem.

Afro-Hispanic Poetry

The Harlem Renaissance of the New Negro writers paralleled a generational preoccupation with the Negro, in lusophone and hispanophone areas of the Americas, that produced a comparable type of literature – denominated variously as *poesía mulata, negroide, afro-americana, afro-antillana,* and *afro-brasileira* – that can be encompassed adequately by the general terms *poesía negra* and *negrismo*. In many, if not most, of the nations of Hispanic America and Brazil, the trend had its practitioners, including Max Jiménez of Costa Rica, Demetrio Korsi of Panama, Andrés Eloy Blanco of Venezuela, Jorge Artel of Columbia, Jorge Carrera Andrade of Ecuador, and Manuel Bandeira, Raul Bopp, Oswaldo and Mário de Andrade, and Jorge de Lima, the Brazilian Modernists of São Paulo and the Northeast. The interest in *poesía negra* was especially intense in the island nations of Cuba, Puerto Rico, and the Dominican Republic, as shown by the work of such poets as Luis Palés Matos, Emilio Ballagas, Nicolás Guillén, Manuel del Cabral, José Zacarías Tallet, Ramón Guirao, Regino Pedroso, Marcelino Arozarena, and Vicente Gómez Kemp.

In the Hispanic Antilles, Fernando Ortiz's ethnographic studies of the African element in Cuban society, particularly his *Glosario de afrocubanismo* (1924), called attention to the artistic and literary potential of Negro folklore, and gave a nativist focus to the international passion for Negro art and culture of the 1920s by renewing interest among Caribbean intellectuals in the variety of African customs and beliefs in the folk life of their mestizo cultures. These African survivals were taken as manifestations of a powerful and elemental Negro essence, and a variety of attempts was made to translate this cultural legacy into literary form. Sorcery, sexuality, masks, herbal medicine, oral traditions, folk religions, and rituals became the common themes of *poesía negra*. Stylistic experiments with the verse forms and rhythms of Afro-Latin songs and dances, the onomatopoeic sound effects of drums and animal sounds, and the perceived African sonority of *jitanjáforas* – nonsense syllables mimicking African dialects – attempted to convey the Negro mileau. The formal roots of *poesía negra* were to be found in the centuries-old traditions of Iberian and Latin American literature about blacks, for Lope de Vega, Lope de Rueda, Quevado, Góngora, and other writers of the Spanish Renaissance had imitated the language and music of Africans in literary works, and Sor Juana de la Cruz followed their example in the New World. As Rose E. Valdes Cruz notes,

> The vogue of the Negro in Europe and in the United States had repercussions in Hispanoamerica and made the artists and writers turn back to that element which was not foreign to them. . . . and it recreated a poetry that was not new, for it had been cultivated since the epoch of slavery, but now was given a modern literary treatment and a distinctly human focus, as an original and American subject in its form of expression.[1]

Richard L. Jackson contributes a necessary perspective, however, when he argues that "poetic Negrism in the Caribbean, which set the tone for the mainland, was, although seldom spoken of as such, primarily an exploitation of black culture by white writers." He continues, "[T]he white practitioners of poetic Negrism in this century were mostly European in their outlook, and they stood in awe of the black man as a curious, exotic, and sensual subject."[2] The Negro vogue in Latin America was a form of vanguardism reforming an outdated European literary heritage, simply one of many elements in the development of a Modernist spirit. An emphasis on Negro sensual and musical vitality was a means to that end. The anti-white, anti-European posturing sought freedom from the lingering domination of outdated cultural modes, in the context of a realignment with the culture of the West. Whereas the generational moment and the international context were shared by the practitioners of *negrismo* and *poesía negra* in Latin America and the New Negro artists in Harlem, the Creole artists' rediscovery of the African aspects of their mestizo culture was a renewed interest in a centuries-old tradition that for the most part had viewed Negroes in terms of their external exoticism, rather than in terms of the developing racial consciousness through which Negroes could explore their own subjectivity and selfhood, in the mode of the New Negro writers. Mário de Andrade's complaint against the "grito imperioso de brancura en mim" (imperious scream of whiteness in me), in his "Improviso do mal da America" (Impromptu on the evil, illness and woe of America) illustrates the point. The speaker catalogs accusations against that scream of whiteness, but the poem ends with a statement that would be impossible for the North American black writers for whom Harlem was a compelling motif:

> Mas eu não posso, não, me sentir negro ni vermelho!
> De certo que essas córes também teçem minha roupa
>   arlequinal
> Mas eu não me sinto negro, mas eu não sinto vermelho,
> Me sinto só branco, relumeando caridade e acolhimento,
> Purificado na revolta contra os brancos, as pátrias, as guerras,
> as posses, as prequiças e ignorâncias!
> Me sinto só branco agora, sem ar neste ar livre de América!
> Me sinto só branco em minha alma crivada de raças![3]

> *But I cannot, no, feel myself black or red!*
> *Certainly these colors also weave my harlequin clothing*
> *But I don't feel black, I don't feel red,*
> *I feel only white, beaming charity and welcome,*

Purified in the revolt against whites, fatherlands, wars,
possessions, indolence and ignorance!
I feel only white now, without air in this open air of America!
I feel only white, white only in my soul riddled with races.

The assertive racial consciousness that Harlem signified was foreign to the aesthetic of cultural *mestizaje,* and the picturesque vitality of the Negro that North American and European whites sought in Harlem was already available in a wealth of native and traditional folkloric forms. Only a few of the relatively large number of Afro-Hispanic poets, and apparently none of the Brazilians, employed the Harlem motif. Significantly, the Latin-American poets who did turn to the symbol of black Harlem were those who identified themselves with a racial as well as a cultural African heritage, by acknowledging a Negro ancestry in themselves and by asserting an ontology of black racial selfhood in Afro-Hispanic poetry that corresponded to the ethos of the New Negro in Harlem. "Casi color," for example, by the Ecuadorian Adalberto Ortiz, asserts the African elements of its speaker's mixed ancestry against the ideal of a colorless *mestizaje* and catalogs Harlem in his spiritual geography of blackness:

Aún recuerdo su voz fraternal que me decía:
Que no quiero ser negro.
Que no quiero ser blanco.
Es mi grito silencioso:
Quiero ser más negro que blanco.
. . . .
He vivido en Congo
y he soñado en Harlem:
He amado en Calidonia
y he dormido en Chicayá
y siempre un mapa de Africa
en todos los ojos enlutados
en todos los ojos sin color.
. . . .
Para olvidarme de todo
Quiero ser negro.
Negro como la noche preñada del día.
Negro como un diamante carioca.
Negro para el azul.
Negro con sangre-sangre.[4]

Although I recall your fraternal voice telling me:
That I don't want to be black.

That I don't want to be white.
My silent scream is:
I want more to be Negro than white.
. . . .

I have lived in the Congo
and I have dreamed in Harlem:
I've loved in Calidonia
and slept in Chicaya
and always a map of Africa
in all their crepe-hung eyes
in all their colorless eyes.
. . . .

I want to be black
to forget about everything
Black like the night pregnant with the day.
Black like a Carioca diamond
Blue-black
Blood-blood black.

And the Afro–Chinese Cuban Regino Pedroso's "Hermano negro" calls
on blacks everywhere, including Harlem, to discover in each other the
subjectivity of their shared racial and existential fraternity and express
their common causes together:

Negro, hermano negro,
tú estás en mí: habla!
Negro, hermano negro,
yo estoy en tí: canta!
. . . .

Negro, hermano negro;
más hermano en el ansia que en la raza.
Negro en Haití, negro en Jamaica, negro en New York,
                                    negro en la Habana,
– dolor que en vitrinas negras vende la explotación –,
eschucha allá en Scottsboro, en Scottsboro, en Scottsboro
                                                      . . .

Da al mundo con tu angustia rebelde,
tu humana voz . . .
y apaga un poco tus maracas![5]

Black man, black brother,
You're within me. Speak!

Black man, black brother,
I'm within you. Sing!
. . . .
Black man, black brother,
brother more in anxiety than race.
black man in Haiti, in Jamaica, New York, in Havana
– the pain hawking oppression in black shop windows –
listen now, in Scottsboro,
in Scottsboro, in Scottsboro . . .
show the world with your rebellious anguish,
your human voice . . .
and give the maracas a rest!

Manuel del Cabral, the celebrated Afro-Dominican poet, has characterized *poesía negra* as "the only literary occurrence until now in Latin America (except, of course, for the unique case of Rubén [Darío]) that has manifested an incontrovertible personality within our literature." Del Cabral distinguishes three levels of *poesía negra,* which he classifies from lower to higher value, as follows:

> First, the racial, with its expressiveness, its folklore, its color, its movement. Second, the magical, the imaginative, the mythical, the ritualized, the religious, the supernatural, etc. The third, the vital, the humane, the social, the universal. . . . [T]he first, animal and elemental, the second, cerebral and abstract. But I think that it is in the third state where *poesía negra* ascends and achieves the stature of universal and eternal poetry. . . . Because it is at this stage where man really is encountered in the living flesh.[6]

Although this hierarchy is questionable – not least of all because it implies that the racial and mythic level is, in some unstated way, separate from and inferior to the humane and universal third level – it is of interest that del Cabral's use of the Harlem motif seems to belong to the highest level of his critical scale. This Dominican poet apparently dedicated no poems to the subject of Harlem, but he consistently employed Harlem as an expressive point of reference for "the vital, the humane, the social, the universal" in some of his many poems about New York, the center of Yankee oppression. In the course of "Viejo chino de Brooklyn" (Old Chinaman in Brooklyn), a rhetorical question about Harlem is directed to Chan, the old Chinaman to whom the monologue is directed:

> Pero, chino,
> ¿sabes tú lo que cuesta todavía
> la piel del hombre hoy?

Oye a Harlem gritando. ¿Sabes lo qué es la tierra
puesta de pie en la voz?

(Manhattan es tu casa,
pero en tu propia casa, negro John,
que barato que compran
tu dolor.)[7]

But, Chinaman,
do you know how much the skin
of a man still costs today?
Listen to Harlem screaming. Don't you hear
the land standing up in her voice?

(Manhattan is your home,
but in your own home, Negro John,
how cheaply they buy your sorrow.)

In "Una carta para Franklin" (A letter for Franklin), addressed to Franklin Delano Roosevelt, New York is questioned in an aside:

Abuelo Nueva York: tú que tiemblas de cosmos
¿con qué noche te ordeña tu diurno metal?
No es la noche de Harlem ni tampoco la nuestra.[8]

Grandfather New York, you who tremble with the cosmos,
with what kind of night do you milk your daily metal?
It's not Harlem's night nor ours.

And in "Lo blanco regresa" (The white one returns), whose title seems
to refer to Christ's double role as sacrificial scapegoat (*blanco*, "target")
and apocalyptic destroyer of worlds (*fuego blanco del cielo*, "white fire
from heaven"), Harlem is an important element in Christ's return. When
New York, depicted allegorically as "un muchacho inflado de confort
. . . con humos de seguro atleta" (a boy puffed up with comfort . . .
with the air of a cocky athlete) asks, "¿Porqué como un perro / que el
amo maltrata, volviste al Planeta?" (Why have you come back to the
planet like a dog abused by its master?), the Christ figure replies that he
has returned to hear the sound of Harlem weeping, a sound to which the
youth is oblivious even though it seethes toward him, passing judgment
and condemning his world to nothingness.

¿Me entiendes? ¿Me escuchas?
¿No sientes que ahora te hierve ya un ruido?
¿No ves las hormigas? Allí Harlem lucha.

De su piel se agarra como un ladrido.
Es aquella barba de social espuma
que da con un rubio sonido sentencia.
y se ven los hombres entrar en la bruma . . .
y se ve tu siglo que va hacia la ausencia.[9]

Do you understand? Are you listening to me?
Don't you feel a noise seething toward you?
Don't you see the ants? There Harlem struggles.
To its skin the weeping clings like slander.
It is that beard of social scum
which passes sentence with a fair sound.
And men are seen entering the mist . . .
and your world moves toward nothingness.

For the Afro-Cuban Nicolás Guillén, Harlem was an equivocal symbol. His early essay "El camino de Harlem" (April 21, 1929) was not
about Harlem but about the challenge of Cuban racism, disguising an
increasing racial separatism beneath a facade of occasional interracial
good fellowship. Guillén used Harlem in this essay as the symbol of a
negative racial problematic:

> Senselessly, we are moving apart in many areas where we ought
> to be united; and as the time passes, this division will be already
> so deep that there will not be space for a final embrace. That
> will be the day when every Cuban settlement – it reaches to all –
> has its "black barrio." And that is the road, that everyone, those
> who are the color of Martí, as well as those of use who have the
> same skin as Maceo, should avoid.
>
> That is the road to Harlem.[10]

The road to Harlem was not to be taken, in Guillén's view, but he came
to respect the effectiveness of the Harlem motif. His consciousness of its
eloquence as a symbol allowed him simply to mention Harlem's name
in the title and repeat it in the essay's concluding phrase to invoke its
powerful associations. This equivocal feeling for Harlem also characterized the two poems by Guillén that employ the Harlem motif.

In "Pequeña oda a un boxeador cubano," Nicolás Guillén brilliantly
evokes an equivocal mix of innocent exultation and cautious disbelief in
Broadway's championship ring and in the metaphoric "rings" of Harlem
and Havana by presenting the voice of a disillusioned social observer
considering the image of a cocky new champion:

Tus guantes
puestos en la punta de tu cuerpo de ardilla,
y el *punch* de tu sonrisa.[11]   (p. 52)

Your gloves
at the tip of your squirrelly body
and the punch of your smile.

The boxer in the ring can be identified with the New Negroes in Harlem
and Havana, for like them he is alert, confident, confrontational, and
victorious. And his new situation feels so good that even Guillén's
speaker is captivated:

En realidad acaso no necesites otra cosa,
porque como seguramente pensarás,
ya tienes tu lugar.   (p. 54)

In reality, perhaps you've got it all
because, as you certainly think,
you've found your niche.

The speaker, whose skepticism is born of centuries of the black experience, cautions the boxer. The Broadway that "unta de asombro su boca
de melón" (oils its melon-mouth with fear), when the boxer leaps "como
un moderno mono" (like a modern monkey),

es el que estira su hocico con una enorme lengua húmeda
para lamer glotonamente
toda la sangre de nuestro cañaveral.   (p. 52)

is the very Broadway
that roots its snout with its moist enormous tongue,
to lap up gluttonously
all our canefields' blood.

But the first flush of the boxer's fame, like the first rush of pride in
other rings of the Negro enthusiasm, after centuries of contempt and
humiliation, overwhelms caution and skepticism:

Es bueno, al fin y al cabo,
hallar un *punching bag*
eliminar la grasa bajo el sol,
saltar,
sudar,
nadar,

y de la suiza al *shadow boxing,*
de la ducha al comedor,
salir pulido, fino, fuerte
como un bastón recién labrado
con agresividades de *black jack.*
Y ahora que Europa se desnuda
para tostar su carne al sol
y busca en Harlem y en La Habana
jazz y son
lucirse negro mientras aplaude el bulevar,
y frente a la envidia de los blancos
hablar en negro de verdad.   (p. 54)

It's great, after all,
to find a punching bag,
to work the fat off in the sun –
to leap,
to sweat,
to swim –
and from the brawling to the shadowboxing,
from the shower to the dining room,
come out polished, fine, and strong
like a newly crafted cane
with the aggressiveness of a blackjack.
And now that Europe strips
to tan its hide in the sun
and looks in Harlem and Havana
for jazz and son:
to flaunt your blackness while the boulevards applaud
and to the envy of the whites
talk black talk for real.

The version of "Pequeña oda a un boxeador cubano" in *Sóngoro cosongo* suppressed a reference which suggests that Guillén's distrust of Harlem applied, at least for a time, also to Langston Hughes: "De seguro a ti / no te preocupa Waldo Frank, / ni Langston Hughes / (el de 'I, too, sing America')"[12] (For certain you are not worrying about Waldo Frank, nor Langston Hughes either, the one of "I Too Sing America").

    The same equivocal feelings about Harlem were articulated also in "Un negro canta en Nueva York" (A Negro sings in New York). The poem is related to several Harlem poems cited previously. Its initial vision of New York as "piedra y humo / y humo y plomo / y plomo y llama / y llama y piedra y plomo y humo" (p. 64) (Rock and smoke / and smoke and lead / and lead and flame / and flame and rock and lead and smoke) recalls the mechanized and dehumanized cityscapes of Federico García Lorca and Manuel del Cabral. The Negro in New York in Guillén's poem, like his counterparts in their Harlems, offers the only human force in the barren setting. And, like the Harlems of many poets in this period (for example, Adalberto Ortiz, who has "soñado en Harlem," or Langston Hughes, whose Harlem was the dreamscape of the blues), Guillén's Negro in New York is associated with a dream of racial amplitude:

> · Tengo un pedazo de sueño,
> paloma,
> que un soñador me dejó:
> con ese sueño, paloma,
> voy hacer yo
> una estrella y una flor.
> (La estrella y su resplandor.
> El resplandor en la flor).
>
> (p. 66)

> *I have a piece of a dream,*
> *dove,*
> *a dreamer left to me:*
> *with that dream, dove,*
> *I'm going to make*
> *a star and a flower.*
> *(The star and its resplendence.*
> *The resplendence in the flower.)*

But Guillén elucidated the progression from dream to actualization of the dream in the Negro's song. Besides "un pedazo de sueño," the Negro in New York has "un pedazo de canto," a piece of song left him by a poet to make a hymn against Jim Crow to give the dream form. He also has "un pedazo de hierro," a piece of steel left by a blacksmith to make a hammer and sickle with which to bring the dream and its cultural formulation to social reality.

Indigenism and Negritude

New Negro poetry in the United States also had its francophone counterpart in the Haitian Renaissance of the 1920s and 1930s and among

black students from West Africa and the Caribbean in Paris in the 1930s.
The international cultural context was the same for the Haitian indigenist
and the negritude movements as it was for the black nascence in Harlem
and Afro-Hispanic poetry in Ibero-America. The postwar interest in Negro sculpture, initiated by Picasso and Matisse, and a Paris vogue for
Josephine Baker and the jazz band of Lieutenant James Europe in Paris,
were reinforced by an extensive literature about the Negro in French,
including Blaise Cendrar's *Anthologie nègre* (1921), René Maran's *Batouala*
(1921), Maurice Delafosse's *Les noirs d'Afrique* (1923), and André Gide's
Voyage au Congo (1927).

Of particular importance to the Black Awakening in Haiti was the
cultural response to the United States's intervention in Haitian affairs
and its occupation of the island from 1915 to 1934, a response articulated
in the ethnological studies of Haitian folklore of Dr. Jean Price-Mars.
The proud, sophisticated Haitian elite had found itself oppressed by the
humiliating racial ideology of the occupiers, many of them Navy officers
from the American South. Dr. Price-Mars demonstrated that Africa was
a center of ancient civilizations and suggested that the popular tales,
songs, legends, proverbs, and beliefs of Haiti proceeding from such ancient roots offered writers a valuable and inexhaustible lore of cultural
value. The founding of the *Revue Indigène* by a pleiade of young Haitian
writers in 1927, with the aim of emphasizing nativist cultural values,
initiated an exceptionally fertile period in twentieth-century Haitian literature. A majority of the poets interviewed by Naomi Garret for her
study of the Haitian Renaissance listed "lectures by Dr. Mars" as the
principal influence on the indigenist generation's racial and cultural *prise
de conscience*.[13] "[The Haitians] turned within themselves and to their distant past to seek what there was, if anything, in their traditions and heritage of which they could be proud," writes Garret. "Here, at least, was
something entirely theirs and inaccessible to the Americans."[14]

The cultural aesthetic now known as "negritude," with roots in the
Paris salon of Mlle. Paulette Nardal and the *Revue du Monde Noir*
(1931–2), as well as in the ethnological writings of Price-Mars, was proclaimed in the single issue of *Légitime Défense* (1932) and given form in
the pages of *L'Etudiant Noir* (1934–6). The Paris manifestos of *Légitime
Défense* constituted a kind of declaration of war against Christian, capitalist, bourgeois culture by young students from the French island of Martinique, who vowed to use surrealism and communism – the most recent
philosophical innovations of Western civilization – against the authority
of Western civilization and its cultural imitators in the Caribbean. The
creation of a literature that bespoke the issues cited in *Légitime Défense*,

however, fell to a different group of young blacks, writing in another periodical: *L'Etudiant Noir,* led by Léon Damas, Léopold Senghor, and Aimé Césaire, who coined the term "negritude" in its pages.

The example of the New Negro movement in Harlem was another important influence on the development of the indigenist movement and the negritude aesthetic, for the writers of New Negro Harlem were known both in Paris and Port-au-Prince. Countee Cullen was the subject of an article by Dominique Hippolyte, in an early issue of the *Revue Indigène.* Langston Hughes had been introduced to the Haitian literati by Jacques Roumain on a visit to Port-au-Prince, and from 1933 until the demise of *La Relève,* René Piquion regularly published translations of Hughes's blues poetry. Frank Schoell's "La renaissance nègre aux Etats-Unis," in *La Revue de Paris* (January 1, 1929), introduced many of the New Negro authors in French translation, and Carl Van Vechten's *Nigger Heaven,* Walter White's *Fire in the Flint,* and Claude McKay's *Banjo* and *Home to Harlem* were available in French translation in Paris.[15] The New Negro movement of black Harlem in the 1920s was an invigorating contrast to the submission to European literary models still marking Antillean literature in French in the early 1930s and foreshadowed the cultural appetite and generational destiny that had yet to be articulated by the Negro poets of French expression. "The wind rising from Black America will soon sweep the West Indies clean, we hope, of all the stunted fruit of its outdated culture," Etienne Léro proclaimed in "Misère d'une poésie."[16] Price-Mars, in "A propos de la 'renaissance nègre' aux Etats-Unis," in *La Relève,* called on Haitian writers to follow the example of the New Negro writers in America.

The figurative use of the Harlem motif by the poets of the Harlem Renaissance anticipated the Haitian indigenists and the negritude poets. Reading Jean-Paul Sartre's genial "Orphée noir," which served as a preface to Léopold Senghor's classic *Anthologie de la nouvelle poésie nègre et malgache de langue française* (1947), one is struck by the observation that Sartre's analysis of negritude can be illustrated in many respects by Harlem poems of the New Negro poets, for Sartre's "prise de conscience" of revolutionary negritude involves a similar perceived black, and even African, subjectivity:

> The black who calls his brothers of color to take conscience of themselves seeks to present to them a model image of their negritude and will plunge into his soul to extricate this image which he is seeking. He wishes to be at the same time a beacon and a mirror. The first revolutionary will be the apostle of black soul, the herald who will tear this negritude from himself to

offer it to the world, a demi–prophet, a demi–advocate, in brief a poet, in the precise sense of the word "vates."[17]

Langston Hughes's identification of Harlem as a landscape of the blues is a prime example of what Sartre defines as one of the two roads that converge toward this original simplicity of racial being:

> An objective negritude which expresses itself in the customs, the arts, the song and the dances of African populations. The poet as a spiritual exercise submits himself to the fascination of primitive rhythms, and allows his thought to run in the traditional forms of black poetry.[18]

And when one considers Sartre's definition of the alternative approach to one's negritude, in the Orphic descent of the Negro "de rentrer chez soi à reculons" (to go home backward), one discovers an elaboration of the very tension between perception and observation, possibility and actuality, and being and becoming that is the common issue of the Harlem poems of the New Negro authors. For the New Negro poet, like the negritude poets cited in Sartre's preface,

> It is necessary to plunge under the superficial crust of reality, of common sense, of reasonableness, in order to touch the bottom of the soul and to awaken the immemorial powers of desire. Of desire which makes man a rejection of all and a love of all; of desire, radical negation of natural laws and of the possible, the call of miracles; of desire which by its mad cosmic energy replunges man into the boiling bosom of Nature and raises him at the same time over nature by the affirmation of his right to dissatisfaction.[19]

Put aside the "surréaliste" label, and we find that Sartre's definition of this alternative method of approaching one's negritude can be substantially applied to the use made of the motif of Harlem in New Negro poetry: in the Harlem wine of Countee Cullen, which "hurtle[s] flesh and bone past fear / Down alleyways of dreams"; in the visions of Helene Johnson's Harlemites, who disdain the urban reality to perceive that "palm trees and mangoes stretch before your eyes"; in the Harlem shadows of Claude McKay, which "bend and barter at desire's call"; and in the pretension to elegance of Maggie from Spartanburg and Tom from Martinique, satirized by Sterling Brown. Speaking of Césaire, Sartre writes: "Perhaps it is necessary in order to understand this indissoluble unity of suffering, of eros, of joy, to have seen the Negroes in Harlem dance frenetically to the rhythm of the blues, which are the most desolate songs of the human race."[20] Sartre's definition of the *méthode surréaliste* (Hughes's "jazzonia," in an altered mode) recalls many lines from *The Weary Blues:* "Does a jazz band ever sob?"[21]; "The rhythm of life / Is a jazz rhythm, / Honey, / The gods are laughing at us"[22]; and "Hey! Hey! / That's what the / Blues singers say. / Singing minor melodies / They laugh, / Hey! Hey!"[23]

Harlem was a motif of the impulse to reassert the legitimacy of blackness, in the paradoxical and ambivalent terms of one's perceptions. In the terms of Sartre's analysis, the motif of New Negro Harlem would be the subjectivity object of a still-unformulated concept of blackness that had preceded negritude and part of what Aimé Césaire calls

> . . . mon originale géographie aussi; la carte du
> monde faite à mon usage, non pas teinte aux
> arbitraires couleurs des savants, mais à la
> géomètrie de mon sang répandu.[24]

> . . . *my original geography also; the map of the*
> *world made to my use, not dyed the*
> *arbitrary colors of the masters, but with the*
> *geometry of my spattered blood.*

Césaire makes an explicit reference to Harlem, in *Cahier d'un retour au pays natal,* as an emblem of black suffering in the geography of oppression that exploits all peoples:

> Comme il y a des hommes-hyènes et des hommes-
> panthères, je serais un homme-juif
>
> un homme-cafre
> un homme-hindou-de-Calcutta
> un homme-de-Harlem-qui-ne-vote-pas[25]

> *As there are hyena men and leopard men,*
> *I would be a Jew-man*
> *a Kaffir-man*
> *a Hindu-man-from-Calcutta*
> *a man-from-Harlem-who-cannot-vote*

And Paul Niger includes Harlem in a geographic litany of injustice, in "Nuit sur les bords de la Mekrou":

> Toi qui n'as pas de nom mais comprends tous
>   les noms
> Ourou, Chabi, Gnon, Moussa, Jacques ou Zinsou

Toi qui n'es pas Batoulé-batoulé mais
Batoulé-Fon, Batoulé-Bambara, Batoulé-Galibi
Corps de Batoulé uni aux corps de tous les
                nègres du monde
Batoulé de Harlem, Batoulé de Louisiane, de
                Port-au-Prince ou de Port of Spain
Nègre à la grandeur du monde, niger-nigrorum,
Pour qui toute honte des nègres est ta honte,
                ta joie toute joie nègre[26]

You who have no name but includes all the
                names
Ourou, Chabi, Gnon, Moussa, Jacques, or Zinsou
You who are not Batoule-Batoule but
Batoule-Fon, Batoule-Bambara, Batoule-Galibi
A corps of Batoules unified in the army of all
                the Negroes of the world
Batoule of Harlem, Batoule of Louisiana, of
Port-au-Prince or Port of Spain
Negro to the grandeur of the world, niger-nigrorum,
For whom all shame about Negroes is your
                shame, your joy all Negro joy

In "Nedje," Roussan Camille reflects that same geography of oppression, using terms specifically shaped by Claude McKay's use of Harlem:

Tes yeux étaient pleins de pays
de tant de pays,
qu'en te regardant
je voyais ressurgir
à leurs fauves lumières
les faubourgs noirs de Londres,
les bordels de Tripoli,
Montmartre,
Harlem,
tous les faux paradis
où les nègres dansent et chantent
pour les autres.[27]

Your eyes are full of countries
so many countries
that when I looked at you
I saw arise

in their wild light
the dark suburbs of London
the brothels of Tripoli,
Montmartre,
Harlem,
every pseudoparadise
where Negroes dance and sing for others.

The latter makes a single reference to Harlem, in a single verse of a rather long poem that echoes and amplifies the prototype of the "falsely smiling face" of McKay's "Harlem Dancer." The repeated phoneme in "fauves" and "faubourgs" echoes and reechoes the falsity of the smiling face of McKay's dancer. It predicts and intensifies the signification of falseness of "tous les faux paradis," among which Harlem is specifically identified with Montmartre and Tripoli, and underscores the gap between appearance and inner reality. The falsely smiling face of McKay's "Harlem Dancer" is also alluded to in a verse from "Satchmo," by Guy Tirolien, whose speaker, like McKay's, distinguishes between inner perception and the superficial observation of Harlem cabaret life:

> joie trúquée des filles noires
> > des filles jaunes
> dans les cabarets noirs
> > de Harlem
> cherchant au fond d'un whisky brun
> > d'un whisky or
> le visage oublié
> > d'un garçon brun / d'un garçon jaune
> > > de Bâton Rouge
> > > ou de Natchez[28]

> *Joy faked by black girls*
> > *by yellow girls*
> *in the black cabarets*
> > *of Harlem*
> *looking in the bottom of a shot of brown whiskey*
> > *of gold whiskey for*
> *the forgotten face*
> > *of a brown boy / of a yellow boy*
> > > *from Baton Rouge*
> > > *or from Natchez*

The "joie trúquee" by Tirolien's Harlem cabaret girls is among the elements expressed in the sobs and strides of Satchmo's cadences, which the reader might prefer not to recognize, so the poem concludes:

> non
> ne fermez pas l'oreille
> aux rires aux soupirs
> aux délires
>
> aux éclats aux oua–oua
> à la joie
> qui se bousculent –
> > ha ha!
> qui s'accumulent –
> > j'te crois!
> > – dans la trompette de Satchmo[29]

> *no*
> *don't shut your ears*
> *to the laughter to the sighs*
> *to the madness*
> *to the peals of the wah-wah*
> *to the joy*
> *that bump –*
> > *ha ha!*
> *that build –*
> > *I believe 'ya!*
> > *– in the trumpet of Satchmo*

Jacques Roumain, Léopold Senghor, and Jean Brièrre were the poets of the generation of the Black Awakening, writing in French, who employed the Harlem motif as specific and sustained subjectivity objects of negritude in major poems. Jacques Roumain's "Langston Hughes" echoes Hughes's "The Negro Speaks of Rivers" with a touch of irony, for the catalog of historic rivers carrying the Negro's history and symbolizing the profundity of the Negro soul is here a bittersweet series of inconclusive, personal encounters over a vast geographic range, which Roumain recapitulates in a verse:

> Tu as promené ton coeur nomade, comme un Baedecker, de
> Harlem à Dakar
> La mer a prêté à tes chants un rythme doux et rauque, et
> ses fleurs d'amertume écloses de l'écume[30]

You have carried your nomad heart like a Baedeker,
From Harlem to Dakar.
The sea lent to your songs its sweet wild rhythm
And its bitter flowers blossoming in the foam

And so Hughes, now back in Harlem, is presented as sitting in a cabaret at dawn, like one of his own subjects in *The Weary Blues,* murmuring, in accented French, "Jouez ce blues pou' moa / O jouez ce blues pou' moa" ("Play those blues for me! / O, play those blues for me!").[31] Roumain evokes the silver trees and shining rivers of the soul of the cabaret in "Jazzonia," as well as the ancient dusky rivers of "The Negro Speaks of Rivers," as he answers Hughes's blues call with a pensive question ("Rêves-tu de palmes et de chants de pagayeurs au crépuscule?" [Are you dreaming of palm trees and the river songs of the oarsmen at dusk?]), completing the poem in the spirit, form, and structure of the blues. "Langston Hughes" is a fitting tribute to Hughes's Harlem, as it is a tribute to the poet himself; Roumain celebrates his friend's already evident commitment to an ancient racial dream, in the face of disheartening actualities, by employing the terms of Hughes's version of the Harlem motif with remarkable exactness. The Harlem that set Hughes's "coeur nomade" to wandering is the very Harlem to which he is shown returning to hear the blues, which revive and sustain his spirit for the journey on the deep rivers of soul.

Whereas Roumain employed the Harlem motif in the precise terms of Langston Hughes's topography, the Haitian Jean Brièrre, and the Senegalese Léopold Senghor, shaped Harlem differently, to serve other literary purposes. Brièrre's "Harlem" addresses the black neighborhood's various moods and experiences, then wonders rhetorically when and where does Harlem do the only thing it has never been observed doing: sleeping. The otherwise all-knowing voice of the speaker can offer only a tentative response to his own inquiry:

> Où dormez–vous, Harlem?
> Peut–être vous appuyez–vous
> doucement à la musique des saxos ivres
> comme à une présence souveraine?
>
> Quand dormez–vous, Harlem?
> Peut–être effeuillez–vous la dernière étoile
> dans votre coupe fragile
> et retrouvez à la porte de l'aube
> la peine,
> le travail,

la fatigue,
la misère,
l'heure qui sonne en glas
et votre coeur las et seul
sur la route hostile et noire.[32]

Where do you sleep, Harlem?
Perhaps you rest
quietly on the music of some drunken saxophones
as if in some sovereign presence?

When do you sleep, Harlem?
Perhaps you pluck the leaves of the last star
in your fragile cup
and find again at the portals of the dawn
the pain,
the travail,
the weariness,
the misery,
the hour which tolls a knell
and your heart weary and alone
on the black and hostile road.

But in Brièrre's "Me revoici, Harlem," the empathic note becomes a chord of racial solidarity as the horror of a lynching in Georgia – the specific inspiration of the poem – rekindles a sense of ancient fraternity between the Haitian speaker and his long-lost African twin. Brièrre's response to a lynching in Georgia, it should be noted, is not addressed to the immediate victims of the incident but to all African-Americans, in the symbolic figure of Harlem. The poem laments the memory of a shared tragedy of slavery that has separated the black brothers since 1600 but announces their reunion:

Me revoici, Harlem. Ce drapeau, c'est le tien,
Car le pacte d'orgueil, de gloire et de souffrance,
Nous l'avons contracté pour hier et demain:
Je déchire aujourd'hui les suaires du silence.
. . . .
Nous avons désappris le dialecte africain,
Tu chantes en anglais mon rêve et ma souffrance,
Au rythme de tes blues dansent mes vieux chagrins,
Et je dis ton angoisse en la langue de France.
. . . .
Quand tu saignes, Harlem, s'empourpre mon mouchoir.

Quand tu souffres, ta plainte en mon chant se prolonge.
De la même ferveur et dans le même soir,
Frère Noir, nous faisons tous deux le même songe.[33]

Here I am again, Harlem. This flag is yours,
For the pact of pride, of glory and of suffering.
We contracted it for yesterday and tomorrow:
I am tearing up today the shroud of silence.
. . . .
We have forgotten the African dialect,
You sing in English my dreams and my suffering.
To the rhythm of your blues my old sorrows dance,
And I speak your anguish in the language of France.
. . . .
When you bleed, Harlem, my handkerchief is stained.
When you suffer, your lament in my song is prolonged.
With the same fervor and in the same evening,
Black Brother, we two sing the same song.

Naomi Garret has noted that Brièrre acknowledged the paramount influence of Langston Hughes on his ideas,[34] and echoes of Hughes resound in both poems. The speakers reflect Hughes's omnipresent and oracular voice of "The Negro Speaks of Rivers," as the panorama of a common black history in "Me revoici, Harlem" elaborates the historical vision of Hughes's first poem. But Brièrre's "Harlem" and "Me revoici, Harlem" also introduced an innovation to the motif, which would be widely imitated in its later phases: Brièrre presented Harlem as the personification of the African-American experience. Prior to Brièrre, the motif of black Harlem had always retained its character, in the imagery of the Black Awakening, as *situs*. Sidney Alexander's Harlem is a strange forest; Federico García Lorca's a surreal kingdom; Salvatore Quasimodo's a transformed storefront church; and William Rose Benét's is an animated landscape. Similarly, Countee Cullen's wine flows in Harlem, and Claude McKay's prostitutes dance and walk in Harlem; Brown's Harlem is a doubtful Mecca, and Helene Johnson's peculiar specters of Africa haunt Harlem's streets. To apostrophize the Harlem River, as does Yvan Goll, is a figurative maneuver that does not alter the understanding of Harlem as a place, and to speak of Harlem's "sons," with Fenton Johnson, is to follow a rhetorical practice that need not invoke a personal image. After Brièrre, however, the Harlem genre would include the idea of Harlem as a human personality representing all of black America.

Léopold Senghor depicted Harlem, on the other hand, as an urban celebration of the negritude of the African personality and its humanizing mission in the mechanized West – an immanent Harlem in the metallic wasteland of New York City, recalling García Lorca's and Manuel del Cabral's New York. But whereas García Lorca's image of Africa in Harlem was the totemic *mascarón* of a destructive dance of death, Senghor proclaimed Harlem to be the vision and the voice of God: "Dieu qui d'un rire / de saxophone créa le ciel et la terre en six jours. / Et le septième jour, il dormit du grand sommeil nègre" (God who with a saxophonic laugh created the heavens and the earth in six days. And on the seventh day, he slept his great Negro sleep).[35] Using the jazz accompaniment popularized by Langston Hughes, and employing James Weldon Johnson's image of God as a Negro laborer in "Creation," Senghor's speaker prophesies of Harlem:

> Harlem Harlem! voici ce que j'ai vu Harlem Harlem!
> > Une brise verte de blés sourdre des pavés labourés
> > par les pieds nus de danseurs Dans
> Croupes ondes de soie et seins de fers de lance, ballets de
> > nénuphars et de masques fabuleux
> Aux pieds des chevaux de police, les mangues de l'amour
> > rouler des maisons basses.

> *Harlem Harlem! Here is what I have seen. Harlem Harlem!*
> > *A breeze green with wheat springing from the*
> > *pavements plowed by the bare feet of dancers in Cresting*
> *waves of silk and breasts of fers-de-lance*
> > *ballets of water lilies and fabulous masks*
> *At the feet of the police horses, mangoes of love*
> > *rolling from the low houses.*

Senghor's prophecy for New York is that the city will find its salvation in the African humanism of black Harlem. Senghor's poetic voice, like one of God's trombones sundering the barriers between New York and Harlem, calls New York to accept the saving gift of Africa and revive its congealed soul:

> Ecoute New York! ô écoute ta voix mâle de cuivre ta voix
> vibrante de hautbois, l'angoisse bouchée de tes larmes
> tomber en gros caillots de sang
> Ecoute au loin battre ton coeur nocturne, rythme et sang
> du tam-tam, tam-tam sang et tam-tam.[36]

Listen, New York, oh listen to your brassy male voice your
vibrant oboe voice, the muted anguish of your tears falling
in great clots of blood
Hear the distant beat of your nocturnal heart, rhythm and
blood of the tam-tam, tam-tam blood and drums.

Thus the ontology of racial being in Harlem, regarded as an atavistic return to primitive modes and perceived in moot and problematic ways by the New Negro writers, evolved into a more formal and fuller thematic articulation by Langston Hughes and was echoed by Roussan Camille, Guy Tirolien, and Paul Niger, evoked nostalgically by Jacques Roumain, transformed fraternally into a bond of solidarity by Jean Brière, and celebrated as the saving humanism of an Africana ethos by Léopold Senghor. Black Harlem was acknowledged and employed by black francophone poets as a shared motif of the African experience, transcending boundaries of geography, language, or nationality – and even of ethnicity, in Senghor's case. It is ironic, therefore, that in the 1930s, when the negritude poets were discovering their art in terms that Langston Hughes and his New Negro contemporaries had anticipated, most of the New Negro voices had fallen silent, and Langston Hughes was employing the motif of Harlem in what Sartre characterized as the opposite "prise de conscience" to negritude – one rooted in the rational, materialistic, positivistic, and antipoetic language of the European proletariat and expressed in such poems as "The Same" (*Negro Worker*, 1932), "Advertisement for the Waldorf-Astoria" (*New Masses*, 1931), and "Air Raid over Harlem" (*New Theatre*, 1936).[37] Perhaps Hughes's return in the 1940s to the blues and jazz motif of Harlem was energized and enabled by the example of the negritude poets, who had amplified his initial impulse to express black soul in the Harlem motif to a degree and an implication beyond the concepts of the New Negro writers of the Harlem Renaissance.

II

The Emerging Ghetto: The 1940s and 1950s

Harlem Riots, 1943.

5

The Emerging Ghetto

A decade after Alain Locke's optimistic prophecies in "The New Negro," Harlem was still a city of migrants, but no longer of refuge and hope.[1] The legendary promise of refuge and cultural hope had been circumscribed by the evident deterioration of the fabled Negro enclave in the 1930s and 1940s, and the Harlem motif that bespoke a racial dream was becoming one more demonstration of denial. On March 19, 1935, barely one decade after the glittering debut of the New Negro renaissance, a rumor of the death of a juvenile shoplifter at the hands of police on 125th Street sparked a violent disturbance in Harlem, which, according to a subcommittee of the New York County Lawyer's Association, "surprised no one who has been in touch with the conditions under which we have permitted our Negro citizens to live."[2] A crowd began gathering at the store for news of the boy and grew angrier as one, then another, speaker denounced police brutality. The police ordered the crowd to disperse, but the arrival of an ambulance with a shrieking siren, followed by the coincidental appearance of a hearse, seemed to confirm the death of the boy and increased the hysteria. "The rumor of the death of the boy, which became now to the aroused Negro shoppers an established fact, awakened the deep-seated sense of wrongs and denials and even memories of injustices in the South," stated *The Complete Report of Mayor LaGuardia's Commission on the Harlem Riot of March 19, 1935*. "One woman was heard to cry out that the treatment was 'just like down South where they lynch us.' The deep sense of wrong expressed in that remark was echoed in the rising resentment which turned the hundred or more shoppers into an indignant crowd."[3] A brick crashed through a store window, and the crowd surged toward the store. Policemen went after the speakers who were inciting the crowd, and fistfights broke out. Eventually mobs spread out along 125th Street, stoning police, breaking store windows, and looting the exposed premises. At least four persons were killed, dozens were hospitalized, and business losses were in the hundreds of thousands of dollars. Later it was established that the juvenile shoplifter had not been shot, but the false rumor had "set aflame the smouldering resentments of the people of Harlem against racial discrimination and poverty in the midst of plenty,"[4] because the probability of a black youth being killed by a white policeman, just for trying to snitch a penknife, seemed reasonable to the expectations of a new mood in black Harlem.

The *Report on the Harlem Riot* documented many of the underlying causes disposing the Harlem community to believe the false rumor and react violently. These evil effects of racial discrimination in the 1930s summarized what Dominic J. Capeci termed the "vicious cycle" of ghetto living. Racial discrimination consigned many lower-class Afro-Americans to the most menial, lowest-paying, and least secure occupations. Economic deprivation and residential segregation, in turn, forced them into dilapidated tenements. High rent consumed much of their already scant income, leaving little for food and clothing. Underfed and ill-clad, living in congested and unsanitary quarters, the ghetto dweller's health suffered, but racial prejudice reduced the quality and availability of medical facilities. Home life degenerated as humiliated and underemployed men found raising a family frustrating, and broken homes, illegitimate children, and mental depression resulted. Inadequate supervision, and an education emphasizing vocational training rather than liberal arts, prepared youngsters only for menial employment, promoting juvenile delinquency and adult crime. In turn, police insensitivity to black people increased resentment, and the cycle was completed.[5]

This vicious cycle of ghetto living was not new in Harlem in 1935. Capeci merely provides a label for a syndrome of social problems that Osofsky had shown to exist in black Harlem even in the glory days of the 1920s. If the stock-market crash on Black Tuesday of 1929 had registered little immediate impact in Harlem, it was partly because the social and economic evils afflicting the nation in the depression had arrived earlier in Harlem as a result of racial discrimination, but the destructive social conditions worsened with the national crisis. Unemployment in Harlem was one-and-one-half to three times the rate for white New Yorkers, throughout the depression. According to most estimates, food prices were higher and quality generally poorer in Harlem than in the rest of New York City. Several of the major black churches had to organize soup kitchens, employment agencies, shelters for the homeless, and other relief services, in addition to coping with the economic burden of carrying the mortgages undertaken in the move to Harlem in more optimistic times. Evictions for nonpayment of rent were a daily event, as were the social disruptions that resulted when families found themselves on the sidewalk. In the first three months of 1931, Abyssinian Baptist Relief Bureau served 28,500 free meals. In 1933, the Brotherhood of Sleeping Car Porters was forced from its national headquarters. In 1934, 19,000 families were on Home Relief. By 1935, black ownership of real estate in Harlem slid from 35 to 5 percent.[6]

The March riot of 1935 was not entirely unprecedented. In 1928, a policeman's attempt to arrest a Negro in Harlem had led to a riot in which 2,500 Harlemites fought with some 150 policemen. The disorder was quelled only after police and firemen turned hoses on the crowd.[7] The 1928 riot had little impact on the general consciousness, and its memory was largely swept away, perhaps by the power of the Harlem mystique, but by 1935 the optimistic spirit had eroded, and the hopefulness had turned bitter and resentful. "Slum shocked" was Roi Ottley's term for Harlem's condition in 1935.[8] Harlem had been swamped by a new wave of economic refugees, fleeing from the even worse conditions of the Black Belt of the South. Its population had long since outdistanced the 204,000 figure given by the 1930 census. Its boundaries were being pushed rapidly toward 110th Street, on the south; 164th Street, to the north; Morningside Avenue and Amsterdam Avenue, to the west; and the Harlem River, to the east. Its black population was overflowing into new Negro enclaves in Brooklyn and Queens. Tuberculosis continued to thrive in the crowded, unsanitary conditions of the tenements, even though elsewhere in the city the scourge was beginning to be contained by improved medical practices. Public schools, chronically underfunded in Harlem, were so overcrowded that they operated on multiple shifts and irregular schedules. The neglect of delinquent or homeless Negro children by municipal authorities was compounded by the fact that many citywide charitable organizations specifically excluded Negroes from their social services.

So bad were the times that blacks were even losing control of the numbers rackets in Harlem. During Prohibition, the white mob had concentrated on the profits of bootlegged liquor and generally disregarded the smaller revenues of the numbers rackets, but as the end of Prohibition seemed politically inevitable, white racketeers began to look for other opportunities, and the Harlem numbers racket came to be of increasing interest to the masters of organized crime. An early shot in the mob's campaign to take over the numbers racket in Harlem may have been fired on September 21, 1928, when Caspar Holstein – the black Maecenas of the Harlem Renaissance, and the model for the bolito king in *Nigger Heaven* – was kidnapped and held for a ransom of fifty thousand dollars.

The kidnapper was widely believed to be Dutch Schulz and the purpose of the exercise the takeover of the numbers trade, although Holstein, who reappeared a few days later, refused to explain. In any case, the trade began to slip gradually from the control of individual black bankers. Judge Samuel Seabury's investigations of municipal corruption spotlighted the wealth of the numbers bankers and the large sums of money paid for protection to politicians and policemen. Dutch Schulz summoned the policy bankers of Harlem and dictated terms for the future. Many of the smaller bankers submitted. Several of the richer ones, some of whom did not wish to be associated with bootleggers and murderers, decided to retire. When Schulz was murdered in 1934, his black enemies in the numbers racket toasted his death, particularly Madam St. Clair, who managed to arrive on the scene of the murder not long after the bullets that ended Schulz's life, but effective control of the numbers racket passed to Schulz's white successors.

The disspiriting shadows over Harlem in the 1930s were not without breaks and bright spots. One of the brightest was Joe Louis. Like many a black American, Louis came from the poverty-stricken rural Black Belt of the South, but in the ring this black youth proved himself in a way that signified hope for black America. Joe Louis was not a native Harlemite, nor did he live in Harlem, but New York was the site of almost all his most celebrated victories, and on those trips the black contender usually stayed in Harlem. Ironically, the rising action of Louis's career coincided with the collapse of Harlem's promise. The fight that made Joe Louis famous, in 1935, was not simply against a white man but against an Italian, and it occurred at a time when Ethiopia was prey to Mussolini's imperialist delusions, just a few months after the March riot in Harlem. Consequently, "the brown bomber," undefeated in more than twenty-two professional fights as he aspired to the heavyweight championship of the world, was a kind of talisman. Wherever Louis went in Harlem, a crowd gathered to admire and touch this symbolic figure. In 1936, Louis fell to Max Schmeling of Germany, and Harlem was dismayed, but in 1937 Louis knocked out Jim Braddock to recapture the crown that had been stolen from Jack Johnson decades earlier. Louis's return bout with Schmeling in 1938, like Jesse Owens's exploits at the Berlin Olympics, carried powerful political overtones. Even more ironical, Joe Louis had become the "great black hope" of segregated America's international prestige as he confronted a challenger identified with Nazi philosophies of Aryan racial superiority, and Harlem felt vindicated by Joe Louis's victory.

Another bright spot among the shadows was the development of black political influence in New York City. African-American citizens, whose impact on the political life of New York City had been negligible well into the first decades of the twentieth century, began, in the 1930s, to exercise greater political power in the midst of social and economic decline. Politics was one arena of relative progress in the 1930s and early 1940s, largely because of the imposing number of voters in Harlem's burgeoning population, but Harlem's early break with the unrequited fealty that blacks had traditionally rendered the Republican Party as the party of Lincoln, its increasing commitment to militant collective action, and its new, independent political leadership were also important factors. Harlem was one of the first black communities to give significant support to the Democratic Party. In 1921, Harlem voted three to one for the Democratic candidate for mayor, John F. Hylan, and enjoyed various benefits as a result. During Hylan's administration, for example, black physicians were appointed for the first time to the staff of a municipal hospital, Harlem Hospital. In 1929, Charles W. Fillmore became the first African-American district leader in the history of New York City,[9] and Hylan's Democratic successor, Mayor Jimmy Walker, gave black doctors unrestricted access to Harlem Hospital in 1930. So, when after a decade of resistance the Republican-controlled legislature finally gerrymandered the divided judicial districts of Harlem into the unified Tenth District, Harlem elected two Democrats to be New York's first black judges.

In the early 1930s, the Harlem Communist Party, whose agitation had been spurned, for the most part, by blacks in the 1920s, moved more quickly than the traditional civil-rights organizations to take up the case of the Scottsboro Boys and began to enjoy direct and intimate contact with ordinary Harlemites. As a militant collective political spirit won greater acceptance in Harlem, the campaign for jobs against the large white-owned Harlem enterprises that refused to employ blacks became one important focus of community organization, and raising political and financial support for the Ethiopian monarchy in its fight against Italian aggression in the late 1930s became another. A new line of "unity against facism" in the mid-1930s, encouraging Communist Party activists to work with black organizations in a united front, positioned the Harlem Communist Party to exploit the campaign for jobs, as well as the support-for-Ethiopia movement, to further expand its membership and credibility in Harlem.

In this progressive political environment, The *Report on the Harlem Riot* offered a large number of recommendations for remedial action, many of which were implemented by Mayor Fiorello LaGuardia. Harlem River Houses, the Women's Pavilion at Harlem Hospital, and two new Harlem public schools were completed in the years following the riot of 1935. The number of black nurses and attendants at Harlem Hospital doubled, and the number of black physicians tripled. Black officeholders received significant mayoral appointments, and – most spectacular – the top-ranking black policeman in New York City was named parole commissioner. Adam Clayton Powell, Jr., emerged as the most prominent of several charismatic, grassroots leaders of boycotts, job campaigns, and protest parades, who concentrated on the voters of Harlem at a time when black leaders typically cultivated a national constituency of influential figures of both races. In 1941 Powell ran for the New York City Council and won, in spite of a citywide system of proportional representation that made it very difficult to elect a black.[10]

Although its reputation for fabulous nighttime entertainment was diminished by the depression and the riots, Harlem's cultural energy crested and surged in new ways. In 1934, Frank Schiffman and Leo Brent acquired Hurtig & Seamon's Music Hall on 125th Street, reopening it as the Apollo Theatre, and new legends continued to be created, in the mid-1930s, as younger blacks and whites were drawn to Harlem. The sounds and style of a new generation were epitomized on the dance floor of the Savoy Ballroom, in the late 1930s and early 1940s, as "jitterbugs," "hep cats," and "hipsters," both black and white, decked out in "zoot suits" and talking "jive," dubbed Harlem the "Big Apple" of a new national craze. The visual arts, which had taken a second place to literature in the Harlem Renaissance, flourished, with the formation in Harlem of "one of the more important groups of black painters and sculptors that have yet emerged in America."[11] This extraordinarily productive group – Romare Beardon, Norman Lewis, Ernest Crichlow, and Jacob Lawrence – was drawn into the orbit of Augusta Savage's workshop, which "attracted the gifted children in Harlem like a magnet,"[12] and of Charles Alston's studio, at 306 West 141st Street, which became a kind of cultural institution in its own right.[13]

A mood of frustration and disillusionment with Harlem was strong among the literati, however. By the mid-1930s, the writers of the New Negro movement had lapsed into silence, but no corresponding Harlem school of Afro-American writers had come into existence. In the "Foreward" to the first issue of *Challenge,* James Weldon Johnson wrote of "a degree of disillusionment and disappointment for those who a decade ago hailed with loud huzzas the dawn of the Negro literary millennium. We expected much; perhaps too much."[14] Countee Cullen wrote to the editor of *Challenge,* Dorothy West, "Lord knows I wish we could recapture the spirit of '26; I hope the bird hasn't flown forever."[15] In another issue, West editorialized, "We were disappointed in the contributions that came in from the new voices. There was little we wanted to print. Bad writing is unbelievably bad. We felt somewhat crazily that the authors must be spoofing and they didn't really mean us to take their stuff for prose or poetry."[16] Alain Locke spoke, in the *New Challenge,* of the "spiritual truancy" and "social irresponsibility" that had "vitiated" the writers of the Harlem Renaissance,[17] and the editors, including West and Richard Wright, eschewed any attempt to "restage the 'revolt' and 'renaissance' of ten years ago."[18]

With the onset of World War II, the status of blacks in the military created additional layers of frustration and resentment. Although some men, like Malcolm X, avoided the draft, and others took a kind of tacit satisfaction in Japanese victories that discredited the myth of white supremacy, many blacks were eager to answer the nation's call to arms. Harlem was proud of its youth in uniform, and the Harlem USO was one of the best organized and most faithfully supported of such facilities in the country. Nonetheless, the armed services restricted black enlistment and segregated those who managed to enter the service. Discrimination was commonplace in the war industries and civilian support efforts. The Red Cross, for example, refused blood plasma from black volunteers, although the concept of transfusing plasma had been developed by an African-American physician, Dr. Charles Drew. "The treatment accorded the Negro during the Second World War," James Baldwin wrote, "marks for me, a turning point in the Negro's relation to America. To put it briefly and somewhat too simply, a certain hope died, a certain respect for white Americans faded."[19] The ironics and contradictions of fighting overseas against second-class citizenship, authoritarian rule, and the belief in the racial superiority of whites, while suffering from those very same abuses at home, were unavoidable, and the plight of the black soldier shattered whatever naïveté blacks still had about the depths of American racism. Indeed, the March on Washington movement (MOWM), which anticipated the agenda and methodology of the Civil Rights movement, more than a decade later, was primarily a demand for an honorable place for blacks in the civilian and military war effort in the early 1940s. Significantly, its call was issued and organized from Harlem.[20]

When Detroit, a major industrial center of the war effort, erupted in a race riot on June 22, 1943, leaders and commentators feared that a similar outbreak might follow in Harlem. The mood of Harlem in the summer of 1943 was brilliantly evoked in *Notes of a Native Son* by James Baldwin, whose nineteenth birthday that year, on August 2, coincided not only with his father's funeral but with a riot in Harlem:

> All of Harlem, indeed, seemed to be infected by waiting. I had
> never known. it to be so violently still. . . . I had never before
> been so aware of policemen. . . . Nor had I ever been so aware
> of small knots of people. They were on stoops and on corners
> and in doorways, and what was striking about them, I think,
> was that they did not seem to be talking. . . . There was cer-
> tainly, on the other hand, between them, communication ex-
> traordinarily intense . . . ; something heavy in their stance
> seemed to indicate that they had all, incredibly, seen a common
> vision, and on each face there seemed to be the same strange
> bitter shadow.[21]

In spite of mutual distrust between Councilman Powell and Mayor La-
Guardia, white and black leaders managed to avert an outbreak in Harlem in July, but on August 1, 1943, when Harlem was swept up in another rumor – this time that a black soldier had been shot by a white
policeman in the Braddock Hotel – 125th Street exploded. People rushed
into the streets by the thousands as the rumor spread. Cars were over-
turned and set on fire. Store windows were smashed. Businesses were
looted and burned. Firemen, policemen, and other officials were stoned.
Appeals for peace and order by black spokesmen like Walter White and
popular white political leaders like Mayor LaGuardia were ignored or
caustically repulsed.

    After the events of March 19, 1935, and August 1, 1943, Harlem could
no longer be considered a unique location in the spiritual geography of
African America. The violence of the riot was an expression of a sense
that Harlem was no longer a haven. By the mid-1940s, Harlem was just
the best-known of the emerging ghettos of America's large urban centers
at midcentury. The historical imperatives of American racism were too
deeply imbedded to be uprooted by the charm and high culture of a
vanguard. The dynamics of racism in Harlem, formerly obscured and
overshadowed in the public imagination by an optimistic reading of
black Harlem's glossy Jazz Age veneer, as well as by the genuine differences between the relative freedom of Harlem's streets and those of the
rest of America, had been gradually exposed to general observation by
the stress of economic depression and the impact of a global war.

    Yet too much was vested in the racial promise of Harlem, proclaimed
by the generations of the Black Awakening. A whole generation of black
Americans had been raised on the legend. Malcolm X, for one, recalled:

> Even as far back as Lansing, I had been hearing about how fabu-
> lous New York was, and especially Harlem. In fact, my father
> had described Harlem with pride, and showed us pictures of the

huge parades by the Harlem followers of Marcus Garvey. And every time Joe Louis won a fight against a white opponent, big front-page pictures in the Negro newspapers such as the *Chicago Defender,* the *Pittsburgh Courier* and the *Afro-American* showed a sea of Harlem Negroes cheering and waving and the Brown Bomber waving back at them from the balcony of Harlem's Theresa Hotel.[22]

Although he understood that "almost everyone in Harlem needed some kind of hustle to survive, and needed to stay high in some way to forget what they had to do to survive," Malcolm X was "mesmerized," for even in the bitter years of the early 1940s, Harlem was "Lansing's West Side and Roxbury's South End magnified a thousand times."[23] "[T]his world," he concluded, "was where I belonged."[24] The idea of Harlem could not be disavowed, even in decline, but if Harlem were to remain the symbolic center of black America in the literature of this new phase, it would have to express some as yet unfathomed meaning. Ottley's *New World A-Coming* sensed the new temper: "Harlem is . . . a cross-section of life in Black America – a little from here, there and everywhere. . . . Harlem! The word itself signifies a vast, crowded area teeming with black men. . . . Though their skins may be black, brown, yellow, or white, they all are seeking a way out of the impasse of Negro life."[25]

6

Go Tell It on the Mountain

In the 1930s and 1940s, Harlem's deterioration created a crisis for the black cultural awakening represented by the literary trope of the 1920s. The trope was rooted in a popular reading of Harlem's rapid transformation into a vital black community as scriptural and prophetic, so fundamental alterations in the enclave's social and historical circumstances were regarded as signs of change to be deciphered and accommodated by the motif's meaning and authority. If Harlem were to survive as an emblem of racial renewal in the spiritual geography of the black world, a process of reinterpretation and revision would have to occur. In contrast to the writers of the Renaissance generation, who had initiated the theme of Harlem in poetry, novelists were the first writers of the new generation to turn their attention in imaginative literature to the decline of Afro-America's cultural capital, for the emerging Harlem ghetto offered rich material for the naturalistic impulse exemplified with such authority by Richard Wright in *Native Son*.

David Dortort's *Post of Honor* (1937)[1] and Carl Offord's *White Face* (1943),[2] by a white and a black writer respectively, are early representative expressions of dozens of naturalistic novels, ranging from forgettable potboilers to compelling popular fiction, set in whole or in part in a Harlem very different from the locale of the novels of the Harlem Renaissance. Both Dortort and Offord locate oppressive conditions of the emerging Harlem ghetto within the political context of global events. In *The Post of Honor* a single episode is set in Harlem. The story follows Max Gerard, a political idealist and struggling author, from the internecine rivalries of New York City leftist politics in the 1930s through wartime service in the South Pacific. Because he cannot get any other work before the war, Gerard takes a job in a large vegetable market in Harlem owned by a Syrian who delights in shortchanging "simple-minded, slow-thinking Negroes, counting their pennies as though they were dollars, never watching the scale, their eyes withdrawn and caught up by something a long way off, their voices soft when they called their selections and full of a ridiculous deference" (p. 103). Gerard is stacking cabbages when Harlem learns the news of Mussolini's invasion of Ethiopia and a black man runs past the store, blaming all white people: "The curse of evil on you! You raping Ethiopia! The curse of evil on you!" (p. 129). Feeling guilty of complicity in the small larcenies of the produce store, Gerard quits on the spot, walks down to the offices of the Harlem section of the Young Communist League, knowing that "the first voice raised in all of America, as in all of the world, would be the militant outcry of the Communist Party" (p. 133), and volunteers. Gerard is assigned to help alert Harlem by distributing copies of the *Daily Worker,* but even in the midst of Harlem's intense reaction to the invasion, the personal animosities of party workers intrude. Gerard is denounced by a white comrade from the Brownsville section of the party in Brooklyn. He is ordered off the streets, and Harlem vanishes from the novel, except for a brief "tug of memory" later, when Gerard, on a troop carrier, is reminded of the New York City ghetto by "the stinging whiplash of power" in the South Pacific.

Offord's *White Face* is rooted in the conventions of the "flight" genre of the 1920s, but the action of the novel develops around a near-murder, whose motivation in the social pathology of Harlem and the conflicts of international politics reflects the new perspectives for fiction about black life in America advanced by Richard Wright's *Native Son,* published only three years earlier, in 1940. The opening chapters of *The White Face* play out in compelling narrative detail the flight from southern peonage summarized by Rudolph Fisher in "City of Refuge." The north star of freedom, for Chris and Nella Woods, as for King Solomon Gillis, is Harlem, where there are "black people with rights just like any white man. Black people riding the trains, walking the sidewalks next-to-next with white folks. Black folks talking back to white folks, man to man. Harlem was paradise" (p. 17). This view is shared by a neighbor, who impulsively joins Chris and Nell in their flight. "I wish I was going to Harlem with you all. A nigger's a man up North" (p. 25). Harlem more than matches its billing. When Chris learns about the riots and the depression relief programs, he is astonished: "Harlem was truly wonderfully different. He tried to picture the scene of black men rioting in defiance of all the white folks and their police. Black men sitting at home by the thousands. Just sitting down and receiving government checks twice a month. It was too much for him. He smiled confusedly" (pp. 55–6). When Chris sees a typical 1930s Harlem political protest in action ("Harlem's a place for meetings," says his cousin), he is disturbed: "Chris walked in silence with his thoughts. Harlem was a strange place. Up here black folks really had freedom, he thought" (p. 77). Additionally, Chris's fear that he will be extradited to stand trial for murdering a white landowner who had tried to block his flight to freedom dominates the mood of this man of the rural South – who does not know how to read the signs of this new environment – and alienates him from those who might have best initi- ated him into Harlem's urban ways. Guilt about his baby daughter's death and secret burial in an empty lot compounds the lonely fear. Mis- trust, even of his wife, who gets cleaning work in the slave markets of the Bronx when he cannot, opens Chris to the resentful propaganda of a cell of fascist thugs operating in Harlem. Convinced of her infidelity, Chris follows Nell to her job in the Bronx, finds her in the company of a Jewish lawyer (who is only trying to help crush the extradition war- rant), and nearly kills the lawyer. With Chris in police custody, the long- ignored warrant gets national attention, as southern racist politicians, civil-rights organizations, and anti-Semites make the captured fugitive a cause celèbre.

In prison, Chris reaffirms his original purpose in fleeing to Harlem's proverbial refuge: "In Harlem, far from the whips of the riders, they were to have built and added forever to the sweetness and goodness. It was easy and good to think this way" (p. 310). Chris also begins to express a consciousness of the pervasive control exercised by what he terms "the white face" over "the black hand," even in Harlem. Unlike his prototype in "City of Refuge," who accepted the ironic figure of justice he saw embodied in a black policeman in Harlem, Chris's

> spirit insisted on a justice of its own making, his own under- standing. In the world that passed before him there was nothing that was his. The white face had taken all that the black hand had produced, had made the laws that governed the black hand and withered it. . . . His spirit lashed out during the black nights of his anguish. That he should die within this pattern made for him by the white face! That he should live and die by it, without smashing it, without cracking it, without even bruising it! (pp. 312–13)

Although Chris realizes that his wife's actions were taken largely on his behalf, his doubts about her fidelity are fed by her reliance on sympa- thetic whites in times of crisis: "She bared herself to the white face, her heart to the white God" (p. 314). After refusing all of Nell's attempts to visit him in prison, Chris consents to a single visit – only in order to commit suicide before her eyes. At its best, *The White Face* achieves some of the narrative power of Wright's *Native Son,* as it locates a somewhat older character of Bigger Thomas's typology, in the prototypical setting of Harlem, undergoing a struggle against social forces largely beyond the scope of his conceptions. Offord's ambitious attempt missteps, however, between the authenticity of the protagonist's paranoia and confusion, so well dramatized in the novel, and the untested political consciousness that is merely stated at the end. Consequently, the resonance of Chris Wood's conclusions with his delusions is puzzling, rather than ironic.

Bucklin Moon's *Without Magnolias* (1949)[3] and Phillip B. Kaye's *Taffy* (1950)[4] are representative of Harlem novels of the period in a different respect. The idea of Harlem remains a pivotal issue in both, although each is set, for the most part, outside of Harlem. Harlem's status as an idea is taken for granted in the use of the Harlem motif by the white author of *Without Magnolias.* Although the main action of the novel is set in the South on the eve of the Civil Rights movement, Harlem is invoked, frequently and consistently, as a kind of platonic form of what black life and thought can be, in a less oppressive if not actually ideal context, in contrast to the abject form experienced in the segregated South of the mid-1940s. For example, Ezekiel Rogers, the president of a struggling black college in Florida, tries to justify himself to the young rising star of his faculty by saying,

> Eric, when I go to New York I go to a lot of parties. I sit around until all hours drinking more than is good for me and arguing about the race question. I like that as much as the next one. But when I come home I'm not one of those Sugar Hill leaders sitting around with a scotch and soda in each hand. Down here I've got a problem. It's all around me and these crackers down here aren't fooling. They really play for keeps. (p. 23)

Harlem is a presence that also defines the philosophy and racial orientation of each of the principal actors in the novel. Alberta, a native of Citrus City, who has taken an advanced degree at Columbia University and has remained in Harlem, is understood to be "doing something for the race" (p. 4), whereas the contributions of Bessie, Alberta's younger sister and secretary to President Rogers, are taken for granted. Harlem is a kind of spiritual and intellectual standard even for one of the college's white trustees, who had advanced his own spiritual liberation as far as he dared in Harlem before returning south to inherit the editorship of the local newspaper. Significantly, the protagonist's crisis of conscience occurs in the novel's only chapter actually set in Harlem. Although Ezekiel thinks that "a nigger's a nigger in New York, the same as in Atlanta, and Harlem's really no different than Hannibal Square or Citrus City"

(p. 123), a fortuitous encounter with Alberta in Harlem forces him to see that he has become "an Uncle Tom bowing and scraping to the white folks for favors" and enslaved to a near-white wife, whom he does not love, "by something too strong for him to have the courage to break" (p. 124). Subsequent plot complications tempt Ezekiel to defy the tyranny of his wife and the oppression of his white trustees and bring him almost to the point of action. He decides to resign his position at Commencement, as a public protest, and to confront his wife, but at the crucial moment his nerve fails him, for the inspiration of Harlem is too distant and too defused to help. Full of self-loathing, Ezekiel Rogers resigns himself to enduring the domineering spouse and the overbearing social system, without warning of the gathering forces of rebellion.

Taffy, by the black author Phillip B. Kaye, begins with a family's flight from Harlem to Brooklyn to escape everything negative that the Harlem ghetto of the 1940s had come to represent, but Harlem remains a focal point of the family's life in the new home. In Brooklyn, the mother prospers. By facing down some white male neighbors who try to bully her out of her new home, she wins a certain celebrity in Brooklyn's developing black community and parlays the force of her personality and organizational skills into economic rewards, social position, and a political career, but her family finds upward mobility more difficult. The widening gap created by her blindness to the various forms of withdrawal exhibited by her husband and children becomes the counterpoint to her rising ambition and social mobility. The novel is centered in the psychological refuge taken in Harlem by her son Taffy, the title character. Right from the start, Taffy is ambivalent about leaving Harlem: "Maybe it wasn't paradise, but eight of his sixteen years had been framed here, and it was what you had. . . . His mother said everything would be different in the new home. Maybe. But he'd have to see if different meant better." Prejudices and misconceptions about Harlem ghetto life complicate his adolescent insecurity as he tries to fit in. Taffy's social successes, as well as his failures, all seem to be perceived in terms of what his mother calls the "dirty Harlem ways" that cling to him, and he cannot imagine himself as one of "the young people who looked sparklingly new, clean, plainly strange to his Harlem shocked eyes" (p. 71).

The novel conveys a sense of the quality of Harlem life that could mislead an unhappy adolescent like Taffy or his Brooklyn sidekick, the unhandsome, socially incompetent son of a rich member of the church who tags along with him.

> Evening is kind to Harlem. . . . Strident voices, harsh noises, and glaring light cut across at noon; but at twilight life has slowed

to the muffled bump of a grinding jukebox. Greed and lust are naked in daylight, but with nightfall mysterious enchantment lures with promises of strange dark pleasures. The bitter line is erased and only sparkling eyes above a sharply curving cheek freely offer a forbidden invitation to alien ecstasy. (p. 12)

In Brooklyn, on the other hand, "It was as though the silence was impatient with waiting; but there was nothing, not like Harlem where voices or cars or taxi horns or radios could fill and keep the gaping hole from being" (p. 91). Harlem's hold on Taffy gets stronger as his mother's political success in Brooklyn alienates her from her family. Taffy develops an obsessive relationship with a Harlem prostitute, who becomes both a lover and a mother to him, but when she eventually rejects him, Taffy acts out his rage, stabbing a white insurance broker only a few doors from the Harlem tenement in which his family had lived before fleeing to Brooklyn. The confused boy is identified with little difficulty and traced to his new home, where he and his only Brooklyn friend are shot and killed while resisting arrest. Ironically, Taffy's death completes the ritual of petty criminality and death at the hands of the police – the classic social nightmare that his mother had tried to leave behind in Harlem.

Among the many novels of the 1940s and 1950s focusing on juvenile delinquency in Harlem, Warren Miller's *Cool World* (1959),[5] and Julian Mayfield's *Long Night* (1959),[6] both later made into movies, represent contrasting attitudes toward the state of community life in the ghetto. *The Cool World,* by the white novelist Warren Miller, is a self-portrait drawn by Duke, the former warlord of the Royal Crocodiles, turned autobiographer in the relative sanctuary of a correctional facility in upstate New York. Duke, born Richard Custis, says he has given up on ponderous questions: "You start figurin out who am I an why am I an why am I here in Harlem – and man they ain't no end to it. . . . They ain't no end to it an you just end up scared" (p. 10). Nevertheless, these considerations remain the focus of his semiliterate yet eloquent narration. Duke's memoir is a narrow, if indisputable, vision of the degradation and despair of the underside of Harlem life. An apartment building is described as a three-flight walkup, with "dogs barkin behin the doors an evry door with an iron flange to keep out the jimmys" (p. 9). The project is a "new bilding it got the Uptown Stink" (p. 20). Harlem's decay is a bitter joke: "Only 9 hundred and 99 thousan left in Harlem now Man. I kill em all. I leavin rats an mice to the City but I killing the roaches myself" (p. 7). His own mother testifies to the despair: "You lose a person in Harlem you never see him again. Any man get adrift in Harlem he sink outa sight forever" (p. 41). One oasis of cleanliness and order in the filth, decay, and disarray typical of Duke's Harlem is the home of a postal worker, but even this exception illustrates the rule, for although one son promises to be a success, the other has become the Royal Crocodile's first junkie. Upon learning of his sibling's drug dependency, Harrison, the brother who attends Fisk University, says "He stand up an go to the window. He say to the window. 'They make us live like animals. Is it any wunder then that some of us act like animals an some of us become animals. The fantastic thing is how few of us succum to their idea of us.' An he went on like that standin there at the window not lookin at us looking out at Harlem" (p. 21). In spite of the diversions of drugs, sex, and violence, the emptiness of Duke's life in Harlem is inescapable: "I wake up Saturday morning with a bad hang over from the wine. Have drunk too much of that stuff jus sitting there by my self after evry body leave. Nothing else to do. I get up an go in the kitchen an make my self some coffee again. I think to my self God dam it here I am makin myself coffee again. Evry day the same an I dont see nothin ahead but the same for me" (p. 148). Duke's recurrent fantasy of a lion in the zoo that grows to enormous proportions and consumes the entire city seems to be his best approximation of hope: "Man. Aint nothin left when he get thru. The whole city jus one big beat up pile of crap when he get thru with it. I laying there on the sofa an I watch it go. He go Chomp an it all fall down in ruin the whole city" (p. 86). Duke's final word on his life in Harlem is a round condemnation: "Some time I think about the old days. . . . At first I miss it. But now I dont so much any more. I mean Man who need it? Man that one sue-cio city an I dont care if I never see it again" (p. 160). Duke's offhand comment about a buddy suggests an oblique meaning for the novel's title and conveys what the boy thinks of Harlem: "An he fool enough to look for a cool breeze in a Harlem summer" (p. 124).

In contrast, *The Long Night,* by the black novelist Julian Mayfield, attempts to limn with affection "the personal I . . . searching in this / hell on earth" alluded to in the frontispiece of Mayfield's earlier Harlem novel, *The Hit* (1957): "In my Harlem, therefore, / find the Race, the Group, but, more / find me" (unpaginated). Mayfield's fictional Harlem is a world of fundamentally good-natured people whose materialistic dreams and petty infractions of law are goaded by the pinch of segregation, rather than by malice or moral decay:

> The sun hung high over Harlem, and its heat was heavy as a white cloak over the flat roads and the gray streets. . . . Preachers napped and dreamed of churches larger than the Abyssinian. Lawyers and petty real-estate brokers planned and schemed and

gamblers figured. A con man dropped a wallet with a hundred-dollar bill in it to the sidewalk in front of the Corn Exchange Bank and waited for a sucker to fall for the age old game. . . . There, near the top of Manhattan Island, Harlem sizzled and baked and groaned and rekindled its dream under the midday sun.[7]

The dreamer in the Harlem of *The Long Night* is ten-year-old Frederick Brown, better known as Steely, a staunch member of the neighborhood gang, with a taste for heroic fantasies. Steely, who imagines himself as a combination of Frederick Douglass, Toussaint L'Overture, and Superman, is given a mission suitable to his adventurous spirit when his mother sends him to pick up what seems like a small fortune, the twenty-seven dollars and change she hit on the daily number. Steely is soon reminded that he is just a little kid that bigger kids can push around, when four older members of his gang hold him up and take the money, but like his heroes, Steely Brown refuses to accept defeat and vows to get another twenty-seven dollars. The boy first tries to borrow the money and then snatches a purse on 125th Street, nearly getting caught for two dollars. Steely feels adrift and confused, as he considers the guilt involved in what he is doing, but he is determined to persist in his misguided quest. On East Eighty-Eighth Street, Steely steals a Silver Streak bicycle, worth at least fifty dollars, from a careless white boy, only to have members of a rival gang beat him up and take the bike when he gets back to Harlem. Late that night, after almost getting into a car with a man who smiles strangely and offers him a dollar, Steely, whose name is beginning to take on a double meaning, decides his last resort is to roll a drunk slumped in a doorway. Improbably, the drunk turns out to be the absent father who originally imbued Steely with a heroic sensibility. Caught face to face in the cage of their mutual betrayals, each of them – the father and the son – struggles to redeem himself in the other's eyes, and the novel ends on a note of understanding and renewal in the midst of the ghetto's debilitating circumstances.

Anne Petry's *The Street*[8] (1943), Ralph Ellison's *Invisible Man*[9] (1952), and James Baldwin's *Go Tell It on the Mountain*[10] (1952), however, are the three novels of this period to rise above typical expression of the emerging ghetto and incorporate the new Harlem of the 1930s and 1940s with transcendent and enduring literary artistry. *The Street* is a keenly observed portrait of the emerging ghetto of Harlem in the early 1940s, and a vivid perceptual rendering as well. The omniscient narrator of *The Street* identifies so convincingly with the perspective of the particular character from whose point of view each specific portion of the story is

told that the illusion of a flow of intimate, overlapping autobiographies is
sustained without compromising the impartial authority of the narrative
voice. Consequently, Petry's third-person narrative reads with the intimacy and perceptual emphasis of a first-person narration. Nonetheless,
precise modal distinctions of point of view are maintained, one of which
is especially germane to our interests. Opinion about Harlem may be
uttered in dialogue by any character and placed on the record, but Harlem is seldom characterized from the vantage of their rich interior lives.[11]
Perceptual interpretation of Harlem in *The Street* is reserved almost exclusively for Lutie Johnson, the novel's protagonist. Lutie's view of Harlem is the one that counts in *The Street,* for her struggle to rebuild her
family is waged against the malevolent phenomenon of Harlem itself.
The microcosmic form of one block of 116th Street is a personage in
its own right, and Lutie's true antagonist. Lutie's battle with Harlem is
established initially in her struggle with the vindictive "cold November
wind" (p. 1) on 116th Street, personified at length in the opening pages
of the novel:

> The wind pried at the red skullcap on her head, and as though
> angered because it couldn't tear it loose from its firm anchorage
> of bobby pins, the wind blew a great cloud of dust and ashes
> and bits of paper into her face, her eyes, her nose. It smacked
> against her ears as though it were giving her a final, exasperated
> blow as proof of its displeasure in not being able to make her
> move on. (p. 4)

Petry's Harlem is developed next by Lutie's sense of the contrast between the perfection of country living, which she recalls from her time
as a domestic worker, and the dark, deteriorating, airless apartment to
which she has had to take her son to live: "All through Harlem there are
apartments just like this one, she thought, and they're nothin but traps.
Dirty, dark, filthy traps. Upstairs. Downstairs. In my lady's chamber.
Click goes the trap when you pay the first month's rent. Walk right in.
It's a free country" (p. 73). Her many impressions of Harlem's debasing
social conditions notwithstanding, Lutie understands, paradoxically, that

> [s]he never felt really human until she reached Harlem and thus
> got away from the hostility in the eyes of the white women who
> stared at her on the downtown streets. . . . These other folk feel
> the same way, she thought – that once they are freed from the
> contempt in the eyes of the downtown world, they instantly
> become individuals. Up here they are no longer creatures labeled
> simply 'colored' and therefore all alike. . . . The same people

who had made themselves small on the train, even on the platform, suddenly grew so large they could hardly get up the stairs
to the street together. (pp. 57–8)

Harlem's nature is also defined for Lutie by the summary of its effect
on her family and her neighbors: "Streets like 116th Street, or being
colored, or a combination of both with all it implied, had turned Pop
into a sly old man who drank too much; had killed Mom off when she
was in her prime." In the very apartment house in which she is now
living, the same combination of circumstances "had pushed [the superin-
tendent] into basements away from light and air until he was being eaten
up by some horrible obsession; and still other streets had turned Min,
the woman who lived with him, into a drab drudge so spineless and limp
she was like a soggy dishrag" (pp. 56–7). The resignation to madness,
violence, and tragedy in Harlem, expressed in the flat, unemotional reaction of a young girl to the sight of her brother's lifeless body lying on a
Harlem sidewalk ("I always thought it'd happen," p. 203) enrages Lutie,
for she begins to see that Harlem is a purposeful consequence. "It all
added up to the same thing, [Lutie] decided – white people" (p. 206).
Lutie is determined not to be defeated by Harlem and the larger forces
that make it what it has become. Money, she thinks, may be the key.
When she was working for a white family, "money transformed a suicide she had seen committed from start to finish in front her eyes into
'an accident with a gun'" (p. 49). In Harlem, she observes that "even if
you're colored, [money] makes a difference, not as much, but enough
to make having it important" (p. 166).

Lutie tries to make money with her modest voice, when Boots, a Harlem bandleader, is attracted to her. She is unaware that the bandleader is
himself little more than a pawn of the malevolent forces of Harlem, embodied by Mrs. Hedges and Junto, two benignly placid puppetmasters
whose bizarre relationship constitutes one of the most inventive details
in *The Street*. Mrs. Hedges is a gigantic black woman, whose scars from
a fire confine her to a comfortably furnished first-floor apartment in the
building to which Lutie moves. Junto is a physically unprepossessing
white man, who first ran across Mrs. Hedges when he was starting out
as a junk dealer in Harlem and recognized her to be one of the few people
of any race with a "self-will" comparable to his own. Junto is not squea-
mish in any way about Mrs. Hedges's scarred and unwomanly figure.
To him, she is uniquely attractive, but her own sensitivity about her
appearance has made any physical intimacy impossible. Instead Junto and
Mrs. Hedges have sublimated their intense feelings into a curious business relationship. From her apartment in a building owned by Junto,

Mrs. Hedges has spent her time looking at the life of the street and, with the insights gained from ceaseless observation, has directed Junto to the best investments in Harlem – places where people dance, drink, and make love, in order to forget their troubles. Together the couple monopolize a substantial portion of Harlem's infrastructure, each profiting in respective ways from Harlem by pacifying the pain of the very oppressions that they conspire to create and sustain. His bar, called the Junto, creates an oasis of warmth in winter and of coolness in summer by giving black men the illusion of dignity and younger black women the illusion of possessing the fine things they lack. One of Mrs. Hedges few pleasures is presenting beautiful, compliant young black women to Junto as symbolic substitutes for herself. After he tires of each stand-in, Junto sets the woman up in one of his classier houses for white clients, and Mrs. Hedges offers up another surrogate to their odd passion. For much of the novel, Lutie is the unwitting target of this bizarrely touching relationship. Mrs. Hedges identifies Lutie for such a role early in the novel and is content to watch and wait, defending Lutie from physical harm while secretly using Harlem to break Lutie's spirit. Only gradually, as circumstances conspire to force her to submit, does Lutie begin to understand that Harlem and Junto are facets of each other. Junto makes Harlem bearable, while Harlem makes the Junto indispensable and profitable. Harlem has become less an instrument of black hopes and aspirations, and more a means of limiting and controlling blacks. As Junto's net closes around her, Lutie kills in desperation and flees Harlem in despair, abandoning the young son whose future was the principal motivation for her struggle with life on the street in the first place.

In Ralph Ellison's *Invisible Man,* Harlem is a complex analog for the self that the unnamed narrator begins to discover as he seeks his destiny in the chaos of possibility of New York. After the drama of his temptation, disobedience, and expulsion from the edenic, if rigidly formal, garden of a southern college for Negroes, our protagonist struggles to hold together the fragments of his disassociating hopes and illusions in New York, where his authentic education occurs in gradually deepening encounters with the full force of the political consciousness of Harlem. In spite of the countervailing manipulations of the Brotherhood, which is better aware of the force of Harlem than he but wishes only to channel it toward their own objectives, the narrator gradually learns that he can find his destiny only in himself, but that self-discovery is so disorienting and dismaying that he flees to the extreme illumination of hibernation in a hole on the edges of Harlem.

The unnamed protagonist's initial attraction to Harlem is part of the impulse to hold onto illusions and shallow hopes, as the Veteran – the

inmate of the insane asylum he first encounters at the "sporting-and-
gambling house" called Golden Day – intimates when they find themselves leaving the college town on the same bus:

> "New York," he said. "That's not a place, it's a dream. When
> I was your age it was Chicago. Now all the little black boys run
> away to New York. Out of the fire into the melting pot. I can
> see you after you've been in Harlem for three months. Your
> speech will change, you'll talk a lot about 'college,' you'll attend
> lectures at Men's House. . . . You might even meet a few white
> folks. And listen," he said leaning close to whisper, "you might
> even dance with a white girl!" (p. 150)

As our unnamed protagonist arrives in New York, the flight north to
Harlem within New York is identified with the proverbial flight north
to freedom, first of the fugitive slaves and later of the disenfranchised
migrants: " 'Sure, but how do you get to Harlem?' 'That's easy,' [the
Redcap] said. 'You just keep heading north' " (p. 155). And the rural
youth's intimate contact with a well-endowed white woman on a
crowded subway car illustrates the Veteran's wit and insight: "The vet
had been right: For me, this was a city not of realities, but of
dreams. . . . And now as I struggled through the lines of people a new
world of possibility suggested itself to me faintly" (p. 157). But he is
overwhelmed by the ghetto's powerful dynamics, when his evident
country-boy innocence, not the passion of a political rabble-rouser, is
what arouses the suspicion of a policeman on the beat in Harlem. He
realizes, "I would have to take Harlem a little bit at a time" (p. 158).

A folk lesson about Harlem comes from a black junk man, whose job
in the Wall Street district is to dispose of the white man's revised and
discarded plans. " 'Man, this Harlem ain't nothing but a bear's den. But
I will tell you one thing,' he said with a suddenly sobering face, 'it's the
best place in the world for you and me' " (p. 171). Discovery of a different sort is offered by a young white man, the scion of a Wall Street
tycoon, who sees himself as a kind of Huckleberry Finn and apparently
regards interracial intrasexual contacts, at Harlem's Club Calamus, as
the cultural equivalent of going down the Mississippi on a raft (p. 182).
Later, after his psychological death, reincarnation, and resurrection following an explosion at the Liberty Paints Company, the delirious protagonist returns to a hallucinatory Harlem. "Lenox Avenue seemed to
career away from me at a drunken angle, and I focused on the teetering
scene with wild, infant's eyes, my head throbbing" (p. 245). "Don't let
this Harlem git you," warns Mary, who rescues the incoherent protagonist when he collapses on the streets, babbling deliriously. "I'm in New

York but New York ain't in me, understand what I mean? Don't get corrupted" (p. 249). But Harlem has been getting to the protagonist, divesting him of his innocence, stripping him of illusions, and exposing him to the possibility of chaos.

After a summer hibernation with Mary, the unnamed protagonist steps into the Harlem winter: "The whole of Harlem seemed to fall apart in a swirl of snow" (p. 255). His emergence is marked by an unexpected assertion of individual consciousness ("I Yam What I Yam") and the development of a personal theme ("dispossession") that attracts the attention of the Brotherhood, Ellison's analog for the Communist Party. The Brotherhood presents the protagonist to the public in a new identity. He scores with his audience by emphasizing the theme of dispossession, but despite his success, the Brotherhood immediately orders him to "stay completely out of Harlem" (p. 343) and undergo a period of indoctrination. Four months later, on April Fool's Day, he is assigned the leadership of the Harlem district. Here he becomes a danger to the Brotherhood, precisely because of the effectiveness of his developing identification with the consciousness of Harlem (p. 393), and again he is ordered to be "inactive in Harlem" (p. 396). The protagonist of *Invisible Man* believes that the Brotherhood is merely mistaken, rather than manipulative, in treating him this way, because he is only dimly aware of the tactical purpose of his periods of exile from Harlem. "Being removed from Harlem was a shock, but one which would hurt them as much as me," he thinks (p. 398). What he does not understand is something that the Brotherhood leaders have always known. The protagonist's notion that "the clue to what Harlem wanted was what *I* wanted" is useful to the Brotherhood – but dangerous as well (p. 398).

Indeed, when changing events of global consequence do make it necessary for Harlem to be "sacrificed" to larger issues and Tod Clifton – the leader of the Brotherhood youth – takes his suicidal "plunge," a new facet of Harlem, "outside the groove of history" (p. 433), is exposed to the protagonist. Without authorization he participates in Tod's funeral, "realizing that I was listening to something within myself," that the words of the old spiritual were "deepened by that something for which the theory of the Brotherhood had given me no name" (p. 442). Harlem is, in fact, a kind of name for "that something" excluded by the Brotherhood theory, and the protagonist is attacked for glorifying a traitor to the Brotherhood. "Does my membership stop me from feeling Harlem?" is his sarcastic retort (p. 460). Brother Jack angrily lectures the young black man, telling him that the Brotherhood expects both sight and insight to be sacrificed to the larger view, and he pops his own glass eye into a glass of water as a graphic illustration.

Only after the protagonist pretends to be chastened and repentant is he allowed to return to the Harlem district. The process of his discovery of himself in Harlem is further deepened, when, by donning a pair of dark glasses to disguise himself from some followers of Ras, the black-Nationalist agitator, he comes face to face with Rinehart, the amoral "spiritual technologist." Rinehart can be anything others want him to be, and Rinehart's existence reveals a facet of Harlem, and of the protagonist himself, that before had only been seen as though through a glass darkly. In discovering Rinehart, he discovers the nature of his own role in the Brotherhood. What they had expected of him in the Clifton affair was to be their "justifier," taking "Harlem's mind off Clifton," affirming them in what they want to believe, demonstrating that "Harlem loves them," that history is on their side. His task had been "to deny the unpredictable human element in all Harlem so they could ignore it when it in any way interfered with their plans" (p. 503). For a time the protagonist tries to exploit his Rinehart identity in the Brotherhood, bending it to his own purposes. "Cherchez la femme" becomes his motto, but he only manages to debase himself to the abject sexual stereotype of a black buck. When he abandons the Brotherhood and commits himself irrevocably to Harlem, he feels that he is stepping into a river of ordure bearing him toward a vision. That vision, when it comes at the end of the riotous final chapter of the novel, is an illuminating, blinding, and liberating castration. The final phase of the protagonist's Harlem education, the reader eventually comes to understand, has been retrospective in process, but prospective in purpose, and it has coincided with the reading of the novel, which ends where it began, with the protagonist in his illuminated hole, where he reappraises his discovery of self in his deepening encounters with the unseen consciousness of Harlem.

In James Baldwin's *Go Tell It on the Mountain,* Harlem is a constant and significant presence in a variety of ways, although it is seldom named directly in the prayers of the born-again congregants of the Harlem storefront church that is the principal setting of the novel. Like so many aspects of their lives, Harlem is rendered in the transformational and allusive diction of the black church, but its presence is palpable and strong even when its reality is distanced or denied by the habits of mind and language of the novel's principal characters. Harlem functions as a kind of secular center of gravity for the narrative voice, which, although it resonates in sympathy and harmony with the rich spiritual and rhetorical heritage of the fundamentalist black church, always places final authorial emphasis on the exactness of social, chronological, and psychological observation in the actuality of time, place, and history.

The "saints" perceive Harlem as an environment of sin, whose manifestations, such as "the sinners along the avenue" on a Sunday morning, should be shunned and resisted. John, the adolescent protagonist, is confined by his parents to the defensive circles of his church and his home, but the sensations of Harlem penetrate all barriers. The refuge of the home is disturbed at night when John can hear the sound of his parents' sexual coupling "over the sound of rats' feet, and rats' screams, and the music and cursing from the harlot's house downstairs" (p. 12). The storefront church has "stood, for John's lifetime, on the corner of this sinful avenue, facing the hospital to which criminals wounded and dying were carried every night" (p. 50), and its sanctuary is violated from time to time by "a curse from the streets" (p. 14). Harlem's inescapable presence infects the home, in the inescapable form of dirt: "The room was narrow and dirty; nothing could alter its dimensions, no labor could make it clean. Dirt was in the wall and the floorboards, and triumphed beneath the sink where roaches spawned" (p. 21). The residue of Harlem's mundane being penetrates even to the church: "In the air of the church hung, perpetually, the odor of dust and sweat; for like the carpet in his mother's living room, the dust of the church was invincible" (p. 49). The school, the only sanctioned locale in Harlem outside the perimeters of church and home, has uncovered John's evident intellect and introduced him to an alternative future beyond Harlem, "opening outward for him on a world where people did not live in the darkness of his father's house, did not pray to Jesus in the darkness of his father's church, where he would eat good food and wear good clothes, and go to the movies as often as he wished" (p. 19). This alluring alternative to church and home in Harlem is embodied for John in the brilliant skyline of New York City, which gives him feelings of exultation and power when he sees it in the distance from Central Park, but on his forays beyond Harlem John senses that he would not be welcome in that glorious world and "his soul would find perdition" (p. 33).

The migration to Harlem – illuminated with the empowering imagery and allusive language of the narrative in the framework of Afro-American history – is the common element among the conflicting motivations and memories of John's aunt, Florence, and his parents, Gabriel and Elizabeth. Harlem lies at the heart of the hope that Florence felt "every day she heard that another man and woman had said farewell to this iron earth and sky, and started on the journey north" (p. 72). She had invested years of sacrifice in "a railroad ticket to New York," had acted in spite of her mother's manipulation of her insecurity and guilt ("Girl, where you going? What you doing? You reckon on finding some man up North to dress you in pearls and diamonds?"), had wagered her dream and lost, ending up with a man "who sang the blues and drank too much" (p. 83) in "a city she did not like." Florence's history is expressed ironically in the congregation's selection of the spiritual "I want to walk in Jerusalem just like John," but her nephew John, who knows little of this, can only sense "an awful silence. . . . a dreadful speculation . . . a deep turning as of something huge, black, shapeless, for ages dead on the ocean floor" (pp. 80–1).

For Gabriel, Harlem is the final refuge from the blood guilt running in "all the cities through which he had passed" (p. 137), the harlotry of "the widow from the North" (p. 95) who had invaded the "defenseless city of his mind" (p. 94), and the memory of the violent death of the son he had conceived but not acknowledged. Gabriel's history is expressed obliquely in the choice of the spiritual "Lord, I'm traveling, Lord, / I got on my traveling shoes" (p. 144), but John, kept in ignorance of his real father and only dimly conscious of the depths of his putative father's antipathy, senses a need for salvation in which he would "no longer be the son of his father, but the son of his Heavenly Father, the King. . . . His father could not cast him out, whom God had gathered in" (p. 145).

For Elizabeth, Harlem had served as the pretext for escape from a domineering aunt, because "coming to New York to take advantage of the greater opportunities the North offered colored people" could not easily be denied in 1920. Harlem also provided the idyllic backdrop to her short-lived romance with John's father, a youth imbued with the faith of the New Negro movement, who "just decided me one day that I was going to get to know *everything* them white bastards knew, and I was going to get to know it better than them, so could no white son-of-a-bitch *nowhere* never talk *me* down, and never make me feel like *I* was dirt, when I could read him the alphabet, back, front, and sideways" (p. 167), but Harlem became the setting for his defeat and despair when the reality of racism overwhelmed the viability of his dreams. Elizabeth's continuing need to make a way for her fatherless son in Harlem is encoded hopefully in the spiritual "Somebody needs you, Lord / Come by here." In this maelstrom of oblique cues and intuitive impressions in the ritual being acted out around him by his mother, his "father," and his "aunt," but of which he knows only fragmentary and evasive versions, John is "astonished before the Lord" at the historic moment of the March riot of 1935, not unlike James Baldwin himself, who, as noted earlier, faced the death and burial of his own father on his nineteenth birthday in the midst of the chaos of the Harlem riot of 1943.

The presence of Harlem penetrates even to the core of John's spiritual ecstasy, an ecstasy that recalls the apocalyptic revelations of the Christian visionary of Patmos for whom he is named. Although the memories of John's father, mother, and aunt encompass the broad reach of Afro-American history, the fictional present moment of John's spiritual initiation is on his fourteenth birthday, on a Saturday evening in the spring of March 1935, dated only days away from the Harlem riots of that year with remarkable specificity, in a novel where other historic incidents are either reflected in cosmic grandeur, or deflected to the vanishing point, by the transformational rhetoric of the charismatic black church. As a result, Harlem becomes a kind of crucible for the turbulent mix of Afro-American social history, from slavery onward, as John flounders spiritually, "searching for something, hidden in the darkness, that must be found" (p. 199) and chokes, in "the dusty space before the altar" (p. 194) of the storefront church, on the invasive dust of Harlem, whose significance has been so carefully elaborated in the novel's opening chapter. Paradoxically, John is rescued from the darkness by familiar Harlem sounds, which he has heard "every where, in prayer and in daily speech, and wherever the saints were gathered, and in the unbelieving streets" (p. 200). The sound is one "that could only come from darkness, that yet bore such sure witness of the glory of the light" (p. 200) and pulls his spirit toward a vision of a future, a number, and a city, which he spies, like Ezekiel's wheel, up in the middle of the air. Awaking from his spiritual crisis, John realizes that the sound he had heard in the darkness was the echo of his spiritual brethren, as "they moved on the bloody road forever, with no continuing city, but seeking one to come: a city out of time, not made with hands, but eternal in the heavens" (p. 204), and as John leaves the storefront church with his family in the early morning, the streets of the real Harlem seem transformed:

> Now the storm was over. And the avenue, like any landscape that has endured a storm, lay changed under Heaven, exhausted and clean, and new. Not again, forever, could it return to the avenue it once had been. Fire, or lightning, or the latter rain, coming down from these skies which moved with such pale secrecy above him now, had laid yesterday's avenue waste, had changed it in a moment, in the twinkling of an eye, as all would be changed on the last day, when the skies would open up once more to gather up the saints. . . . He was in battle no longer, this unfolding Lord's day, with this avenue, with these houses, the sleeping, staring, shouting people, but had entered into battle with Jacob's angel, *with the princes and the powers of the air.*
> (pp. 215–16; Baldwin's italics)

Thus, a literary ideology for the emerging Harlem ghetto began gradually to find new imaginative terms of order with the outpouring of novels set in black Harlem during the 1940s and 1950s, particularly Anne Petry's vivid perceptual rendering of Harlem in *The Street,* Ralph Ellison's employment of Harlem as a complex analog for the self experiencing the chaos of possibility in *Invisible Man,* and James Baldwin's transformation of the streets of Harlem with the allusive vocabulary of the black church in *Go Tell It on the Mountain.* Reformulation of the idea of black Harlem came more slowly and with greater difficulty in poetry, which seemed shocked into silence by the culture capital's decline as a symbol of hope.

7

Montage of a Dream Deferred

The implications of the depression years and the epoch of global war for the Harlem motif were only slowly digested and assimilated in poetry. Indeed, for a time in the late 1930s and early 1940s, few poets seemed able to sing about Harlem, re-weaving the actuality of this new black ghetto into the earlier song of the culture capital. Melvin B. Tolson's was the single new voice to attempt to rise to the theme of Harlem between the riots of 1935 and 1943, but his *Gallery of Harlem Portraits*, completed in the late 1930s, remained unpublished in Tolson's lifetime.[1] Robert Hayden and Gwendolyn Brooks, the major Afro-American poets to emerge in the 1940s, seem never to have employed the motif, and Margaret Walker referred to Harlem only fleetingly in "For My People." It was left to Langston Hughes – more than any other figure shaping and elaborating the theme of Harlem in this new phase – to take the lead in confronting in poetry the fact that the city of refuge, associated initially with optimism, success, and racial amplitude, had deteriorated so rapidly into a setting for ghetto riots.

Shakespeare in Harlem (1942)[2] – the first major poetry volume about Harlem that Hughes published after spending nearly a decade away from the enclave – identifies the Harlem environs as a landscape of jazz and blues, as had his Harlem poetry of the New Negro period, but the texture and flavor were very different. Harlem was nocturnal, as in *The Weary Blues,* but now the Harlem night was often oppressive and dangerous rather than nurturing and liberating. The volume's title specified Harlem, as did many of the poems, but Hughes's introductory note described it as "a book of light verse. Afro-Americana in the blues mood. Poems syncopated and variegated in the colors of Harlem, Beale Street, West Dallas and Chicago's South Side" (unpaginated). Harlem – the unique black city – now, one year before the Harlem riot of 1943, had become merely typical. The volume begins and ends with two reveries in the new mood: "Twilight Reverie" (p. 3) presents a speaker "with a bitter old thought, / Something in my mind better I forgot," thinking about guns and violence; "Reverie on the Harlem River" (p. 123) dwells on a question of suicide. "Harlem Sweeties" celebrates the colorations of female pulchritude in Harlem with a sensuous innocence that seems out of place in the new atmosphere in which love, clotted with desperation, is always on the verge of turning "into a knife / Instead of a song" (p. 49). "Statement" speaks of Harlem's capacity for cruelty and violence: "Down on '33rd Street / They cut you / Every way they is" (p. 28). The intertwining of love and death is a major theme of the collection. "Death in Harlem" is the narrative of Aranella's murderous revenge when she is betrayed by her meal ticket while on a trip to the ladies room (pp. 57–64). The death of the title character of "Sylvester's Dying Bed" (pp. 67–8) is made easier by the presence of all his "sweet mamas," but other deaths in *Shakespeare in Harlem* occur in abject loneliness and despair. Three poems are about a dying lover, a hearse, and a suicide, respectively. Others are about loneliness and abandonment or a cynical, unhoping search for love. "Love" is defined as "the little spark" of John Henry's hammer, "dying in the dark" (p. 124).

In *Shakespeare in Harlem* the character of the blues has changed as well. The volume's title poem juxtaposes the conventional folk-babble of traditional English lyrics with the sardonic call–response of the blues, in a verse that is cruelly disorienting:

> Hey ninny neigh!
> And a hey nonny noe!
> Where, oh, where
> Did my sweet mama go?
>
> Hey ninny neigh
> With a tra-la-la-la!
> They say your sweet mama
> Went home to her ma.
>
> (p. 111)

In "Hey Hey Blues," which echoes the blues laughter of "Blues Fantasy" in *The Weary Blues,* it now takes good corn whiskey for the singer to "HEY-HEY-HEY – and cheer" (p. 53). In "Ballad of the Gypsy," a variation on a traditional blues topic, the fortune-teller says what the speaker wants to hear but cannot believe, for hope seems no longer to be possible in this Harlem. In "Reverie on the Harlem River," the blues singer's answer–response is oddly defeatist, lacking the traditional resilience of blues: "Lord, I wish I could die – / But who would miss me if I left?" (p. 123). Escape seems to be the only alternative in the actuality of this Harlem. Escape – the solution in so many country blues, which lured blacks from the rural South to the city – had, ironically, become the only option in the blues landscape of the city of refuge itself. The dynamic Jazzonia of the blues in *The Weary Blues* had lapsed into the debilitating tension of unrelieved loneliness, isolation, abandonment, and despair, but *Shakespeare in Harlem* was simply Hughes's first view of a strangely altered black city. After a decade in which he had traveled around the world and through many controversies, the bitter poems captured the existential change but were not his final word. The promise of his earlier vision would not so easily surrender to this new, disheartening Harlem.

Hughes's vision of Harlem in *Fields of Wonder* (1947) and *One-Way Ticket* (1949) was consistent with his earlier apprehension of his chosen environs. Harlem continued to be conceived above all as the landscape of the urban Negro folk, observed with empathy and understanding and perceived in terms of their music and dreams. The Jazzonia of *The Weary Blues* (1926) was still present but now organically fused, rather than exotically juxtaposed. The bitterness and despair of *Shakespeare in Harlem* (1942) was balanced by irony and transformed in expression.

The Harlem poems in *Fields of Wonder*[3] resisted the note of despair and bitterness at Harlem's decline sounded in *Shakespeare in Harlem* and even reasserted Hughes's New Negro belief in the possibility of the race capital, while acknowledging Harlem's obvious decline into a ghetto only in muted and indirect terms. The "Stars over Harlem" section opens with "Trumpet Player: 52nd Street," a poem set by its subtitle outside the boundaries of Harlem, in Tin Pan Alley, but that returns to the Harlem issues of "Jazzonia." Hughes's description of the trumpet player recalls the dual views of his long-legged jazzers in a Harlem cabaret of two decades earlier, but here the lifted gowns of gold and shining rivers of the soul have fused in a single apprehension, and the spontaneous eroticism and magical idealism have been reduced to a profound fatigue. The music of "Jazzonia" had been an invitation to eroticism; the music of "Trumpet Player: 52nd Street" arises from the musician's mastery of desire. The gap between the ideal to which he is attuned and the reality to which he is attached is synthesized imaginatively and distilled harmonically to a tensile, expressive musical interval:

> The music
> From the trumpet at his lips
> Is honey

Mixed with liquid fire
The rhythm
From the trumpet at his lips
Is ecstasy
Distilled from old desire –

Desire
That is longing for the moon
Where the moonlight's but a spotlight
In his eyes,
Desire
That is longing for the sea
Where the sea's a bar glass
Sucker size.   (p. 91)

And actuality, if not changed by his music, at least is transformed, as "the music slips / Its hypodermic needle / To his soul."

But softly
As the tune comes from his throat
Trouble
Mellows to a golden note.

"Dimout in Harlem" expresses death by silence, the converse of Harlem's transformation through desire and the instrumentality of music:

Silence
No one talking
Down the street your Harlem
In the dark
Is walking.   (pp. 95–6)

But "Stars," whose first line echoes the heading "Stars over Harlem," challenges the oblivion of silence with the admonition to dream.

Hughes's lyric posture, tone, and modulation were quite different in the six Harlem poems of *One-Way Ticket,*[4] as he bluntly protested segregation and racial discrimination there and in the rest of the United States, but his view of Harlem's potential remained fundamentally unchanged. "Visitors to the Black Belt" contrasts the habitual phrases "across the railroad track," "up in Harlem," and "Jazz on the South Side" with "here on this side of the tracks," "here in Harlem," and "hell on the South Side" (p. 65–6). In this way, the speaker confronts ghetto tourists not simply with the unreality of their perceptions of black people but also with the unconscious egotism of their own sense of self. "Puzzled" confronts the speaker himself, just as bluntly, with the quandary of Harlem, "Here on the edge of Hell" (p. 71) and with the challenge of "What we're gonna do / In the face of / What we remember" (p. 73). "The Ballad of Margie Polite," one of the rare poems about the riot of 1943, celebrates the historic anger of the woman who chose to belie her name in the lobby of the Braddock Hotel. "Negro Servant" identifies Harlem with a sense of liberation and release for the black worker on the job:

> Dark Harlem waits for you.
> The bus, the subway –
> Pay-nights a taxi
> Through the park.
> O, drums of life in Harlem after dark!
> O, dreams!
> O, songs!
> O, saxophones at night!
> O, sweet relief from faces that are white!
>
> (p. 70)

"Deceased" makes it clear that Harlem can be vicious, too: "Harlem / Sent him home / In a long box – / Too dead to know why: / The licker / Was lye" (p. 116), and "Could Be" implies that, after all, Harlem is now much like Any Ghetto, USA. Yet the speaker's very emphasis on the hypothetical usage "could be" calls into question the idea proposed – that Harlem is like Hastings Street, Eighteenth and Vine, and other ghetto streets – and betrays a lingering faith.

Langston Hughes's *Montage of a Dream Deferred* (1951), however, is the volume that developed a credible lyrical approach to the Harlem ghetto of the 1940s and 1950s and provided a new key to the Harlem motif for younger poets by identifying Harlem with the deferred dreams of black people in America. Hughes's statement of purpose at the beginning of the volume established the mode and technique for the drama of Harlem presented in *Montage of a Dream Deferred*:

> In terms of current Afro-American popular music and the sources from which it has progressed – jazz, ragtime, swing, blues, boogie-woogie, and bebop – this poem on contemporary Harlem, like bebop, is marked by conflicting changes, sudden nuances, sharp and impudent interjections, broken rhythms, and passages sometimes in the manner of a jam session, sometimes the popular song, punctuated by the riffs, runs, breaks, and distortions of the music of a community in transition.[5]

One critic sees *Montage of a Dream Deferred* as a kind of jam session of "many voices that speak about the myriad ways in which Harlem's dreams are deferred . . . , like instruments played by musicians who range over Harlem's experiences with a freedom authorized by their artistry."[6] Another characterizes *Montage of a Dream Deferred* as "a guided tour of microcosmic Harlem, day and night, past and present,"[7] "a ritual drama,"[8] and "a vibrant seriocomic ceremony in which a community of voices is orchestrated from a multiset or multilevel stage."[9]

The term "montage" also recalls the motion-picture technique in which the camera cuts rapidly from one shot to another, juxtaposes disparate images, and superimposes one frame of film over another without transition. The poems are voices of America's ghettos, refracted by Hughes's jazz montage into an evocation of the dream deferred in the particularity of Harlem. They represent Hughes's evolution of the figurative postulations about Harlem and the instrumentality of dreams that he had initially introduced through the vehicle of jazz and blues in *The Weary Blues*. The vast majority of the individual pieces in the volume are not restricted by their particulars to the Harlem environment. Nearly seventy of the eighty-seven pieces in *Montage of a Dream Deferred* are unspecified as to setting. The thematic issue of deferred dreams is defined, moreover, as broader than either race or place in such pieces. In "Comment on Curb" one speaker asks: "You talk like / they don't kick / dreams around / downtown," but the retort is sharp and pointed: "I expect they do – / But I'm talking about / Harlem to you!" (p. 271).[10] The theme of Harlem reformulated with the times, in *Shakespeare in Harlem, Fields of Wonder,* and *One-Way Ticket,* is elaborated here in *Montage of a Dream Deferred* in the contemporary jazz modes of boogie-woogie, bop, and bebop.

"Boogie Segue to Bop," the first of *Montage of a Dream Deferred*'s six divisions, presents poems about the love life of ordinary people, shaped by the limits of life in Harlem. "Juke Box Love Song," which echoes the invitation of "Harlem Night Song" in *The Weary Blues* ("Come, / let us roam the night together / singing"), fashions a contemporary kind of romantic love with the common elements of Harlem life, when the speaker seduces his beloved in the terms of boogie-woogie neon:

> I could take the Harlem night
> and wrap around you,
> Take the neon lights and make a crown,
> Take the Lenox Avenue busses,
> Taxis, subways,
> And for your love song tone their rumble down.
> Take Harlem's heartbeat,
> Make a drumbeat

Put it on a record, let it whirl,
And while we listen to it play,
Dance with you till day,
Dance with you my sweet brown Harlem girl.

(p. 227)

"Dream Boogie," the first poem in the "Boogie Segue to Bop," intro-
duces the theme of the dream deferred in the form of a mocking interro-
gation that insinuates itself throughout *Montage of a Dream Deferred:*
"Good Morning, Daddy. / Ain't you heard / The boogie-woogie rumble / Of a dream deferred?" (p. 221). The thematic interrogative "Ain't
you heard?" and the corollary question "You think it's a happy beat?"
restate *The Weary Blues*'s ambiguous aside, "Does a jazz band ever sob?"
Harlem is not mentioned in "Dream Boogie," but the poem's mocking
insinuations foreshadow the eighteen poems in *Montage of a Dream Deferred* that iterate, modulate, and recapitulate the numerous and disparate
instances of the rumble of the deferred dreams of black America specifically in their unifying and comprehensive emblem, the symbolic locus
of Harlem. "Dig and Be Dug," *Montage of a Dream Deferred*'s second
section, which voices the volume's most explicit protest against racial
injustice, is framed by several poems that specify Harlem. At the beginning are "Movies" and "Not a Movie." In "Movies," Harlem personi-
fies the black community's ironic consciousness of Hollywood's exclu-
sion and falsification of authentic black images from the medium that
articulates America's dreams: "The Roosevelt, Renaissance, Gem, Al-
hambra: / Harlem laughing in all the wrong places / at the crocodile
tears / of crocodile art / that you know / in your heart / is crocodile" (p.
230). On the other hand, "Not a Movie" presents an aspect of Harlem's
historical role as a city of refuge, in spite of its now-degraded circumstances. Callous 133rd Street, whose reputation for violence earned it the
street name "bucket o' blood" and was the subject of "Statement," in
Shakespeare in Harlem ("Down on '33rd Street / They cut you / Every
way they is"), can still be a haven from the violent Jim Crow repression
on the wrong side of the Mason–Dixon line: "Six knots was on his head /
but, thank God, he wasn't dead! / And there ain't no Ku Klux / on
133rd" (p. 231). Between "Movies" and "Not a Movie," "Tell Me" asks
Montage of a Dream Deferred's thematic question: "Why should it be my
loneliness, / Why should it be my song, / Why should it be my dream /
deferred / overlong?" (p. 231).

Vignettes of hope and frustration constitute the majority of the poems
of "Dig and Be Dug," of which the most famous is "Ballad of the Land-
lord," whose riotous implications get it banned from time to time. In

"Neon Sign," Hughes's stylistic freedom "yields a poem almost totally comprised of the names of Harlem bars and night clubs."[11] The neon signs' luminous aura and the numinous suggestions of the mythic designations Minton's, Small's, Shalimar become "Mirror-go-round / where a broken glass / in the early bright / smears re-bop / sound" (p. 233). "Corner Meeting" captures the atmosphere of a period charged with protest and calls for political action, but it is "Projection" whose animation (in the cinematic as well as figurative sense), whose startling juxtaposition of disparate Harlem institutions, and whose title make a pun on "Movies" and "Not a Movie":

> On the day when the Savoy
> leaps clean across Seventh Avenue
> and starts jitterbugging
> with the Renaissance,
> on that day when Abyssinia Baptist Church
> throws her enormous arms around
> St. James Presbyterian
> and 409 Edgecombe
> stoops to kiss 12 West 133rd,
> on that day –
> Paul Robeson
> will team up with Jackie Mabley,
> and Father Divine will say in truth,
>
> Peace!
> It's truly
> wonderful!   (pp. 240–1)

"Early Bright," the third section, specifies Harlem in two poems placed at the center of the section and the midpoint of the volume, as if they were *Montage of a Dream Deferred*'s vertical and horizontal axes, like the north–south and east–west avenues – the subjects of the respective poems – that intersect at the geographic and social center of Harlem. The poem entitled "125th Street" sketches the elusive face of Harlem with three provocative images – a chocolate bar, a jack-o'-lantern, and a slice of melon – suggesting the black community's resources and inner strengths, as well as its false and often bizarre exterior, and "Dive" identifies the precipitous quality of the Harlem night world with Lenox Avenue, as it plunges across the map face of Harlem like a river emptying into the sea of Central Park.

Montage of a Dream Deferred's fourth section, "Vice Versa to Bach," focuses on those middle-class Harlemites whose aspirations are more attuned to Bach than to bop, but whose dreams are also deferred. "College Formal: Renaissance Casino" reprises the diction and romanticism of "Juke Box Love Song" in a different social context. "Deferred" sketches the material, middle-class dreams of some blacks: to graduate, study French, buy two suits at once, see the furniture paid for, pass the civil-service examination, and take up Bach. "High to Low" contrasts St. Philip's and 409 Edgecombe Avenue's Sugar Hill strivings "to uphold the race" with the casual down-home ways of the brothers in the Harlem valley in "Low to High," but "Shame on You" cautions all strivers to consider that there is only "a movie house in Harlem named after Lincoln, / Nothing at all named after John Brown. / Black people don't remember / Any better than white" (pp. 254–5). "Theme for English B," one of the principal achievements of this section, is an essay offered by a student to his instructor in fulfillment of the following assignment: *"Go home and write / a page tonight / And let that page come out of you – / Then, it will be true"* (p. 247). The truth that issues from this young City College of New York student[12] is this: "Harlem, I hear you: / hear you, hear me – we two – you, me, talk on this page." The youthful persona of the speaker in "Theme for English B," written when Hughes was at least in his late forties, poses a striking contrast to the historical and geographic sweep of the omniscient persona in "The Negro Speaks of Rivers" written when Hughes was still in his teenage years, but the young speaker's discovery of Harlem's universality recalls Hughes's "Aesthete in Harlem" ("Strange / That in this nigger place / I should meet Life face to face").

"Dream Deferred," the fifth section of *Montage of a Dream Deferred*, strikes many different notes that express the "boogie-woogie rumble of a dream deferred." "Passing" plays a particularly ironic riff on the dream deferred. Harlem of the dream deferred includes even those who have realized their dreams of escaping their blackness, for on sunny Sunday afternoons, "the ones who've crossed the line / to live downtown / miss you, / Harlem of the bitter dream, / since their dream has / come true" (p. 258). "Night Funeral in Harlem" almost turns the theme of deferred dreams on its head, when everything that is required for the funeral of a destitute Harlemite simply materializes out of the generosity of Harlem's common humanity, and when even the mechanical objects of the cityscape contrive to give the poor man a dignified departure: "the street light / At his corner / Shined just like a tear" (p. 261). Echoes of the preceding sections insinuate themselves throughout this extended excursion – by far the longest section of the volume – winding up with "Dream Boogie: Variation," which returns to where *Montage of a Dream Deferred* began and prepares us for its thematic finale.

"Lenox Avenue Mural," the book's sixth and final division, is the most thematically direct section of the volume. The opening poem, "Harlem" – perhaps the most famous individual work in the volume – explicitly identifies the dream deferred with Harlem. The poem simply but eloquently poses what has become the classic formulation of the question "What happens to a dream deferred?" but offers answers only in the form of other interrogatives: "Does it dry up / like a raisin in the sun? / Or fester like a sore – / And then run? / Does it stink like rotten meat? / Or crust and sugar over – / like a sugary sweet?" The final possibilities constitute a kind of climactic moment in *Montage of a Dream Deferred,* for the ominous kinetic potential of "the something underneath" is finally made explicit. "Maybe it just sags / like a heavy load. / Or does it explode?" (p. 268). In "Good Morning," whose title recalls the volume's opening poem, a native Harlemite reminisces about how his community has grown, populated by blacks from all over the Americas, who have come "to Harlem / dusky sash across Manhattan / I've seen them come dark / wondering / wide-eyed / dreaming," but his revery concludes with the classic question of "Harlem" ("What happens / to a dream deferred?") and the mocking interrogative of "Dream Boogie" ("Daddy, ain't you heard?"). "Comment on Curb," cited earlier, erases any lingering doubt that Harlem and the dream deferred are illustrations of each other, in Langston Hughes's lyric vocabulary, and in "Island" the poet of "The Negro Speaks of Rivers" triangulates the *situs* of the dream deferred in the narrow stretch of Manhattan between the Hudson River and the Harlem River above 110th Street in Harlem:

> Between two rivers
> North of the park,
> Like darker rivers
> The streets are dark.
>
> Black and white,
> Gold and brown –
> Chocolate-custard
> Pie of a town.

The Harlem–dream deferred identification is, then, perfected with a restatement of the theme that reveals the final implication of the theme for Harlem's physical and spiritual geography. Harlem – the great black metropolis – within New York City – the great white metropolis – symbolizes the deferred dream of black America within the American dream: "Dream within a dream, / Our dream deferred" (p. 272). Finally,

Hughes's book ends where it began, with the same jazzy interrogative: "Good morning, daddy! / Ain't you heard?" (p. 272).

After *Montage of a Dream Deferred* a new generation of Afro-American poets began to turn to Harlem for inspiration, for, among Langston Hughes's achievements in this volume of poems, was his rehabilitation of Harlem as an Africana motif offering some promise in spite of the ghetto's decline, just as, a generation earlier he, more than any other New Negro poet, had established Harlem's emblematic relevance and potential. By characterizing Harlem as a montage of the dream deferred, Hughes not only presented a valid new concept of Harlem but also issued an implicit challenge: "Ain't you heard?" Younger blacks, indeed, began hearing the music of the dream deferred and responded in poetry in the late 1950s, after a period of relative silence on the theme. "Young Negro Poets," for example, by Calvin C. Hernton, one of the founders of the Umbra Workshop in New York City in the late 1950s, issued a call to

> Wake up o jack-legged poet!
> Wake up o dark boy from 'way down South!
> Wake up out of Central Park, and walk
>   through Harlem Street.
>
> Walk down Seventh Avenue, Eighth,
> Madison, Lenox and St. Nicholas,
> walk all around –
>   It's morning in Harlem.[13]

Younger poets, in the literary constellations of the Umbra Workshop in New York and of *Dasein: Quarterly Journal of the Arts* at Howard University in Washington, D.C., turned, slowly at first, and then with increasing frequency and intensity, to Harlem, as the Civil Rights movement took hold in the black American consciousness and as the dream deferred threatened to explode. Their Harlem poems, anthologized in such ground-breaking collections as *Beyond the Blues: New Poetry by American Negroes* (1962),[14] *Sixes and Sevens: An Anthology of New Poetry* (1963),[15] and *Burning Spear: An Anthology of Afro-Saxon Poetry* (1963),[16] were often landscapes of clashing disparates that conveyed the ghetto's oblique beauty while also depicting its desperation. Their images of Harlem, published on the eve of the Harlem uprising of 1964, prepared the way for a vision of racial possibility within the landscapes of the inner city that would be sifted from the ashes of 1964. Ray Johnson's "Walking East on 125th Street (Spring 1959)" is about a suicide's last walk along 125th Street to a terminus at the bottom of the East River:

> Walking to the edge of the river I remove everything except
>   my chastity belt and keep on strolling
> Walking down on the bottom of the east river scaring
>   the catfish
> Walking lazily by the mafia boys in hip concrete bennies
>   doing a swinging tarantella
> Walking with a orange peel in my ass a condom in my mouth
> Walking[17]

But this surrealistic conclusion to the stroll is preceded by a seriocomic catalog of bizarre, violent, loveless, degraded, unjust, oppressive, and self-destructive features of Harlem life, observed along the way, that make it impossible to read the poem's theme as literal suicide, in spite of the westward stroll's weird terminus in the depths of the East River. This poem is, rather, a scathing, prophetic denunciation of the corruption and debasement in which black men and women have to exist.

William Browne's sketches of Harlem articulate the same "something underneath" that Langston Hughes identified in the boogie-woogie rumble of the dream deferred, in the Harlem of *Montage*. In Browne's "Harlem Sounds: Hallelujah Corner," for example, the "annulled jazz" of Harlem religionists "rages, / stumbles, / and lies exhausted," stretched to the limits of faith and "strung like Jesus." The diction of jazz ("riffs," "runs," "breaks," "tuba snorts") is orchestrated with down-home, Baptist Church sounds ("weeping amens and applauding tambourines"), in the jargon of cinematographers ("superimposed"), to evoke "the / boogie-woogie / voice / of God."[18]

The existential intensity of the Harlems of Oliver Pitcher and William Browne is summarized in the opening statement of "Return of the Native," the only Harlem poem by Amiri Baraka / LeRoi Jones:

> Harlem is vicious
> modernism. BangClash.
> Vicious the way it's made.
> Can you stand such beauty.
> So violent and transforming.[19]

Baraka makes much the same point in "City of Harlem," from his volume of essays entitled *Home:*

> The legitimate cultural tradition of the Negro in Harlem (and America) is one of wild happiness, usually at some black man's own invention – of speech, of dress, of gait, the sudden twist of a musical phrase, the warmness or hurt of someone's voice. But

that culture is also one of hatred and despair. Harlem must contain all of this and be capable of producing all these emotions.[20]

Harlem was a pivotal issue for Baraka as he made the transition from the antibourgeois individualism of his Greenwich Village bohemianism of the 1950s to the consciousness of a group identity in the black nationalism of the 1960s. In the earlier phase, Baraka's attitude toward the cultural significance of Harlem had been negative: "Harlem is today the veritable capital city of the Black Bourgeosie. The Negro Bohemian's flight from Harlem is not a flight from the world of color but the flight of any would-be Bohemian from . . . 'the provinciality, philistinism and moral hypocrisy of American life.' "[21] By the late 1950s and early 1960s, though, Baraka's view of Harlem was changing:

> In a very real sense, Harlem is the capital of Black America. . . . But even the name Harlem, now, means simply Negroes (even though some other peoples live there too). The identification is international as well: even in Belize, the capital of predominantly Negro British Honduras, there are vendors who decorate their carts with flowers and the names and pictures of Negro culture heroes associated with Harlem like Sugar Ray Robinson. Some of the vendors even wear t-shirts that say "Harlem, U.S.A.," and they speak about it as a Black Paris.[22]

This is the Harlem of "vicious modernism": "The place, and place / meant of black people. Their heavy Egypt. (Weird word!)." Harlem's value is a consciousness of self that is loving, hoping, celebratory, significant, and, therefore, joyful, for all its pain. With this Harlem the poet can identify without reservation:

> Their minds, mine.
> the black hope, mine. In Time.
> We slide along in pain or too
> happy. So much love
> for us. All over, so much of
>
> what we need.

Thus, after a period of uncertainty in which the theme of black Harlem was avoided by almost all the emerging African-American poets, Langston Hughes renewed the symbolic linkage between Harlem and black America in the spiritual geography of African-American poetry. The now-classic formulation of the dream deferred, identified with Harlem in *Montage,* reclaimed Harlem's microcosmic place for the literary iconography of black America by reasserting the moral and cultural imperatives of the black experience using the contemporary terms of Harlem in the 1930s and 1940s. After Hughes, younger black poets began to evoke the desperate image of the decaying Harlem ghetto as an emblem of racial oppression and injustice, to prick the conscience of America and to animate their own resistance. This order of expression, common to the Harlem novels of the 1940s and 1950s, was possible in Harlem poetry only after *Montage*. Without compromising its initial optimism or denying its contemporary anxiety, Langston Hughes's revision and reinterpretation of black Harlem as the montage of a dream deferred redefined a path of affirmation and hope for the motif, which could blossom with the flowering of Harlem poetry after the uprising of 1964.

8

Negro de todo o mundo

The decades of the dream deferred in African-American poetry corresponded to the period of liberation struggles throughout the colonized world, from Cuba and Kenya to Indochina and Palestine. Liberation movements of all sorts, quiescent in the face of the Axis threat to "non-Aryan" races during World War II, resumed diplomatic and paramilitary resistance to imperial domination and colonial exploitation after the war. Ironically, self-determination and national autonomy had been advanced by the global war that debilitated the colonial powers, spotlighted the illogic of racist rationalizations for colonialism, and shattered the illusion of Europe's right of dominion. In Africa, the 1950s marked the decisive stage of the liberation struggle. In this same period, the possessions of France and Britain in the Caribbean moved toward autonomy within the French Community and independence within the British Commonwealth. Resistance movements in Cuba and the Dominican Republic challenged, and eventually toppled, dictators sustained by the United States, and Puerto Rico and the Virgin Islands evolved semiautonomous political identities under the Stars and Stripes.

The Harlem motif's legendary character – established in the international glamour of the Harlem vogue and developed in literature by the nativist and negritude movements of the Black Awakening – was affected by these global forces of liberation, as well as by Harlem's disillusioning decline from culture capital to quintessential ghetto. Harlem was evoked in its new status in poetry by the new generation of Africana poets coming of age after 1943, who took the emerging ghetto of Harlem as a legendary instance of racist oppression and employed it as an internationally recognized emblem of solidarity in the Pan-African struggle for political and social justice, just as the previous Africana generation had mythologized New Negro Harlem for its legendary role in initiating the

114

awakening of a black consciousness in the cultural vortex of the West.
The Columbian Marco Fidel Chavez's "Mi corazón permanece en penumbra," for example, identifies the anguish of the black barrio of Puerto
Tejada with the common injustices suffered in Harlem and other African–American ghettos:

> Puerto Tejada, mariposa negra,
> camarada de Hill District, de East Side, de South, de
> > Harlem,
> Puerto Tejada de betún y orillas,
> oloroso a cacao, a paredes carcomidas y húmedas.[1]

> *Puerto Tejada, black butterfly,*
> *comrade of Hill District, East Side, of the South, of Harlem,*
> *Puerto Tejada made of tar and breezes,*
> *smelling of cocoa, of damp and worm-eaten walls.*

Similarly, Chavez's fellow countrywoman Irene Zapata Arias calls Afro-
Americans in Harlem and Alabama to arms as partisans in a common
cause, in "Negro, no mueras por las calles":

> Negro de Nueva York o Alabama
> vecino de mi sangre, . . .

> No te mueras . . .
> No, sin antes quitar [*sic*] hasta con sangre
> que tu pellejo negro vale.[2]

> *Negro of New York or Alabama*
> *neighbor of my blood, . . .*

> *Don't die . . .*
> *Not without shouting, even with blood,*
> *that your black hide is worth something.*

Bernard Dadié's three Harlem poems, in *Homme de tous les continents,*
corresponds to his description of segregated black life in Harlem in his
prose travelogue *Patron de New York:*

> In this country of lighting cells, of flows of dammed-up light,
> Harlem tries vainly to introduce a little life, a little tam-tam.
> Each evening the windows which light up seem like some glanc-
> ing radiance braving the daily darkness. The Negroes on their
> island make signs to the ship *America,* passing at a distance. The
> nation observes them, studies them and opens its portholes any-
> thing but wittingly.[3]

Dadié's image of Harlem as an island recalls the final poem of Hughes's *Montage of a Dream Deferred,* and "Jour sur Harlem" mirrors the circadian reversal, in Harlem, of Hughes's "Negro Servant" in *One-Way Ticket:*

> Une lumière
> > deux lumières
> > > Trois lumières
> > > > Harlem entre
> > > > dans la nuit.
>
> > Dix lumières
> > > Vingt lumières
> > > > trente lumières
> > > Harlem s'installe
> > > > dans la nuit.
> > > > Trente lumières
> > > > > soixante lumières
> > > > > Harlem devient
> > > champ de coton pour Wall Street
> > Cent lumières
> > > mille lumières!
>
> Non! C'est le soleil.
> Harlem
> tombe sa livrée et
> reprend ses rêves.[4]

> *One light*
> > *two lights*
> > > *Three lights*
> > > > *Harlem enters*
> > > > *the night.*
>
> > *Ten lights*
> > > *Twenty lights*
> > > > *thirty lights*
> > > *Harlem sets up for night*
> > > > *Thirty lights*
> > > > > *sixty lights*
> > > > > *Harlem turns*
> > > *fields of cotton for Wall Street*
> > *One hundred lights*
> > > *one thousand lights!*

No! It's sunlight.
> *Harlem*
is taking off its work clothes
> *and putting on its dreams.*

Dadié's "Harlem" presents eleven paired statements of the pain and the paradox of Harlem's isolation from and intimacy with the rest of New York:

Il est une prison dans New York
Un Zoo pour touristes
> Harlem!

Il est des guenilles dans les atours de New York
Un rictus dans les rires
> Harlem!

. . . .

Il est un cimetière de songes dans New York
Un village de fantômes
> Harlem!

. . . .

Il est un enfer dans le paradis de New York
où les flammes d'or savourent du Nègre
> Harlem![5]

It is a prison in New York
A zoo for tourists
> *Harlem!*

It's rags and tatters in the high style of New York
A grin among the smiles
> *Harlem!*

. . . .

It's a cemetery of songs in New York
A community of spooks
> *Harlem!*

. . . .

It's a hell in the heaven of New York
where the golden flames smell of Negroes
> *Harlem!*

A sympathetic sky watches, and "il pleut sur Harlem / Le vieux ciel nègre pleure sur ses enfants.[6] (It's raining over Harlem / The old sky is crying over her children). However, Dadié's Christian prophecy, in "Christmas," of an apocalyptic salvation of the downtrodden, which includes "peuples de Harlem" (peoples of Harlem) in an "Arc-en-ciel du Grand Rêve" (rainbow of the great dream) in its litany of the oppressed,[7] is challenged by his fellow African Tchicaya U'Tam'si, in "Le contempteur" (The scoffer), which accuses Christ of ignorance of the pain of black women everywhere, including Harlem:

> Christ je crache à ta joie
> Le soleil est noir de nègres qui souffrent
> de juifs morts qui quêtent le levain de leur pain
>
> Que sais–tu de New Bell
> A Durban deux mille femmes
> à Pretoria deux mille femmes
> à Kin aussi deux mille femmes
> à Antsirabe deux mille femmes
> Que sais–tu de Harlem[8]

> *Christ I spit at your joy*
> *The sun is black with Negroes suffering*
> *With dead Jews begging leaven for their bread*
>
> *What do you know about New Bell*
> *At Durban two thousand women*
> *at Pretoria two thousand women*
> *at Kin also two thousand women*
> *at Antsirabe two thousand women*
> *What do you know about Harlem*

Particularly intriguing manifestations of the Harlem motif were displayed by the generation of poet-revolutionaries born during the 1920s in lusophone Africa. With their work the complementary phases of awakening and liberation, which crested as separate waves elsewhere in the Africana world, occurred within a single generation. Their emphasis on Pan-Africanism, negritude, and the African personality resembled the Black Awakening of the generation of Claude McKay, Langston Hughes, Jacques Roumain, Léopold Senghor, Léon Damas, Nicolás Guillén, and Manuel del Cabral, but the role of their art as a tool of revolution for their respective nations identified them with age cohorts of the liberation generation. With this generation of poets, influenced by Brazilian Modernism and the literary movements of the Black Awakening, the literatures of lusophone Africa moved to end a general subservience to classical Portuguese cultural and literary trends,[9] but these Afro-Portuguese were motivated by the same sociohistorical forces affecting their contemporaries in the African colonies of Belgium, England, and France. Although Portugal had been on the margin of World War II, this generation born in the 1920s could not have been unaware of the war's lessons for the colonial order: the vulnerability of Europe's might to non-white races such as the Japanese, as well as to Hitler's Aryans; the dependence of Europe's victory at home on the assistance of subject peoples overseas; and the debilitation of the postwar powers, which prevented them from continuing to hold colonial hegemony by sheer economic dominance and force of arms.

The affirmation of African cultural values in the awakening of a Pan-African identity, and the affirmation of African social and political prerogatives through liberation movements, became, for this generation, simultaneous and mutually reinforcing objectives. As the nativist tone intensified, its accompanying note of black identity and social protest was met with official disapproval. *Lusotropicalismo,* the so-called traditional Portuguese mystique that seeks to assimilate all colonial peoples into one multiracial family, was never more explicitly paternalistic than in Angola and Mozambique, where educated blacks were expected to forsake their African past entirely, in favor of a Portuguese identity, and the dictatorial regime in Lisbon seemed determined to hold absolute sway over its ultramarine provinces at any cost. A protracted struggle ensued, in which the nativist poets did not remain neutral. Literature was censored and suppressed from Lisbon, Afro-Portuguese writers were imprisoned, and poets such as Amilcar Cabral and Agostinho Neto became heroes of the revolution.

To this literary generation of poet-patriots in lusophone Africa, for whom the usually distinct phases of Black Awakening and liberation struggle were compressed into the span of a single lifetime, Harlem was a motif of both the legendary assertion of racial consciousness of the 1930s and the struggle for civil rights of the 1940s and 1950s. In major poems, José Craveirinha, Francisco José Tenreiro, Agostinho Neto, Viriato da Cruz, and Noemia de Sousa employed black Harlem as a motif of awakening Pan-African consciousness and as a symbol of racial solidarity in a common struggle. In José Craveirinha's "Africa," Harlem is merely an item in the litany of evils perpetrated by the civilized West:

> E aprendo que os homens que inventaram a cadeira lectrica
> a tecnica de Buchenwald as bombas V2

acenderam fogos de artificio nas pupilas de ex–meninos vivos
de Varsovia
criaram Al Capone, Holywood [*sic*], Harlem.[10]

And I am learning that the men who invented the electric
chair
the technology of Buchenwald the V2 bombs
shot off fireworks in the pupils of ex-young men from
Warsaw
created Al Capone, Hollywood, Harlem.

More characteristically, among the Afro-Portuguese poets of this gener-
ation, black Harlem was considered a leading voice in the global frater-
nity of black men and women crying out for justice. Often this cry for
justice was associated with sorrow songs of the black diaspora, as in
"Fragmento de Blues" and "Negro de todo o mundo," by Francisco José
Tenreiro, who is generally acknowledged as the primary exponent of
Portuguese negritude. In "Fragmento de blues," dedicated to Langston
Hughes, Tenreiro associates black pride in Joe Louis's victory over
Buddy Baer with Harlem and with a blues piano recalling Hughes's
"Weary Blues":

Vem até mim
ao cair da tristeza no meu coração
a tua voz de negrinha doce
quebrando-se ão som grave dum piano
tocando em Harlem:
– Oh! King Joe
King Joe
Joe Louis bateu Buddy Baer
e Harlem abriu-se num sorriso branco[11]

It comes to me
when sadness falls into my heart
your voice of sweet blackness
breaking in the grave sound of a piano
playing in Harlem:
– Oh! King Joe
King Joe
Joe Louis beat Buddy Baer
and Harlem opened up in a white smile.

The Pan-African dimension of Tenreiro's Afro-Portuguese negritude is
also expressed, in the global vision of "Negro de todo o mundo," with

references to blacks in Bahia, the Cape Verde Islands, and Harlem, although in this instance Harlem is confronted with the defeat, rather than the triumph, of the Brown Bomber:

O som do gong
ficou gritando no ar
que o negro tinha perdido.
                    Harlem! Harlem!

América!
        Nas ruas de Harlem
        os negros troçam a vida por navalhas

América!
        Nas ruas de Harlem
        o sangue de negros e de brancos
        está formando xadrez.

Harlem!
        Bairro negro!
            Ring da vida.[12]

The gong of the bell
hangs in the air, screaming
the negro's defeat.
                    Harlem! Harlem!

America!
        On the streets of Harlem
        The blacks mock life with razor blades.

America!
        On the streets of Harlem
        the blood of blacks and whites
        makes a checkerboard.

Harlem!
        Black quarter!
            Ring of the life!

Tenreiro's awakening to blackness involves Harlem in his search for African values, his fusion of blacks and nature, his sense of the unity of the Africana experience throughout the diaspora, and his pride in the African contribution to a cosmopolitan humanism.[13] In addition, Tenreiro's universal sense of the brotherhood of black people evokes a shared experience of international scorn and abuse, expressed in shared musical motifs:

Só as canções longas
que estás soluçando
dizem da nossa tristeza e melancolia![14]

Only the plaintive songs
that you are sobbing
tell of our sadness and melancholy!

Agostinho Neto, Viriato da Cruz, and Noemia de Sousa, like Tenreiro, include Harlem in a global Africana kinship of experience and solidarity, expressed in a common musical vocabulary to transcend national and geographic boundaries. The voice of Tenreiro's "Negro de todo o mundo" is heard by Agostinho Neto, the revolutionary poet-leader and first president of liberated Angola. In Neto's "Voz do sangue," the Harlem black lends a cry of anguish to the global lament:

Palpitam-me
os sons do batuque
e os ritmos melancólicos do *blue*

Ó negro esfarrapado do Harlem
ó dançarino de Chicago
ó negro servidor do South

Ó negro de Africa

negros de todo o mundo

eu junto ao vosso canto
a minha pobre voz
os meus humildes ritmos.[15]

The sound of the batuque
and the melancholy rhythm of blues
palpitate me.

Oh, ragged Negro of Harlem
oh, dancer from Chicago
oh, black servant of the South

Oh, African black

blacks of all the world

I join to your song
my poor voice
my humble rhythms.

Harlem is part of the worldwide chorus heard in Mother Africa's voice in Viriato da Cruz's "Mamã Negra": Tua presença, Minha Mãe – drama vivo duma Raça / drama de carne e sangue / que a Vida escreveu com a pena dos séculos! / Pela tua voz . . . / Vozes de Harlem District South / . . . Vozes de toda America! Vozes de toda África! / Voz de todas as vozes, na voz altiva de Langston / na bela voz de Guillén[16] (Your presence, my mother – the living drama of a race / drama of flesh and blood / which Life writes with the compassion [quill] of centuries / Through your voice . . . / Voices of Harlem District South . . . / Voices of all America! Voices of all Africa! / Voice of all the voices, in the proud voice of Langston / in the beautiful voice of Guillén). The voice of Mother Africa joins in a "canto de esperança" (song of hope), as the poem is subtitled, and, in spite of oceans of pain and bloody landscapes, the light in her eyes "ora esplende / demoniacamente tentadora – como a Certeza . . . / cintilantemente firme – como a Esperança . . . / em nós outros teus filhos, / gerando, formando, anunciando / – o dia da humanidade / O DIA DA HUMANIDADE" (now shines / demonically tempting like Certainty . . . / scintillatingly firm like Hope . . . / in us your children, begetting, forming, announcing / the day of humanity / THE DAY OF HUMANITY).[17]

Noemia de Sousa's "Deixa passar o meu povo" (Let my people go) is the most sustained and developed instance by an Afro-Portuguese poet of the association of Harlem and black music with the universal brotherhood of blacks in the diaspora. The poem opens with the mournful, distant sounds of the Mozambican night, as the poet, in her wood and galvanized-metal hut, turns on the radio to help her drift off to sleep:

> Mas vozes da America remexem-me a alma e os nervos.
> E Robeson e Marian cantam para mim
> *spirituals* negros de Harlem.
> *Let my people go*
> – oh deixa passar o meu povo,
> deixa passar o meu povo – ,
> dizem.
> E eu abro os olhos e já não posso dormir.
> Dentro de mim soam-me Anderson e Paul
> e não são doces vozes de embalo.
> *Let my people go.*[18]

> *But voices from America stir my nerves and my soul.*
> *And Robeson and Marian sing*
> *Negro spirituals for me from Harlem.*

Let my people go.
– oh, let my people go,
let my people go – ,
they sing.
And I open my eyes and now I cannot sleep.
Anderson and Paul resound within me,
and they are not sweet lulling voices,
Let my people go.

The sounds of spirituals from Harlem inspire and compel the poet to write, and, as she writes, familiar forms from the black past seem to peer out of the shadows:

Minha Mãe de mãos rudes e rostro cansado
e revoltas, dores, humilhações,
tatuando de negro o virgem papel branco.
E Paulo, que não conheço
mas é do mesmo sangue e da mesma seiva amada de
                                       Moçambique,
e misérias, janelas gradeadas, adeuses de magaiças,
algodoais, e meu inesquecivel companiero branco,
e Zé – meu irmão – e Saul,
e tu, Amigo de doce olhar azul,
pegando na minha mão e obrigando a escrever
com o fel que me vem da revolta.[19]

My mother with rough hands and tired face,
and the uprisings, oppressions, humiliations
tattooing with blackness the virgin-white paper.
And Paul, who I never met,
but is of the same blood and spirit beloved by Mozambique,
and the sufferings, jailhouse windows, bewitching farewells,
cottonfields, and the inescapable white associate,
and Ze – my brother – and Saul,
and you, my friend with the sweet blue radiance,
seizing my hand and forcing me to write
with the rising disgust it brings me.[20]

The poem concludes with the resolve to keep the faith of the Negro spirituals, presumably in revolutionary activity in Mozambique, "enquanto me vierem de Harlem / vozes de lamentação / e meus vultos familiares me visitarem / em longas noites de insónia" (as long as haunting voices come to me from Harlem and my familiar figures visit me from the shadows on long insomniac nights).[21]

Francisco José Tenreiro's idea of the "negro de todo o mundo" (blacks of all the world), repeated almost verbatim by Agostinho Neto in "Voz do sangue" and paraphrased in the title of Bernard Dadié's *Homme de tous les continents* (Man of all the continents), attested to the same global experience of racial oppression and pan-African solidarity expressed by Marco Fidel Chavez, Irene Zapata Arias, and Tchicaya U'Tam'si, as well as by Viriato da Cruz and Noemia de Sousa. The geographic components of this common global vision varied considerably from author to author – from Hill District, Puerto Tejada, and the South, in Chavez's poem; to New Bell, Durban, Pretoria, Kin, and Antsirabe in Tchicaya U'Tam'si's; to Bahia and Cape Verde, in Tenreiro's – but the motif of black Harlem was common to all, even – or perhaps especially – after the Harlem riots of 1935 and 1943.

In the same colonial context, the white Angolan poet Ernesto Lara Filho's use of black Harlem corresponded, in broad terms, to the conception of Harlem of non-black poets in the 1950s as a primary landscape of black oppression, but in his actual adoption of the lifestyle of the *musseques* (native quarters or slums),[22] he resembled his close counterparts among the white bohemian poets of the Beat Generation in the United States. In "Sinceridade" (Sincerity), Lara Filho interpreted the symbolic locus of Harlem as expressing the alienation of a bohemian identity by sharing in the black experience directly, partaking of black suffering and oppression as well as black music and other black cultural creations:

> Sou sincero
> Eu gostava de ser negro
> viviendo no Harlem,
> nas plantações do Sul
> trabalhando nas minas do Rand,
> cantando ao luar da Massangarala
> ou nas favelas da Baia:
>
> Eu gostava de ser negro.
>
> Eu sou sincero.[23]

> *I really mean it.*
> *I wish I were black*
> *living in Harlem,*
> *in the plantations of the South*
> *laboring in the Rand Mines,*

singing in the Massangarala moonlight
or in Bahia's slums

    I wish I were black

    I really mean it.

Clichés of Harlem's Jazz Age reputation outlived Harlem's fabled night-world, and more than a few poets continued to stereotype Harlem as a world of uninhibited joy and sensuous laughter, long after the legendary cabaret life of Harlem had expired. After 1943, though, Harlem was depicted more typically by non-black poets as a landscape of preternatural suffering, tinged with the nimbus of martyrdom. Leo Liberthson's "Summer in Harlem" and Luis Oyarzun's "La canción de Harlem" are cases in point. Liberthson showed Harlem exhausted and defeated, in bleak, primordial submission:

> The heat hangs heavy in the air
> Like dragon's breath. The squalid
> Caves of brick expel their pallid
> Ghosts. Eyes bloodshot stare
> In curiosity at passersby.[24]

and Oyarzun saluted the quality of Harlem's ordeal with diction of consecration and transfiguration:

> Sentí avanzar tu sangre imaginada
> de dormido soñar por todas partes,
> tu sangre terrible arrodillada
> como un ángel.
>
> Tus casas levantadas como brazos
> eran ruina de rostros, dedos rotos,
> la santidad del pan ya devastado
> de abandono.
> . . . .
>
> Vi tus sombras en sombra coronadas
> de dulces manos amorosas, tantas,
> que callando tu gloria, la besaban
> como santas.[25]

> *I felt your blood advance imagined*
> *in sleeping dreams everywhere,*
> *your terrible blood genuflecting*
> *like an angel.*

Your houses stretched out like arms
were a ruin of facades, broken fingers,
the sanctity of the hearth now desecrated
by neglect.
· · · · · · ·

I saw your shadows crowned by the shadow
of so many loving hands,
that concealing your glory, kissed it
in veneration.

Harlem was comprehended as a setting for suffering also by Russian-born New Yorker, Aaron Kurtz; American Edward Field; Mexican Efraín Huerta, and Spanish-born Cuban Eugenio Florit. All of them viewed Harlem's tortured circumstances as part of broader, more pervasive tensions, neither unique nor endemic to Harlem, for Harlem was understood to symbolize all the oppressed, exploited territories around the globe. In his own translation from the Yiddish original, Aaron Kurtz summarizes the history of outrages perpetrated against blacks in the symbol of Harlem, which his speaker identifies with the anti-Semitic insults and atrocities inflicted by Christian bigots on his father in Russia and on his people at Dachau: "I saw the scabrous walls of Harlem cry the cry of your clean heart."[26] Edward Field's "Ode to Fidel Castro" celebrates the hero of the Cuban revolution for the allegorical promise of a new social order expressed in Castro's gesture when, in 1960, he deserted the Waldorf-Astoria and held his meeting with Khruschev at the Hotel Theresa, on 125th Street in Harlem. The Theresa, "a dumpy landmark in a slum," is deemed an appropriate setting for Castro and Khruschev's newsworthy kiss, which put Harlem on the front page once again and made it, if only for a moment, "the capital of the world / And the true home of the United Nations."[27] Just as Harlem's former status is restored by Castro's newsworthy kiss, so may the other Harlems of this world be transformed.

Eugenio Florit's "Los poetas solos de Manhattan" takes a fellow Cuban poet's failure to find in either Langston Hughes, at home in Harlem, or Florit himself on Park Avenue, an epiphany of the angst and alienation of New York's daily round:

Pero es que aquí, por aquí arriba,
lo mismo da que vivas
en la calle 127
o en el número 7
de la Avenida del Parque.

Aquí todos andamos solos y perdidos,
todos desconocidos
entre el ruido
de trenes subterráneos, y de bombas de incendio,
y de sirenas de ambulancias
que tratan de salvar a los suicidas
que se tiran al río desde un puente,
o a la calle desde su ventana,
o que abren las llaves del gas,
o se toman cien pastillas para dormir
– porque, como no se han encontrado todavía,
lo que desean es dormir y olvidarse de todo –
olvidarse de que nadie se acuerda de ellos,
de que están solos, terriblemente solos entre la multitud.[28]

But it's that here, up here,
it is the same whether you live
on 127th Street
or at number 7
Park Avenue.
Here we all walk alone and lost,
all unknown
in the noise
of the subway trains, and the fire trucks,
and the sirens of the ambulances
that try to save the suicides
who dive into the river from a bridge,
or into the street from their window,
or who turn on the gas,
or take one hundred sleeping pills
– because, since they haven't found themselves yet,
all they want is to sleep and forget about everything –
to forget all about how nobody remembers them,
how they are alone, terribly alone in the crowd.

Efraín Huerta's "Harlem negro," on the other hand, celebrates a temporary interruption of Harlem's misery by the singing voice of Phyllis
Branch, who has come uptown to Harlem from Greenwich Village to
honor the birthday of Joe Wells, the proprietor of Wells' Musical Bar at
135th and Seventh Avenue:

Hoy es el cumpleaños de Joe Wells.
Y en el Harlem negro, el corazón de los asesinatos,
del misterio a vuelta de esquina, del calosfrío y el miedo,

hubo un comienzo de alba, un alba negra
que se dejó arrastrar por esta voz de Phyllis.
Gran noche fue la noche de Joe Wells.
Gran noche para el cielo de Harlem,
Gran noche, ¿por qué no?, para todo Manhattan.[29]

Tonight is Joe Wells' birthday.
And in Negro Harlem, the heart of assassinations,
from the mystery around the corner, from the chill and fear,
there was the beginning of sunrise, a black sunrise,
that let itself be impelled by this voice of Phyllis
It was a great night for Joe Wells.
A great night for the Harlem sky,
a great night, why not, for all Manhattan.

Like Ernesto Lara Filho, Leo Liberthson, and Luis Oyarzun, the Beat poets who wrote of Harlem associated the emerging ghetto with suffering and oppression. Like Aaron Kurtz and Edward Field, they saw Harlem as victimized by global ideologies of bigotry. Like Eugenio Florit and Efraín Huerta, they understood that Harlem's pain was a share of the larger society's angst. Like Ernesto Lara Filho, their inclination to identify with Negro life in Harlem was a measure of their own alienation from the values of the mainstream of their culture. Unlike these poets, however, who were distanced from Harlem in significant ways – by Liberthson's primal imagery, by Oyarzun's elegiac tone, by Kurtz's, Field's, Florit's, and Huerta's limited perspectives as occasional visitors or observers, by Lara Filho's geographic isolation – the Beat poets related to Harlem in direct and personal ways, playing out their identification in behavior as well as in art.

A significant formulation of the hipster identification with the Negro can be found in Norman Mailer's essay "The White Negro": "In such places as Greenwich Village, a menage-a-trois was completed – the bohemian and the juvenile delinquent came face to face with the Negro, and the hipster was a fact in American life."[30] The Negro's dowry in this union of white and black, according to Mailer, was an "existential synopsis," the Negro's cultural intimacy with constant danger, as he lived "in the enormous present" and "subsisted on Saturday night kicks, relinquishing the pleasures of the mind for the more obligatory pleasures of the body, and in his music . . . gave voice to the character and quality of his existence, to his rage and the infinite variations of his joy, lust, languor, growl, cramp, pinch, scream and despair of his orgasm."[31] Seymour Krim, writing about what he calls his "uptown education," locates the quintessential hipster environment in Harlem:

> I sincerely doubt that even God could marry the discrepancies: namely the boots and joys of Harlem life for soul-as-well-as-penis-starved human beings like myself, who could get the needed equivalent nowhere else in this greatest city on the globe, along with its ugliness, .45 calibre toughness, and kick-him-when-he's-just-getting-up attitude (not when he's down – that's too easy). The life scarred pavement that reaches from 110th and Lenox to 155th breeds the one intergrown with the other. And yet if you look at Harlem without morality at all, from a strictly physical and blindly sensuous point of view, it is the richest kind of life one can ever see in American action as far as fundamental staples of love, hate, joy, sorrow, street-poetry, dance and death go. The body and texture of its solid reality is a 100 times stronger, sharper to nostrils, eye, ear, heart, than what we downtown greys are used to. And within a decade (some say two) it will probably end as Negroes become increasingly integrated and sinewed into the society around them. I will truly hate to see Harlem go – where will I seek then in my time of need, O merciless life? – and yet I would obviously help light the match that blows it out of existence. . . . So long, dark dream mistress of my adolescence and educator of my so-called manhood![32]

Not a few observers have indicated that for all its reversals and revisions of classic stereotypes of Negroes – a kind of hip awareness replacing their primal innocence, and their emotional expressiveness attributed to an acute awareness of civilization's constant dangers rather than to ignorance of civilized values – the hipster updated the fundamental axioms of the myth of the primitive Negro, which had fueled some aspects of the Harlem vogue in the 1920s. "Crow-jimism" was Kenneth Rexroth's term for this reversal, by the bohemian cult of the Negro, in the 1950s.[33]

Jack Micheline's writings demonstrate another ironic reversal of meaning in the Beat version of black Harlem. Micheline's "O' Harlem" is an apostrophe to a scene of extraordinary suffering and is "dedicated to the damned":

> O' Harlem smoke rises forever in a dream
> your toothless mother selling flowers
> your junkies gone with sugar
> mulatto death beds of crimson
> your rose of blood above the moon
> Harlem of tears and blood
> your princess eats with watermelon eyes

no cemetery grass
no refuge
only the blood racing time
your glance eats neon with children's eyes
and death knows no tomorrow.[34]

Ironically, this territory of the damned is viewed by Micheline, in other contexts, as a kind of retreat. "Harlem was a place in itself, a country in itself, far different from any place he had seen before," Micheline's narrator states, in the short story "Nigger"; 125th Street was a haven for the tortured, "where the lost souls of the night, without home, room, shelter, family or friends – the junkies, the hustlers, the two-bit pimps, the con men, the lost whites – were waiting for dawn to come up on the street where they could crawl, hide somewhere and wait for another night and another dawn."[35]

An apartment in East Harlem was Allen Ginsberg's retreat from Columbia University, where in Aram Saroyan's delightful phrase, "Harlem and Lionel Trilling intersect in an extraordinary urban mambo."[36] Ginsberg's sojourn in Harlem is recalled in many of his poems as a crucial moment in the development of his vision of "angelheaded hipsters . . . / who dreamt and made incarnate gaps in Time & Space through / images juxtaposed, and trapped the archangel of the soul / between 2 visual images."[37] In *Naked Angels: The Lives and Literature of the Beat Generation,* John Tyrell describes Ginsberg's sweepingly blissful, visionary experience of "a deep, grave voice sounding like 'tender rock' reciting 'Ah! Sun-Flower,' and a few minutes later, 'The Sick Rose,' " while he was masturbating and reading William Blake in an East Harlem apartment in 1948.[38] Ginsberg's "Psalm IV" records the same "secret vision, impossible sight of the face of God. / It was no dream, I lay broad waking on a fabulous couch in Harlem"[39] and describes how Harlem looked in the aftermath of his vision:

> . . . red walls of buildings flashed outside endless
>   sky sad in Eternity
> sunlight gazing on the world, apartments of Harlem standing
>   in the universe –
> each brick and cornice stained with intelligence like a vast
>   living face –
> the great brain unfolding and brooding in wilderness![40]

The Blake visions of 1948 were evidently a threshold experience in the evolution of Ginsberg's literary identity. "Catalyzed to the vitality of the universe," Tyrell states, "[Ginsberg] would now see his own poetic attempts as part of a tradition of magic prophecy."[41] Wherever Harlem is referred to in Ginsberg's poetry, between 1948 and the mid-1960s, it is associated with the idea of madness or visionary awareness, or both. The poem "Vision: 1948," whose title refers directly to the Blake visions, is a revelation of ironic coincidence between the poet and Harlem:

> Outside, great Harlems of the will
>   Move under Black sleep:
> Yet in spiritual scream,
>   The saxophone the same
> As me in madness call thee from the deep.[42]

The saxophone of Harlem, like the madness of the poet, calls to the same "dread spirit in me that I ever try / with written words to move."[43] Here Ginsberg equates the Harlem saxophone – often associated with authentic black soul – with his own anguish, anticipating the line in "Howl," "eli eli lamma lamma sabacthani / saxophone cry that shivered the cities,"[44] which conflates the "spiritual scream, / The saxophone the same / As me in madness" with the despairing call of the crucified Christ.

In "Sunflower Sutra," Harlem is summoned up in San Francisco from memory, when Jack Kerouac points to a sunflower: "Look at the Sunflower, he said, there was a grey shadow / against the sky, big as a man, sitting dry on top of a pile of / ancient sawdust – / – I rushed up enchanted – it was my first sunflower, memories of / Blake – my visions – Harlem."[45] In "My Sad Self," as he gazes at his world from the top of the RCA Building, in New York City, Ginsberg's "history summed up" in the places he sees and remembers includes another reference, "my absences / and ecstasies in Harlem."[46] In "The Lion for Real," Harlem is recalled in the phrase "real lion starved / in his stink in Harlem": here the lion symbolizes the "roar of the universe" and the "starved and ancient presence" of the Lord, which the poet seeks again, after "a decade knowing only your hunger."[47] Harlem was more than simply the place where Ginsberg's Blake visions occurred, however, for his references to Harlem assert a spiritual identification, in addition to specifying a locale. In "Howl," "the negro streets" – by inference Harlem – constitute the spiritual cosmos, as well as the physical environment, of the "best minds of my generation destroyed by madness," for "on the sixth floor of Harlem crowned with flames / under the tubercular sky surrounded by orange crates of / theology,"[48] Ginsberg's "angelheaded hipsters burning for ancient heavenly connection" are touched by Pentecostal fire, like the Apostles, who fled to an upper chamber in fear after Christ's Ascension. Although the Harlem motif can hardly be described as a central focus of

Ginsberg's art, the identification of the visionary spirit with Harlem is a fundamental thread. A quarter-century after his Harlem visions, Ginsberg still characterized his life and his work in the same basic terms in "Who": "From Great Consciousness vision Harlem 1948 buildings standing in Eternity / I realized entire Universe was manifestation of One Mind / My teacher was William Blake – my life work Poesy, / transmitting that spontaneous awareness to Mankind."[49] Furthermore, Ginsberg's use of the Harlem motif was echoed by other poets of the Beat Generation. In "Writ on the Steps of Puerto Rican Harlem,"[50] for example, Gregory Corso identifies Harlem similarly as the place in which the speaker achieved a comprehensive revelation of himself and the order of things, and, in "Altar Piece," Hugh Romney associates Harlem with visions of William Blake: "Having had an illumination of Blake in my hotel room in / Harlem / I am for Buddha and bumming around Park Avenue."[51]

Whereas the Harlem vogue of the 1920s had celebrated the uninhibited, primitive quality of Negro joy and perceived in Harlem a freedom from the self-alienated persona that constituted the only identity offered by Western civilization, the hipster poets of the 1950s regarded Harlem, in its altered circumstances after the Great Depression and World War II, as an icon of suffering, alienation, and perdition. Now it was Harlem's capacity to endure affliction that was significant to individual artists who nurtured the unique core of their personal being. Poets such as Oyarzun, Kurtz, Huerta, Florit, and Lara Filho approached Harlem with great sympathy but observed its circumstances with a detachment born of considerable cultural, psychological, and geographic distance. This Harlem of the damned, ironically, served a need of the Beat Generation. Beats turned to the Negro in Harlem as avatar because of the completeness with which he seemed to oppose the values of society. They emphasized what they took to be Negroes' self-conscious awareness of their outsidership and identified with what they interpreted as the emotional openness of Negro pain. Harlem's very suffering and perdition made it an effective spiritual buffer zone, on the fringes of which Ginsberg and other bohemian poets could seek a kind of peace in which to develop personal visions. In the very period when black authors felt compelled to revise the trope of Harlem as a city of refuge from American racism, the oppressive New York ghetto could be taken by Beat poets as a haven from the inhibiting values of bourgeois American life at midcentury. This view of black Harlem's hip awareness of constant danger and of its peculiar capacity for suffering reversed the stereotypes of primitive innocence and joy that had been projected by the Harlem vogue of the 1920s, but the Beats' reading of the cultural significance of the Harlem motif still rested on assumptions about the fundamental otherness of Negro life. Thus, as African-American authors rose, in their respective ways, to the ideological challenge to the culture symbol of black Harlem by reinterpreting the spiritual imperatives of the Harlem motif using the contemporary terms of the 1930s and 1940s, Africana writers outside the United States incorporated the emerging ghetto of black Harlem in a vision of Pan-African solidarity in the struggle against a global experience of racial oppression, and non-black poets revised the myth of Negro primitivism in response to Harlem's changing circumstances but without challenging their premises and assumptions about the Negro's unalloyed primal qualities.

III

The Inner City:
The 1960s and 1970s

National Memorial African Bookstore, 1964.

9

The Inner City

In the 1950s and early 1960s, the Harlem ghetto was plumbing the nadir of its decline. "Harlem was getting fucked over by everybody, the politicans, the police, the businessmen, everybody," Claude Brown wrote in his autobiography, *Manchild in the Promised Land* (p. 198).[1] The dream seemed permanently deferred. Most of the celebrated figures who had made the Harlem legend either were no longer alive or no longer lived in Harlem. The residual energy and optimism of the legendary spirit of Harlem had been exhausted. Harlem had lost its nighttime cachet. A few survivors of Harlem's once-glamorous cabaret life, such as Small's Paradise, where Malcolm Little had spent several years as "Harlem Red," lingered on, in reduced circumstances. People were still stomping at the Savoy, but the most talented musicians were playing in the jazz spots of West Fifty-Second Street and Greenwich Village, rather than in Harlem, and the Cotton Club had long since moved downtown to Broadway and Forty-Eighth Street. Only the Apollo Theatre, supported by a faithful black clientele, was flourishing. From 1941 to the mid-1950s, the relative position of black workers, compared with that of white workers, improved generally, and economic progress kept pace with the expectations of the black masses, but after the recession of 1954–5, living conditions declined steadily for the majority of Harlemites,[2] who lacked the resources to escape the ghetto by moving to integrated neighborhoods or the new black neighborhoods of choice, or who simply did not wish to abandon the place they had made their home.

By the 1960s, Harlem was notorious for its negative extremes. *Youth in the Ghetto* noted that central Harlem ranked extremely high on six of seven indices of social pathology. The rate of juvenile delinquency, over a ten-year period, consistently had been twice as high as the rate for the city as a whole and was increasing more rapidly. The proportion of habitual narcotics users was from three to eight times that of the city in general. Venereal disease among youth was six times the citywide norm, and infant mortality was twice as high. Proportionately three times as many youth under the age of eighteen were supported wholly or in part by Social Security Aid-to-Dependent Children funds, and Harlem's homicide rate was over six times the city's. "Only with respect to suicide [did] the community rate approximate the city."[3] In a sense, these high indices of social pathology were part of an old story in Harlem. The stages in the evolution of the Harlem ghetto had been drawn, with similar indices and demographic tables, from census tracts by Osofsky for the 1920s and by Capeci and Ottley for the 1930s and 1940s. In the numbers for the 1950s and 1960s, however, one or two new elements stood out. The population of central Harlem, which had grown steadily since the early decades of the century, had dropped nearly 10 percent in a decade. More significant, the major loss occurred in the twenty-one- to forty-four-year-old group, the portion of the population at the peak productive years and most involved in social and civic affairs, whereas the youth population had remained fairly stable.[4] Furthermore, the educational profile of this youthful population presented "a picture of cumulative deterioration": the longer pupils were in school, the greater the proportion who failed to meet established comparative norms of academic competence.[5]

Manchild in the Promised Land reflected the human situation of many young Harlemites in this period with a personal eloquence. Fear was the keynote in *Manchild,* and psychological escape explained the appeal of heroin to the strung-out young men of Brown's generation: "We understood this whole thing about Harlem, but we didn't mind it too much then. You could get high, sit down, and talk about it, even laugh about it" (p. 198). "The only thing that seemed to matter now, to my generation in Harlem, was drugs," Brown remembered. "Everybody looked at it as if it were inevitable. If you asked about somebody, a cat would say, 'Oh, man. he's still all right. He's doin' pretty good. He's not strung out yet' " (pp. 271–2). The ironic reference to the Book of Exodus in Brown's title carries an allusive twist, for the promised land of Harlem had become a new Egypt, where the visitation of drugs was being inflicted on the oppressed, rather than on the oppressor: "It was like a plague, and the plague usually afflicted the eldest child of every family, like the one of the first born with Pharaoh's people in the Bible" (p. 188). Looking back, with an elegiac feeling, on the violent episodes of his puberty for their relative innocence, Brown lamented, "Young Harlem, happy Harlem, Harlem before the plague" (p. 224).

Harlem's hopelessness was even more poignant when compared with the momentum of achievement of the Civil Rights movement in the South. The decade following the end of World War II was an eventful and relatively productive era in the struggle for black rights in the United States, particularly in the Jim Crow South, from which the typical Harlem migrant had fled. Obstacles to racial progress continued to be formidable, but more racial progress had been made in that short period than in the rest of the earlier history of the Republic. In 1946, in *Morgan* v. *Commonwealth of Virginia,* the Supreme Court found for Irene Morgan, a black woman who had refused to move to the rear of a Greyhound bus, and ruled that segregation was an unreasonble burden on interstate travel. In 1947, Jackie Robinson became the first African American to be signed by a major-league baseball team in modern times. In 1948, President Truman issued Executive Order No. 9981, barring segregation in the armed forces. In 1949, discrimination in the U.S. civil service was forbidden, by federal law. In 1950, a Negro, Ralph Bunche, received the Nobel Peace Prize. In 1951, the last all-black unit of the armed forces was deactivated. In 1952, the University of Tennessee was ordered to admit Negroes to its graduate and professional schools. In 1954, the Supreme Court issued a unanimous ruling, in *Brown* v. *Board of Education,* declaring that "separate educational facilities are inherently unequal" and ordering the end of segregation in the public schools with all deliberate speed. On December 1, 1955, Rosa Parks refused to give up her seat in a Birmingham bus, and a boycott was declared that resulted in victory within the year. The Supreme Court ruled, in November 1956, that segregated buses were unconstitutional, and in December the City of Birmingham announced compliance. In 1957, President Dwight D. Eisenhower resolved a deepening Constitutional crisis by ordering the 101st Airborne into Little Rock, Arkansas, to enforce an integration order at Central High, and the Civil Rights Act of 1957 established a commission on civil rights. In 1958, the Southern Christian Leadership Council (SCLC) was founded, as a result of the success of the Birmingham bus boycott, to consolidate the gains and coordinate the next phase of the nonviolent assault on the structure of custom and law that constituted southern apartheid.

Harlem had marked its own racial milestones in the same period, especially in politics. In 1945, Harlem was represented in the Congress of the United States for the first time by a black man, Adam Clayton Powell, Jr., and in 1953 Hulan Jack, a black assemblyman, was elected Manhattan borough president. Nonetheless, a disturbing contrast between atrophy and torpidity in the already extreme social conditions of the Harlem ghetto, and vigor and anticipation in the national pursuit of civil rights, provoked a new emphasis on various forms of direct community action. In the late 1950s, probably no incident was more expressive of this dynamic potential of Harlem than the protest of the Black Muslims, directed by Malcolm X, which occurred in 1959, when a black man named Johnson Hinton was beaten up by police and held without medical care in a Harlem precinct house. In a short time, some fifty members of Temple 7 were standing in rank order outside the precinct house, as the police temporized with Malcolm X inside. First they denied that Hinton was in their custody; then they conceded his presence but refused Malcolm X access to him; finally, as a crowd of Harlem residents began to gather around the Muslims, the authorities backed down. Malcolm X demanded immediate medical attention for Hinton, who was taken to Harlem Hospital in an ambulance as the Muslims marched behind, attracting a crowd of Harlem residents from shops, restaurants, and bars. As Malcolm X described it, the scene at Harlem Hospital became even more ominous:

> The crowd was big, and angry, behind the Muslims in front of Harlem hospital. Harlem's people were long since sick and tired of police brutality. And they had never seen any organization of black men take a firm stand as we were. A high police official came to me, saying "Get those people out of there." I told him that our brothers were standing peacefully, disciplined perfectly, and harming no one. He told me those others, behind them, weren't disciplined. I politely told him those others were his problem.[6]

When Malcolm X was satisfied that Hinton was receiving the needed care, the Muslims dispersed, and the crisis was defused. The Muslim demonstration received wide coverage and commentary as an epiphany of angry possibilities within the black community. The Muslims were "something, I suppose, that most cats in Harlem could accept, because it was an angry thing," Claude Brown recalled in *Manchild*. "If [the Muslims] don't do anything more than let the nation know that there are black men in this country who are dangerously angry, then they've already served a purpose" (pp. 342–4).

The growing influence of Black Muslims on the social landscape of Harlem was one of many signs of change evident in a series of boycotts, rallies, protest meetings, and other events in Harlem that ran parallel with the decisive phase of the Civil Rights movement in the South and accelerated to a climax after the March on Washington in August 1963. The growing influence of the Muslims amid the economic deterioration of the urban ghettos in the late 1950s, and their increasing visibility in Harlem under the leadership of Malcolm X, signaled a change in goals and tactics, from Constitutional rights to economic and social concerns; from middle-class protest to mass action, involving all social classes of the black community; from appealing to white America's sense of fair play to making demands based on the power of the black ghetto.[7] Harlem's endemic problems of deteriorated housing, inadequate segregated schools, police brutality, and structural underemployment proved to be largely impervious to the nonviolent protests, the demonstrations, and the legal and legislative strategies of the national civil-rights organizations. Increasingly, anger and frustration defined the mood of Harlem, and more radical tactics and goals began to be advocated and implemented. Time and sentimentality have emphasized the soaring quality of Martin Luther King's rhetoric and blurred the sharp-edged conviction of a need for fundamental social change expressed in his memorable "I Have a Dream" oration, delivered during the March on Washington in the summer of 1963. Radical action and revolutionary change were the agenda, nevertheless, in Harlem in the immediate aftermath of the Washington march. On November 1, 1963, a major rent strike began. On February 3, 1964, and March 16, 1964, a school boycott protesting the segregated character of New York City schools and the failure of negotiations to integrate the schools, produced a 92-percent absentee rate. On April 22, 1964, the World's Fair Stall-In attempted to make the black freedom struggle in America the theme of the opening date of the World's Fair in Flushing Meadow. Finally, what John O. Killens would later call "the moment of truth in the summer of 1964"[8] initiated a turbulent second phase to the Negro Revolution of the 1950s and 1960s in the United States. On July 18, 1964, a mere fortnight after the enactment of the Civil Rights Act of 1964 marked the culmination of a decade of racial achievement for the nonviolent philosophy, Harlem exploded as it had twenty years earlier, and this time the violent uprising lasted for four days, setting the pattern for a historic series of similar outbreaks across the nation over the course of the next five summers.

The Harlem Riot of 1964 was attributed to racial tensions, inflamed by an incident on July 16 in which a black teenager was shot and killed by an off-duty white police officer. The rioting began in Harlem after a rally on July 18, sponsored by the Congress on Racial Equality (CORE), at which Negro leaders accused the New York City police department of brutality. After the rally, CORE representatives gave the platform to speakers from the crowd, who denounced police, city officials, and the white community. It was time for Harlem to stop talking and start acting, at least one speaker declared. When the crowd marched to a nearby police station, police barred the marchers and tried to set up barricades between the protesters and the precinct house. When the marchers refused to disperse, scuffles broke out. Angry crowds began to gather on street corners, and additional policemen were called into the ghetto. Roving bands of blacks broke plate-glass windows and looted stores. Police attacked the crowds with nightsticks and fired into the air, as the angry protest spread through the streets of central Harlem. From the rooftops, Harlemites battled hundreds of policemen with streams of bottles, bricks, and debris.[9]

Since Harlem was still the symbolic center of the black world, the social and cultural impact of the riot was immediate and stunning. Similar outbreaks followed on July 20, in Brooklyn's Bedford-Stuyvesant neighborhood; on July 24, in Rochester's North Side; on August 2, in Jersey City; on August 11, in Patterson and Elizabeth; on August 16, in the Chicago suburb of Dixmoor; and on August 28 in North Philadelphia. The Harlem uprising, the first of the northern riots of the 1960s, was read as a social and cultural statement. The trope of Harlem had been edited in the streets of Harlem, and its revisions were authorized by rituals of formal repetition in ghetto after ghetto, summer after summer, for five years. Beginning with Harlem, in 1964, a wave of ghetto disorders swept across the nation each summer for the next five years. The riots were repeated in the ghettos of the North, while the Civil Rights movement struggled to consolidate its achievements in the South. The march in the spring of 1965 from Selma, Alabama, to the state capitol at Montgomery had its counterpart in Watts in the summer of that year. James Meredith's 1966 march through Mississippi, in the course of which the slogan "Black power" was first reported by network television, had its counterparts later in the year again in Watts, Atlanta, Chicago, Cleveland, San Francisco, Omaha, Detroit, Dayton, Oakland, North Philadelphia, and east New York. The rhythms of the ghetto riots and the civil rights movement alternated and intertwined, as nonviolent demonstrations were brought to the North and riots occurred in southern cities, and their alternating rhythms were linked, tragically and ironically, when the assassination of the leader of the Civil Rights movement precipitated major riots in Washington, Baltimore, Pittsburgh, and Chicago. By 1968, ghetto rioting had become a convention of collective behavior, its forms and patterns so well elaborated and defined that the murder of Martin Luther King, Jr., immediately sparked disturbances in one-hundred-twenty-five cities in twenty-nine states, resulting in 46 deaths, 2,600 injuries, and 21,270 arrests.[10] It is interesting to note that although there were violent incidents in Harlem after Dr. King's assassination, there were no riots. The preeminent black ghetto that had initiated the wave of series rioting in 1964 did not join in the worst and most widespread of the revolts in 1968, and, perhaps only coincidentally, the spasms of ghetto rioting ended. The subsequent riots of the 1960s involved the Chicago police, at the Democratic presidential convention; New York City's Finest, on the campus of Columbia University; and the Ohio National Guard, at Kent State University.

By 1968, very few urban areas with black ghettos of any appreciable size had been spared the insurrections. Predictably, journalists, commentators, and social scientists were moved to describe, classify, and explain what had happened. The most comprehensive attempt came in the form of the *Report of the National Advisory Commission on Civil Disorders,* issued less than one month before the assassination of Martin Luther King, Jr., in the spring of 1968. The *Kerner Commission Report,* as it came to be called, after Chairman Otto Kerner, noted, "What white Americans have never fully understood – but what the Negro can never forget – is that white society is deeply implicated in the ghetto. White institutions created it, white institutions maintain it, and white society condones it."[11] In his introduction to the Bantam Books paperback edition of the *Kerner Commission Report,* Tom Wicker said, "Reading it is an ugly experience but one that brings, finally, something like the relief of beginning. What had to be said has been said at last, and by representatives of that white, moderate, responsible America that, alone, needed to say it."[12] Nonetheless, the *Kerner Commission Report* was faulted for failing "to consider the disorders as forms of communication in which a political message was being delivered."[13] The *Kerner Commission Report* had asked sociological questions: "What happened? Why did it happen? What can be done to prevent it from happening again?"[14] According to Peter H. Rossi, however, the crucial but unasked question was a hermeneutical one: "What does it mean?" Rossi explains,

> While the "causes" of the civil disorders may be properly sought in the history of the treatment of blacks in our society, the meaning of the civil disorders has to be sought in the disorders themselves. That is to say, that the behavior of the ghetto residents in the disorders themselves contains a message expressing substrata of attitudes and values which are exposed in the suspension of everyday behavior that took place.[15]

In the early 1970s, a spate of new studies and surveys finally began to probe the "substrata of attitudes and values" underlying the ghetto uprisings of the 1960s,[16] but the question of the meaning of the riot, posed at last by social scientists, had been asked and answered in the wake of the Harlem riot by writers and artists, particularly by poets, who had sensed immediately that Harlem had been speaking for blacks everywhere in the 1964 insurrection and that Harlem's violent statement had been affirmed resoundingly in the ghettos across America.

Harlem's status as a trope had been long established in Africana literatures, but the reenactment of the events of July 18, 1964, in Harlem across America's ghettos gave the motif of black Harlem a rare immediacy. The dynamism of the ghettos in revolt galvanized artists of all categories, and an extraordinary outpouring of black creativity followed that recalled the cultural expansiveness of the period of the Black Awakening in the 1920s and 1930s. The burning ghetto of Harlem was invoked as a primary motif in the fine arts, in music, and in literature. Harlem became the landscape, more than any other, through which writers turned to the theme of the ghetto, although almost every urban center in America had its own riot-torn landscape by 1968.

Just as the birth of black Harlem in the early decades of this century had been taken as a sign of cultural rebirth in the 1920s, the Harlem revolt of the 1960s was taken as a sign of cultural revolt. The "journey toward a black aesthetic" that characterized the decade following the ghetto riots of the 1960s was explicitly equated, by Hoyt W. Fuller and others, with the turmoil that had erupted in Harlem and spread across the nation. "The Black revolt is as palpable in letters as it is in the streets," Fuller wrote, in "Towards a Black Aesthetic,"[17] for both the rioters and the authors are "infected with a fever of affirmation. They are saying, 'We are black and beautiful' and the ghetto is reacting with a liberating shock of realization which transcends mere chauvinism."[18] The spirit of cultural revolt was framed not only in the writing but in the publishing of the young writers. Unlike the literary rebirth of the New Negro movement, which had been reshaped and redirected by the tastes and views of the mainstream commercial press, the cultural revolt of the new writers of the 1960s was reinforced by the emergence of a new black audience and new black cultural institutions, especially black-owned book publishers and bookstores. Liberated from a virtually total dependence on mainstream publishers by a flowering of new black-owned publishers (such as Dudley Randall's Broadside Press, Haki Madhubuti's Third World Press, Joe Goncalves's Journal of Black Poetry Press, Ahmed Alhamisi's Black Arts Publications, LeRoi Jones's Jihad Press, Robert Hayden's Counterpoise Series, and Paul Breman's Heritage Series) and by a proliferation of black bookstores or bookstores that stocked black literature, which afforded outlets for their books, the new black writers enjoyed greater freedom to create as they chose than had earlier generations. "Writing for a black audience out of a black experience, the poets seek to make their work relevant and to direct their audience to black consciousness, black unity, and black power," stated Dudley Randall of Broadside Press, a leading publisher of black poetry. "This may be called didacticism or propaganda, but they are indifferent to the labels put upon it. They consider such labels as part of white standards and they reject white standards. They are indifferent as to whether their work survives, just so it is effective today."[19]

After the uprising of 1964, the symbol of Harlem crystallized questions of racial being in America once again, and the Harlem motif was associated with the riot itself. In the decade after 1964, the fact of rioting in Harlem was a pervasive historical influence and a dominant metaphoric presence associated with the motif of black Harlem. It seemed difficult for writers, regardless of race, to fathom Harlem except in some dimension of the insurrection. Poets, who formerly had scarcely acknowledged the disorders of 1935 and 1943, were quick to interpret the riots as events of mythic dimensions after 1964, but the reading of the rioting differed markedly between black and non-black poets. Black poets once more made Harlem a primary motif of black racial consciousness in a plethora of new works, as they reached out for a new sensibility of the inner city as an element of nation building within the riot-torn landscape of the ghetto. Non-blacks generally projected Harlem in their poetry, after the riots, in demented counterpoint to their views of a grasping, self-destructive America gone wrong. Still, the riot of 1964 was not the whole story of the Harlem literature of this period, particularly within the narrative forms in which some of the most inventive African-American fiction writers looked to the cultural past, as well as the violent present, to rediscover the resonance of the Harlem motif's special tradition and began to imagine the Harlem landscape anew.

10

Jitterbugging in the Streets

The motif of black Harlem, reinvigorated as a significant Africana motif in the 1950s by the example of Langston Hughes, blossomed in the decade following the Harlem riot of 1964, when a generation of Afro-American poets, born in the 1930s and 1940s, began writing a new kind of black literature with a collective spirit and racial voice. In "The Black Arts Movement, 1965–1975: A Bibliography," Vashti Lewis states that this new kind of writing was characterized by (1) a more nationalistic assertion of blackness than earlier Afro-American literature; (2) a heavy concentration on the present; (3) a conscious effort to motivate black Americans toward changing their condition; and (4) a style whose language is conversational and whose images are concrete. "In short, in 1965, Black American writing turns from Western tradition in concept, language, images, and structure and moves towards a literature which is both about and for the American of African descent."[1] The identification by this new generation of the riots as a theme for poetry, in the aftermath of the ghetto disturbances of the 1960s, constituted a major innovation in the patterns developed for the Harlem motif over two generations. The riots of 1919 and 1943 had affected the mood and attitude of poets, with consequences for the motif in its first and second phases, but the riots themselves had gone virtually unmentioned in poetry. Yet the Harlem insurrection of 1964 became apocalypse and revelation of the temper of the times in poetry.

In Johnie Scott's "The American Dream," for instance, the articulate character of the riots is asserted: "Speech, or dark cities burning: / For a nation of illiterates / historically unable to master / The white Man's speech / Black people learned well."[2] In Bobb Hamilton's "Brother Harlem Bedford Watts Tells Mr. Charlie Where Its at," the rioting ghettos voice an allegorical street rap that runs down whites' infirmities of character, appearance, and religion, as well as their predatory relationship to black people: "Man you been taking / One big piss / On me for / Four hundred years / And them / Calling me / Nasty!"[3] In Conyus's "i rode with geronimo," the burning ghettos of Harlem and Watts ("i'm the riot running through the streets / throwing bricks setting fires looting stores") are a part of the etiology of the sickness of America ("your hemorrhoid problem").[4]

Lucia Martin and Bob Allen describe the Harlem ghetto with musical images. Lucia Martin's "The Drum" figures Harlem as "a black drum / Over which / Black skin / Is taut. / 5 white fingers / Beat that rhythm / 5 more make / That sound."[5] Bob Allen's "Musical Vietnams" declares, for those unable to really dig Vietnam's "polyphonic symphony of napalm bombs / . . . Harmonizing bombers in azure skies":

> Don't sweat it man let me clue you in
> There is a combo in Watts
> and a quartet in Harlem
> rehearsing groovy sounds
> for a spectacular jazz blast
> right in your
> back yard.[6]

Calvin C. Hernton's "Jitterbugging in the Streets" works with the same musical imagery for the Harlem insurrection, but, with the precision of his imagery, Hernton emphasizes that the music for the jitterbugging in the streets is the rhythm of anti-black terrorism and genocide:

> You say there is violence in Harlem, niggers run amuck
> perpetrating crimes against property, looting stores,
> breaking windows, flinging beer bottles at officers
> of the law
> . . . .
> TERROR is in Harlem
> A FEAR so constant
> Black men crawl the pavement as if they were snakes,
> and snakes turn to sticks that beat the heads
> of those who try to stand up –
> A GENOCIDE so blatant
> Every third child will do the junky-nod in the whore-scented
> night before semen leaps from his loins
> And Fourth of July comes with the blasting bullet in
> the belly
> of a teen-ager

Against which no Holyman, no Christian housewife
In Edsel Automobile
Will cry out this year

Jitterbugging
        in the streets![7]

Harlem also was modified as a legendary setting not for cabarets and high living but for black heroes, with legendary reputations among the people. In *Montage,* Langston Hughes had noted that Harlem took little notice of heroes, white or black. There was only "a movie house in Harlem named for Lincoln / Nothing at all named after John Brown. / Black people don't remember / Any better than white" (pp. 254–5). After 1964, poets began celebrating both contemporary and historical black heroes in verse equivalents of the ubiquitous "walls of respect" – the huge outdoor murals, depicting the giants and role models of the black experience, that were being painted in ghettos all over the country. Larry Neal's homage to Melvin B. Tolson, "Harlem Gallery: From the Inside," reformulates the idea of the walls of respect as imprints on the asphalt memory of the streets (that is, the collective psyche of Harlem) made by the fallen faces of black heroes:

. . . ghosts booga
        loo against the haze, Malcolm eyes in the yellow glow
        blood on black hands. compacted rooms of gloom. Garvey's
        flesh in the rat's teeth. Lady day at 100 centre street
        Charlie Parker dying in the penthouse of an aristocratic
        bitch. Carlos Cook, Ras, Shine, Langston, the Barefoot
        Prophet. Ira Kemp, the Signifying Monkey, Bud Powell.
        Trane, Prez, Chano Pozo, Eloise Moore – all
        falling faces in the Harlem rain
        asphalt memory of blood and pain.[8]

The heroes most often associated with the Harlem setting, in Black Arts poetry, are Duke Ellington, Langston Hughes, and Malcolm X. The affinity for Harlem that Duke Ellington expressed in his music is honored by Bill Harris, Sarah Webster Fabio, and Ted Joans. Bill Harris's "Griot de la Grand (for Duke)" crystallizes the impulse to memorialize the Duke:

You got it.   Down.   On
& between the lines.

                                Riffs

& rhapsodies.

  Storefronts

To Abyssynian.   Jungle to
Sugar Hill.

                                          All.   Right

for the hip.   Square business.
Quick cutters.   Sharp as tacks
Nailed to their tracks.

Harlem ought to be
writing you suites.[9]

Sarah Webster Fabio's "Tribute to Duke," orchestrated to be declaimed
to specific Ellington works, also celebrates the Duke's vision of Harlem:

"Harlem Airshaft"	*Ain't*
"Rent Party Blues"	*got no*
jangling jazzed tone	*money*
portraits of life	*Ain't go no bread.*
in the streets.	*Ain't got*
"Harlem" – a symphony	*no place*
of cacaphonous sound,	*to lay my Afro head.*
bristling rhythms,	*I got*
haunting laments	*those low down*
trumpeting into the air	*blues.*
defiant blasts blown solo	*Chorus: hot-and-Cold-*
to fully orchestrated	*Running-Harlem*
folk chorus.	*"Rent Party Blues."*[10]

Ted Joans's "Duke's Advice" acknowledges Ellington as the cultural and
artistic mentor who directed Joans to Harlem:

I live uptown in Harlem I took Dukes advice
and took the "A" Train Now I'm surrounded by my tribe
                                         again in Harlem
I sleep in bed between two dream queens black naked women
                                          in Harlem
I dream this same dream every night Uptown "A" Trainland
                                          in Harlem
What I'm trying to not say is Uptown I have erotic dreams
                                          it seems about
Bessie Smith and Billie Holiday When I close my eyes they
                                          stay and we lay
Uptown in "A" Trainland in a big black bed in Harlem[11]

Many lyric tributes to Langston Hughes emphasize the poet's special kinship to the Harlem locale with which he is irrevocably identified. Mari Evans's "Langston" says of Hughes: "standing on 127th the / smell of collards / the sound / of cueballs and the / Primitive Church / of The Universal God he / told it like it / was."[12] James Emanuel's "To Harlem: Note on Langston Hughes," captures the quality of Hughes's death in Harlem in the image of the early-morning exit of a lover from his beloved: "Your mannerly, / Your soft light tipping, / Soundless waving / At his window. / Third-floor rear. / Harlem. / U.S.A. of him. / Backyard of his soul, / Basement, attic, all, / Who took him in / And up and where / He meant to go."[13] Conrad Kent Rivers's "For All Things Black and Beautiful" recognizes the centrality of Harlem in Hughes's spirit and work in the lines that open and conclude this extended tribute to Hughes: "For all things black and beautiful, / The brown faces you loved so well and long, / The endless roads leading back to Harlem."[14] Ted Joans's "Promised Land" lauds Hughes's unequivocable commitment to the blackness embodied in all the Harlems of America ("LANGSTON HUGHES / PAID HIS DUES / IN THE HARLEMS / OF THE U.S.A."), and Joans's "Passed on Blues: Homage to a Poet" praises Hughes for "the sonata of Harlem / the concerto to shoulder bones / pinto beans / hamhocks IN THE DARK / the slow good bouncing grooves / That was the world of Langston Hughes."[15]

The assassination of Malcolm X inspired a number of poems, collected by Dudley Randall and Margaret G. Burroughs in *For Malcolm: Poems on the Life and Death of Malcolm X* (1967), many of which associate Malcolm X with the motif of black Harlem. Larry Neal's "Malcolm X – An Autobiography" makes Harlem pivotal in the transformations by which Malcolm Little evolves into Malcolm X. First Malcolm becomes "Big Red," in a Harlem that is characterized as "neon madness," "death oozing across the room," and "smelly / with white / sex flesh and dank sheets, and . . . / blood and money," but Harlem also offers the possibility that Malcolm eventually discovers:

> through the Harlem smoke of beer and whiskey, I
> understand the
> mystery of the signifying monkey,
> in a blue haze of inspiration, I reach for the totality
> of being.[16]

Raymond R. Patterson's "At That Moment," perhaps the most powerful of the poems in *For Malcolm,* depicts the death of Malcolm as a liberating baptism of Harlem. Malcolm's vital force is described as seeping through the wooden boards of the stage on which he was standing when he was shot, beginning a journey that pervades the bowels of the city and transforms Harlem, as Harlem had transformed him:

> At that moment,
> Those who drank water where he entered . . .
> Those who cooked food where he passed . . .
> Those who burned light while he listened . . .
> Those who were talking as he went, knew he was water
> Running out of faucets, gas running out of jets, power
> Running out of sockets, meaning running along taut wires –
> To the hungers of their living. It is said
> Whole slums of clotted Harlem plumbing groaned
> And sundered free that day, and disconnected gas and light
> Went on and on and on . . .
> They rushed his riddled body on a stretcher
> To the hospital. But the police were too late.
> It had already happened.[17]

The grammar of the lyric use of Harlem altered, in the black poetry of the 1960s and 1970s, as the meaning of black Harlem changed in the public imagination after the riot. Before 1964 there had been only a hint, in an occasional poem such as Ricardo Weeks's "Harlem Junkman,"[18] that "Harlem," as an adjective, could signify more than simply "of Harlem" or "from Harlem," but after 1964 Harlem was regarded as a social or spiritual condition or state of being, and the term "Harlem" was employed with greater complexity in the diction of Africana perception. Under the intensification of poetic compression and the presumption of an intuitively shared post-riot sensibility, Harlem was inflected in a variety of ways in the grammar of Black Arts poetry. Formerly a synonym for "black," Harlem now also became an intensifier of states of being associated with blackness, in Arnold Kemp's "A Black Cop's Communion":

> Such a Harlem waste
>   white
>   Alabama soil
> lies virgin and fertile
>   in the Easter glow;[19]

and in June Jordan's "All the World Moved":

> Blessing a fear of the anywhere
> face too pale to be family
> my eyes wore ribbons

for Christ on the subway
as weekly as holiness
in Harlem.[20]

Henry Dumas's "Mosaic Harlem" and "Harlem Gulp" are the titles of
poems that are not linked in any specific way to the physical, geographic,
or political reality of the New York ghetto but that employ Harlem to
evoke the state of being of blackness in the diaspora. "Mosaic Harlem"
(that is, the composite status of being black) is illustrated by an accumu-
lation of concrete images of "news"of black life:

what news from the bottom?
Jesus learning Judo
I scratch giant lice and ghetto
fleas in the gutter of my mind
the sucking boll weevil concerts to blood
when will the mosquito fear the rage under the sweat?

what news from the black bastille?
ram of god busting up shit
unicorning the wolf, panthering the fox
the old shepherd is himself lost
the ram will not stop, what news from the bottom?
the east!   the west!   and the top![21]

Similarly, a series of images illustrating the condition of black life surviving in the omniverous gulp of whiteness is entitled "Harlem Gulp":

like black pearls
trapped
in the white cerebellum
we glisten out of reach

of gun drum and talking bird[22]

As Harlem was inflected in the syntax of perception, the idea of black
Harlem as an interior landscape pervaded the use of the Harlem motif,
and the sociological and journalistic term "inner city" came to be understood also to mean the inner city of the black spirit. In "Eclipse," by
Albert E. Haynes, Jr., the speaker, declaring that the darkness in the
open mouth of marble statues "speaks of caves and mines / and ghettos,"
defines Harlem's inner landscape of "dreams / formed within / by the
slow inertia of infinite numbers / blended, crawling on black heaven:
Black Harlem / questing for a soft lap / to place his body."[23] In Edward
S. Spriggs's "For Brother Malcolm," Harlem's inner city memorializes
the martyred Malcolm X by nurturing and sustaining his ideals:

there is no memorial site
in harlem
save the one we are building
in the street of
our young minds
till our hands & eyes
have strength to mould
the concrete beneath our feet[24]

In "Every Harlem Face Is AFROMANISM Surviving," Spriggs conceives of a collective landscape of the spirit, "a jointtenancyincommon" of inner cities, including Malcolm's Harlem.

Haki Madhubuti (Don L. Lee), who, in the view of some critics, stands as the exemplary figure of the Black Arts movement, evokes the motif of black Harlem in a program for black people everywhere, in "To be Quicker / for Black Prisoners / on the inside & outside – real":

anything working to save us to pull us
closer to Tanzania to Guinea to Harlem to the West Indies to
closer to momma to sister to brother closer to closer to
FRELIMO to Rastafory to us to power to running run to
build
to control lifelines to Ashanti to music to life to Allah
closer
to Kenya to the black world to the rays of anti-evil[25]

He warns those blacks who may be ambivalent about their blackness in "We Walk the Way of the New World":

& he will catch all the new jojo's as they wander in and out
and with a fan-like whisper say: you ain't
no tourist
and Harlem ain't for
sight-seeing, brother[26]

He blesses all black men in the name of Harlem, in "Marlayna":

Harlem's night upon the world
women there
are drops of algerian sand
with joyeyes overworked to welcome.
beauty flows the curves of her natural,
hangs
on out like saturday night skipping sunday
she walks / moves the natureway.

to a hungry man
she's his watermelon.[27]

Clarence Major's "Harlem '67" perceives Harlem as a spiritual nexus where destinies intersect and the interior necessity of the race informs unlikely surfaces with unexpected inner meanings. Major asserts there the mysterious, all-encompassing dominion of black life:

Strong people and weak
We are here
Drenched in blackness
And tears
    Why are we here
    Why do we reach
    Why do we die

        Why do we seek
        Where do we come from

Where do we go
Have we forgot
Tell if you know
If you know
Please tell me . . .
I know that Harlem
Is mysterious everywhere
  Our dominion
    our dominion
      our dominion
Is what?[28]

Julia Fields's "Harlem in January" challenges the simplistic misunder-standing of the inner city reflected by journalists and politicians when they ponder the last, or the next, long hot summer. In Harlem's winter, a different understanding is to be found:

There at the top of the world
Frozen like a star
All winter long
Whose silent nightmare
Are you now
Whose themes for headlines
For legislation or reform?

There at the top of the
Indifferent world

Frozen like a star
All winter long you are.[29]

Nikki Giovanni's "Walking down Park" proceeds, from a series of nostalgic imaginings about the sylvan condition of the ghetto before it suffered man's technological and social debasement, to a vision of possibility for that same landscape, possible if only black people's inner resources of the spirit were allowed to flower:

ever think what Harlem would be
like if our herbs and roots and elephant ears
grew sending
a cacophony of sound to us
the parrot parrotting black is beautiful black is beautiful
owls sending out whoooo's making love . . .
and me and you just sitting in the sun trying
to find a way to get a banana from one of the monkeys
koala bears in the trees laughing at our listlessness

ever think its possible
for us to be
happy[30]

The interior landscape of black Harlem is not always a positive or a nurturing one in Black Arts poetry. For some black poets, Harlem's state of inner being could also mean constriction and spiritual impotence. Habib Tiwoni characterizes Harlem as "my Harlem / my split level cave" in "Wavelengths Away."[31] And Ntozake Shange's "Lady in Blue" experiences abuse and depersonalization in Harlem:

i used to live in the world
a woman in the world
i hadda right to the world
then i moved to harlem
for the set-up
a universe
six blocks of cruelty
piled up on itself
a tunnel
closin[32]

Harlem's vitality does not penetrate the isolation of Shange's Lady in Blue, for Harlem represents fear, insecurity, exposure, victimization, and cruelty. In Shange's poem the multiplicity of human reactions under the pressure of oppression in Harlem does not bring intimacy, only with–

drawal. Askia Muhammad Touré's "Dago Red (A Harlem Snow Song)"
is an attack on Italian crime syndicates burying the vibrant, summer
landscapes of Harlem's inner city of the soul in a winter avalanche of
"snow" (narcotics):

> Summer in Harlem in bright tropical colors:
> Blackfaces alive in hot pinks / flaming reds / golden orange
> crowning strong Blackbodies in rhythm in motion like a
> constant boogaloo, a James Brown masterpiece, a drumsong
> in colorful Harlem – ebbing and flowing rising and falling
> in summertime, hot sweaty summertime in our captive pain-
> years.
> But winter is present and snow is falling over Harlem
> rooftops,
> hallways, down basements tenements swirling blizzards:
> cold chill winter-death being brought to you raw – the New
> Hawk-
> in-summer – by the same people who brought you
> Prostitution
> Gambling Numbers Bootleg Likker in livid color.[33]

And "the edge of Harlem" is Audre Lorde's phrase, in "Dear Toni Instead of a Letter of Congratulation upon Your Book and Your Daughter
Whom You Say You Are Raising to be a Correct Little Sister," for those
blacks who have made themselves a place of honor or achievement.
Lorde celebrates the achievement that a fellow artist has made in her life
and in her art but warns of the impact of the cities we carry inside us on
the children in the next generation: "for we are landscapes, Toni, /
printed upon them as surely / as water etches feather on stone."[34]

The Black Arts movement's use of Harlem as an inner landscape of
the spirit echoed black Harlem's oldest and most fundamental employment: the often ironic disjunction between possibility and actuality in
Harlem, which had characterized the motif from its earliest formulation
by New Negro poets in the 1920s. Some Black Arts poetry illuminated
the reality of Harlem with a manifold sensibility of the urban landscape,
akin to Claude McKay's, which emphasized perception of Harlem's essential spirit and truth rather than observation of its physical and social
reality. Hurley X's "Harlem River," for example, begins with the statement "I can see you / River of green glass / And Mystic algae." But the
river is "seen" only in terms of the "shadowy glow [which] Haunts a
room of my mind / Where I stand numb and blind / Watching your
subtle joy dance, / Your bristling ecstasy."[35] Similarly, Horace Mungin's
"Harlem" is a landscape of perception: "The capital / of Black thought

. . . an awakening / mind becoming accustomed to truth."[36] And "Theme Brown Girl," by Abu Ishtak (Elton Hill), declares, in terms recalling Claude McKay's "Harlem Dancer" and Roussan Camille's "Nedje,"

> I have watched you
> > in Haiti
> crowned with bandanna & bathing in coolness
> and in Harlem
> > lonely on midnight corners;
> . . . . : . . . . .
> Yet,
> > I still see Africa in your eyes
> > girl with the spirit of a leopard
> > tell the world that time
> > will never mark your face[37]

Harlem is evoked also as a standard of perception in poems by Gayl Jones, José-Angel Figueroa, Maya Angelou, and Welton Smith. In "Tripart," Gayl Jones exalts Harlem as a Moslem ideal of positive humanist values: "May you go to Chicago when you die, / i'll be in Harlem with Allah's / blessings / in a restaurant / dealing with humanity."[38] Using Spanish Harlem as the norm, in "East 110th Street," José-Angel Figueroa berates his nuyorican compatriot, Piri Thomas, with perceptual failure: "not knowing that his days out of harlem / have created / manteca in his mind."[39] In "Harlem Hopscotch" Maya Angelou asserts Harlem's victory over conflicts of perception by equating the pivots and spins of belief against reality in Harlem to a sidewalk game that little girls play: "Both feet flat, the game is done. / They think I lost. I think I won."[40] Welton Smith's "phat" senses images of Harlem in the stroll of a black woman: "moving those hips / like that down lenox like a confusion / of savannahs and cypresses and violets / stopping at an african village."[41] In Smith's "new york, new york," the speaker returns from Harlem, after "relating to my superiors / the blues," like "one turned inside out, revealing lost cities."[42] In his "malcolm," the landscape is felt rather than seen: "in harlem, the long / avenue blocks. the miles / from heart to heart."[43]

The inner city of Black Arts poetry evoked Harlem as it had been from the first in Africana poetry, as an archetypal setting for the collective activities of the race and a key location in the moral and historical geography of the black experience in America and the diaspora – what thirty years earlier Césaire had called "mon originale geographie . . . la carte du monde faite a mon usage" (my original geography . . . the map of the world made for my use). This poetry imagined Harlem in terms of the global and historical extension of the black presence in Gladstone Yearwood's "I Am the Soil (A Poem for My Mother)":

> I am Harlem.
> My name is Isis,
> Osiris,
> Tubman, Douglass, Turner,
> Nkrumah, Cabral.
> I will rise as I have risen
> Countless times before
> Against the evil tyrant.
> I am the soil.[44]

and Tauhid Mshairi's "Spiritual Unity":

> from lower Egypt
>   to upper Egypt
> from lower Harlem
>   to upper Harlem[45]

the moral panorama of black loving in Quincey Troupe's "You Come to Me":

> the taste of your sweetness
> permeates my lips and my hair
> with the lingering sweetness of Harlem
> with the lingering sweetness of Africa
> with the lingering sweetness of freedom[46]

and of black endurance in Rob Penny's "be cool, baby":

> hillharlemhough. . . .[47]

and also in James Kilgore's "Black Centennial":

> Your own children lie down hungry
>   in Newark and Paterson, New Jersey;
>   in Harlem, New York City;
>   in Inner-City, U.S.A.[48]

and Alicia Loy Johnson's "Long March":

> up michigan & 38th through englewood and lawndale
> past jackson county in carbondale through
> cleveland, mississippi up through harlem down
> through cairo we marched[49]

In this geography of the race, the inner city of Black Arts Harlem could be a source of pride, inspiration, and anger, or even of bitter truth. Charles Cobb's "Mekonsippi" projects a map of the moral geography of American oppression in which the Mississippi runs into the Mekong Delta near the docks of Harlem.

> Yeah,
> the mississippi
> runs into the mekong
> get the boat at harlem
> sail red rivers
> black seas
>
> or walk
> from cotton to rice
> from cement to silt
>
> Vietnam
> and
> Amsterdam
>
> avenues of whitey's wars
> Mekonsippi
>
> the 17th isn't parallel
>
> doesn't divide.[50]

Very different from the civilizing rivers celebrated by Langston Hughes in "The Negro Speaks of Rivers," Cobb's rivers bespeak the violence of racism inflicted on non-whites, black or yellow. And Eugene Redmond's "barbecued cong: OR we laid MY LAI low" identifies the atrocities of American soldiers against Asian civilians in the Viet Nam War with genocidal attacks on blacks in the United States:

> i lay down my life for My Lai and Harlem.
> i lay down my burden in Timbuctu and Baltimore.[51]

Simply by naming Harlem, a poet could invoke the archetypal milieu as a setting of collective significance appropriated for meaningful activities of the race, in such poems as "Tempting," by Ali Bey Hassan Jamal (Joseph Kitt),

> In the summer night cool,
>   she can be seen on any Harlem street,
>   for she is Black woman
>   and her name is tempting.[52]

Nikki Grimes's "Untitled,"

> Walking down 125th street "Hey baby."
> Ain't seen you in a long time. You sure
> do look good and smiling at inflated abdomen
> saying "Don't tell me" and me saying yes,
> five months and him saying that's beautiful
> and I know you got a good man and eyes wandering
> through empty sky and imaginary man and smiling
> always smiling and as fine as you are, I know
> you got a good man, a true brother and the looking
> inside at other sisters smiling cause the
> revolutionary fathers of their revolutionary
> babies got in the wind and some sister saying
> "yeah, that's what being a black woman is about"
> and meaning the coincidence and all and me asking why?[53]

Mae Jackson's "(To Someone I Met on 125th Street, 1966),"

> I saw you there in that dark hole
>
>   which is really your home
>
> No longer fighting
>   just
> Submitting and existing
> And even the bitter wind
> Nor the cold concrete ground
> Would bring on those systems of death
>   which is really what you wanted[54]

and Bobb Hamilton's "Poem to a Nigger Cop":

> Hey there poleece
> Black skin in blue mask
> You really gonna uphold the law?
> What you gonna do when you see
> Your Mama
>   Running down 125th street with
> A t.v. set tied up in a bandana trying to catch a train to
>   Springfield Gardens?[55]

This persistence of earlier patterns of the Harlem motif in Black Arts usage suggests a greater degree of acceptance of a received Afro-American literary legacy than many of the younger Black Arts poets and theorists may have realized or been prepared to acknowledge at the time.

One measure of Harlem's importance to the imagery of Black Arts poetry was the motif's employment by some young poets as a recurring and unifying element, in poetry collections during the period after the Harlem riot of 1964. Harlem is employed as a self-explanatory racial emblem in the titles of poetry collections, even when the volumes are not specifically focused on Harlem but rather on the range of the black experience, as are Antar S. K. Mberi's *Song out of Harlem,* Gil Scott-Heron's *Small Talk at 125th and Lenox,* and Conrad Kent Rivers's *Still Voice of Harlem.* Mberi's volume contains several very brief references to Harlem, in five poems – "Rivers," "In Spain in Harlem: It Is the Night of the Horses," "Charles Street," "Second (Minuet in Duet) Movement: African Twist, Latin Boogaloo then Shingaling," and "Song Out of Harlem"[56] – but Harlem is less a theme than a fixed point of spiritual reference from which the poet ranges across the modern experience of oppression against persons of all races:

> In all this, through all this
> I must confess, i am never idle
> tirelessly mining a music
> fiery as a heart of bitumen
> my song rises out of Harlem
> blazing[57]

Gil Scott-Heron's *Small Talk on 125th and Lenox* contains only four poems that even imply a Harlem setting. The title poem is a sequence of revealing lines of typical street dialogue that could be heard in any black ghetto.[58] Although "Paint It Black" and "Riot" specify Harlem, in a detail or two, they too are composite views of the ghetto as concept or condition rather than of Harlem per se.[59] "Harlem: The Guided Tour" is more an image of all ghettos than a poetic visit to Harlem:

> . . . climb the stairs and listen
> to the joyful noises your neighbors are making
> and say hello to the rats that have so long been
> a part of your life that they all have names.
> . . . climb the stairs to soul music
> and soul food and souls lost in Harlem
> who no longer even sing about heaven.
> Get a good night's sleep because
> you're on the air again at six
> tomorrow morning.[60]

For Conrad Kent Rivers, as for Mberi and Scott-Heron, Harlem sits at the spiritual center of the map of the Afro-American experience. Har-

lem is valorized in the poem "Africa" as the essence of the black home-
land in America:

> Surely some part of you
> blows a saddened dusky breeze across the sea
>
> and walks the streets of Harlem
> lifting a veil of ignorance from our faces
>
>> to remind us there once was a homeland[61]

The title poem of *The Still Voice of Harlem* portrays what in another
poem Rivers calls "Harlem's honeyed voice"[62] as a welcoming, nurturing sound of hope for the future, because all of Afro-America's possibilities, for better or worse, are identified with Harlem:

> Come to me
> broken dreams and all.
> Surrender the glory of your wayward souls.
>
> I shall find a place for them in my gardens.
> Weep not for the golden suns of California,
> nor your mother twisted by the washing board.
>
>> I am the hope
>> and tomorrow
>> of your unborn.
>
> Truly, when there is no more of me
> there will be no more of you.[63]

Mberi, Scott-Heron, and Rivers locate their volumes of poetry at the
spiritual center of black life by identifying their books through their titles
with Harlem, the crossroads of the interior geography of the Afro-
American experience in this century, figuratively associated with international Africana being in the world, thereby invoking the spirit of Harlem in all the poetry in the collection.

More than any other of the young poets of his generation, David Henderson most thoroughly and extensively utilized the thematic and stylistic patterns of the motif of black Harlem after the 1964 riot in his volume
of collected poetry, *De Mayor of Harlem, 1962–1966.* "Walk with De
Mayor of Harlem,"[64] the first of twenty-seven poems in "De Mayor of
Harlem" sequence, invokes the reader to "enter Harlem / to walk from
the howling cave / called the 'A' Train / from columbus circle / (find
america discovered)." The subway to Harlem is characterized as an "existential TWA nightcoach / rome to auschwitz express / where multi-

tudes vomit," echoing the title of a poem by García Lorca from *El poeta en Nueva York*. But Harlem, "black mass / black land," is also a "sight for those / who live away / a new land! / no dream stuff." "Walk with the mayor of Harlem," Henderson's invocation continues: "talk to me talk to me / tell me like it is." He predicts, "there will be monsoon rains / over Harlem / black panther bonnevilles prowling / from block to block. / helicopters colliding with tenements / in orange surprise" (pp. 13–15). The poems that follow in the sequence capture the tone and texture of black Harlem, both in the specifics of its gritty actuality in the 1960s and on the level of its historical and figurative associations elaborated over half a century.

"Bopping" recalls the ritualized violence of adolescent males in street-gangs, who earn self-love in the only way their ghetto-hardened concepts of manhood permit:

> I remember the arm pumping cap crowned blades
> of my boyhood
> their elemental gait talking
> deep beneath my eyes . . .
>   the list at waist and trunk
>   whip of an arm
> abrupt then long wing-tipped stride
> of days when we had to show ourselves love
> in difficult pretensions
>   as if speaking words of self-love
>   was too remote a performance
>   when before the fact
> we understood all too well
> the action of the thrust.   (p. 16)

"So We Went to Harlem" offers the Rabelaisean low comedy of an occasion when Henderson and two male poet-friends, one black and one white, "went to Harlem to get some pussy":

> So in going to Harlem and being meandered throughout
> We: the chick, Richard, Cal and I
>   Getting Black
> Market wine.   Cal talking nigger-shit, Richard jealous
> of his tax free purchase.   Cal cajoling at last
> To a final reluctance.   Me sopping wet and dripping,
> Knowing Richard's fate   Not knowing if I felt exultation
> Pain or guilt submitting generously to the wine
>   (p. 20)

Other poems in *De Mayor of Harlem* touch on the visit of Pope Paul, on dope, on Malcolm X's assassination, and on white fear and black rage in Harlem.

"Keep on Pushing" explores Harlem right after the riot, emphasizing the police occupation, the numbers of unemployed black males who constitute the police's equal-and-opposite reactive force, and the tension between them. Harlem is observed, in the faces of children, as a territory under military occupation:

> I walk and the children playing frail street games seem
> like no other children anywhere
> they seem unpopular foreign
> as if in the midst of New York civilization existed
> a cryptic and closed society.
>   Am I in Korea?   (p. 32)

Harlem is also seen as exploited by opportunistic journalism:

> The *Journal-American* in my lap
> headlines promise EXCLUSIVE BATTLE PHOTOS
> by a daring young photographer they call Mel Finkelstein
> through him they insure "The Face of Violence – The
>   Most Striking Close-ups" /
> WWRL the radio station that serves
> the Negro community
> tools along on its rhythm n blues vehicle

The poem's final vision is a flash of residual violence:

> a flaming bottle bursts on Seventh Avenue
> and shimmies the fire across the white divider line
> helmets
> and faces white as the fluorescence of the streets
> bob by
> Prowl cars speeding wilding wheeling
> the loony turns of the modulating demodulating sirens
> climb the tenements window by window
> Harlem moves in an automatic platform
> The red fish lights swirl the gleaming storefronts
> there will be no Passover this night
> and then again the gunfire high
> in the air   death static
>   over everything . . .
> ripped glass

```
shards          sirens          gunfire
down towards 116th                          (pp. 35–6)
```

Poems after "Keep on Pushing" in Henderson's sequence declare a more committed resistance. In "Yarmuul Speaks of the Riots," the speaker declares:

```
but i am also a man of color
            the third world
            has got to stand now
i got to be here
to see this thing go down
do what i can /            (p. 38)
```

In "Marcus Garvey Parade," the speaker gets caught up in the spirit of the Back to Africa movement:

```
is it proud? is it fun? is it serious? is it political?
is it
ALL OF HARLEM STRAINED OUT OF WINDOWS
STANDING ON FIRESCAPES
STANDING ON SIDEWALKS STANDING IN THE STREETS
AS THE BUSES THE CABS THE TRAINS BOATS &
            PLANES HALT
AS THE MARCHERS MARCH BACK TO AFRICA
                        once more
                                    (p. 40)
```

And in "The Last Set Saga of Blue Bobby Bland," Blue Bobby falls from grace at Harlem's Apollo because he sticks with slicked-back, "processed" hair, when the times call for the political statement of a "natural":

```
poor blue bobby
a headline star
on an uptight stage /
like the phalarope
you were one verse
too late.      (p. 42)
```

Three poems dedicated to Langston Hughes intersperse the final poems of the title sequence of *De Mayor of Harlem*. "Sketches of Harlem," dedicated to Hughes, delineates the experience of "tripping out" on drugs. "Do Nothing Till You Hear from Me, for Langston Hughes" depicts Hughes's wake, at a funeral home "on saint nicholas avenue /

between the black ghetto and sugar hill / where the slick black limousines await yr body / for the final haul from neutral santa claus avenue / harlem usa," then catches details of Hughes's funeral as Hughes would have done it: "In writing the fine details / of your last production / you would have the black sapphires / there / guardians of yr coffin / yr argosy / in life and death / the last time blues / with no hesitation" (pp. 56–7). "Harlem Xmas," the third poem dedicated to Hughes, concludes *De Mayor of Harlem* by evoking Harlem in winter:

> cold druid seasons
> approximate the age
> > huge fires of midwinter
> > or whiskey-fire mid-belly
> > los indios called firewater
> dont burn like sun
> or sit
> > on cold stoops /

In *De Mayor of Harlem,* Henderson summarized the characteristic treatment of the Harlem motif by the young generation of Black Arts poets. Like his contemporaries in the third phase of the motif of black Harlem, he recapitulated many of the patterns elaborated in the first and second stages. By employing Harlem as an archetypal milieu, making it a setting of collective significance for the communal activities of the race and emphasizing Harlem's inner spirit as well as observing the tension and the paradox of its physical and social reality, Henderson accepted and continued the Afro-American literary legacy of the motif of black Harlem. In addition, he innovated in the manner of his generation, employing the motif also as a symbol of the temper of the times, depicting the Harlem riot of 1964 as apocalypse and revelation, establishing Harlem as a legendary setting for legendary black heroes, and projecting the interior landscape of the inner city of the spirit on the physical and social reality of the racial ghetto.

Older poets, who had emerged in the periods of the Black Awakening (1919–1943) and of the Dream Deferred (1943–1964), were affected by the new spirit of the youthful generation of poets of the Black Arts movement, who were under thirty-five – in most cases under twenty-five – when the Harlem riot of 1964 occurred, and they too turned, or returned, to the theme of black Harlem after 1964. Born of an earlier generation, and published before the 1960s, writers such as Ted Joans, James Emanuel, and Raymond R. Patterson gained greater recognition with the new interest in Black Arts poetry after 1964.

James Emanuel employs the motif of black Harlem in poems with the mood and spirit of the 1960s in *The Treehouse and Other Poems* (1968). In "For 'Mr. Dudley,' a Black Spy," "Harlem dud," is the lead-off insult in a string of epithets characterizing the duplicitous Mr. Dudley, who is despised for currying favor with influential white folks.[65] Harlem is the setting for epiphanies of the new self-assertiveness of black Americans, in "Animal Tricks" and "Stop Light in Harlem." In "Animal Tricks," the speaker, "on the A Train leaving Harlem," observes a white man – referred to as "Whitey" – reading a wildlife magazine, while two black men – each referred to as "a brother" – read about rifles and the Black Panther Party. The white man's interest in how birds pick vitamin D from beneath their feathers is interpreted by the speaker as an instructive precaution:

> Yeah . . . see what this cat doin?
> watching crows beneath they wings
> he gettin in the mud seein how beavers live
> figurin what he gonna do
> if he gotta hide
> if he gotta get hisself a cave
> if he gotta live without no sun
> if all this crap he putting down
> knock out the WORLD.[66]

The black brothers, though, are getting their vitamin D from the pamphlets about guns and black power that they carry underneath their wings:

> Them brothers
> gettin they Vitamin D
> gettin they 7–de/hy/dro
> cho/les/ter/ol –
> yeah –
> when that blacknes come
> THEY
> gonna live.[67]

And "Stop Light in Harlem" captures a provocative confrontation between a passing Harlemite and a white driver halted by a Harlem stoplight on his way from midtown Manhattan to his suburban community. The newly self-assertive attitude of blacks toward whites, and the retreating, guilty fear of whites in the presence of blacks, are again expressed:

Don't look at ME.
I got money.
Got a HOME, too. . . .
Hello, Honey!
Can I talk to you?. . .
Road Buddy! Why you rushin' off?
Martin Luther King? Old whatcha-nov?
You gonna live, or you gonna die?

I dig you, Old Road. And I'll tell you why:
The TIMES is outa joint.
(Yeah, I been to school,
Though I mostly act a fool.)
Hey! Got a quarter on a pint?[68]

In "A Harlem Romance," from *A Black Man Abroad: The Toulouse Poems* (1978), the funk of Harlem's vitality acts like smelling salts, reviving Emanuel's speaker from the bitterness and self-pity of a failed romance, with the stimulant of Harlem's pungent resilience:

As I stood long to beg
this crust of pity.
a short black dog pissed on my leg.
Revived. I smelled my Harlem street
of magic stains.
its muscled colors bubbling in the sun.
behind The Veil its broken cups
usable as rain.
its splintered stairways peakable as trees.
windows never empty.
betrayals never wept.

Get a leg up otherwhere. I thought.
It's Harlem.
where streets keep walking.[69]

Raymond R. Patterson's "At That Moment," his tribute to Malcolm X cited earlier, is one of several Harlem poems in *26 Ways of Looking at a Black Man* (1969). Patterson's "Riot Rhymes, USA #15" contrasts the ironically different outcomes of similar historical activities of blacks and whites:

You dumped tea in Boston Harbor.
We dumped junk in New York streets.

Now you're the law and we're the robber.
Strange how history repeats.[70]

"Pope Paul VI Visits Harlem, A.D. 1965" employs Harlem in an ironic cosmology, in order to criticize mainstream Christianity's indifference to, not to say complicity in, black oppression:

Do, Jesus! Lord, we thought you'd
     never send word home!
Shouldn't take so long
     getting from Heaven to Harlem –
Even coming by way of Rome![71]

In "New York, New York: A Shell Game," three New York streets – 43rd, 53rd, and 125th – are settings for different styles and emotions. "Forty-third Street / where colored girls don't come on sweet," and "Fiftythird / where colored girls are few and blurred," are the empty shells in the metaphoric shell game of New York streets, but 125th Street contains the winning pea:

While way uptown, near One Twenty-fifth,
Where colored chicks don't act so stiff,
Us black boys are never quiet. All day we riot
In the streets, TV, all night we hang around
Sharp corners, winter, summer, playing cards
The cops in numbers, checkers, welfare
Fire engines, out-of-work, and women. We brag
We fight, drink wine, eat ribs, and sing, we
Church, we cuss like anything in the streets
African Nationalists, Muhammad Speaks up
To our hips, strung out, up tight, mainline, out loud
Outside, bearded, banging, transistorized; jive and jaw –
Are dispossessed, jungle naked; a clenched
fist

    Razor sharp with fears; ragged
    On the raw chalk cliffs of living, hanging on
    By our tough roots.
    – Are alive![72]

And in an unpublished poem, "Emma, 1925," Patterson evokes the relationship of Harlem to black America in a poignant lyric:

Song and sorrow full
you came.
Harlem never asked your name.

Wanting nothing
you possessed,
Harlem took you to its breast.

That first sunset
made you cry.
Harlem never asked you why.[73]

Ted Joans's tributes to Ellington, Hughes, and Malcolm X are among
many other testimonials by Joans to black heroes (and one white one)
that employ the motif of black Harlem. Three such appeared before 1964
in brief references, in *All of Ted Joans and No More* (1961). In "Soul
Brother Seymour," Joans's affectionate celebration of Seymour Krim as
a kind of white Negro, a "jive Jew / Swinging Manhattan Cat," and
"kosher spade," Krim's attributes include stereotypical bohemian traits
in his relationship to Negroes:

> You flashy openfly rock & ready he-cat
> daily and nightly living it up
> smoke that pot & drink that drink
> screw that nut & expose that fink
>   & have your babes black & white[74]

Krim is honored also, however, as "you who dug Harlem when others /
were afraid or unable." In "Freedom," one of Joans's wishes is

> for the George Washington Bridge to be renamed (since it is
> so close to Harlem) the Booker T.[75]

In "Love a Big Bird," Joans's paean to Charlie Parker includes the following:

> and he was notoriously known in Harlem. He
> had urinated on the borough president of
> Manhattan twice.[76]

Harlem did not emerge as a frequent and fully developed theme in
Joans's poetry until his later volumes, published after the Harlem riot of
1964. In *Afrodisia* (1970), "Way Down Yonder" contrasts Harlem with
Africa:

> When I walked
> across the Senegal-Mali
> savannah
> no Harlem gal tagged
> along with me

Perhaps Saphire knew
there was no scene
in Timbuctoo
no juke box loud blare
no salon to fry the hair
no big shiny cars
no mixed drink bars
   Just Sudanic houses and
   black people galore[77]

The voice of Harlem in Joans's "Harlem to Picasso" taunts Picasso by speculating about the reason he was able to transform his work with African influences:

Hey PICASSO aren't those Moorish eyes you have
could there be a drop of Africa in your Malaguena soul
Hey PICASSO why'd you drop Greco-Roman &
other academic slop then picked up on my
black ancestors sculptural bebop
Hey PICASSO dig man how did you know
the black thing would make the modern art world
lively / sing and actively swing
How Did You Know Huh PICASSO PICASSO?[78]

And Harlem is represented in "Wild West Savages" as an African village set in a modern urban jungle, a white metropolis that Joans depicts in terms of white stereotypes of the jungles of darkest Africa:

An African village in Harlem
yes but surrounded by electric steel palms with no leaves
concrete and asphalt
steamy manholeswamps
screaming monsters with whirling red eyes
more dangerous than lions elephants leopards
these mechanical hyenas that spit death from their metal gun
                paws
enforcing their technical order and laws
metal skyscraping jungle
inhabited by colorless wild savages
clad in grotesque clothing
a dangerous group god forgot to give color[79]

In *A Black Manifesto* (1971), Joans's speaker lists Harlem as part of his personal geography of black history. In "Egosippi," he proclaims,

i've lived at TIMBUCTOO / TANGIER / HARLEM / &
                                          HAARLEM
HOLLAND too double crossed the Atlantic which I shall
rename THE AFRICAN OCEAN blue
NOW I read my poem in 'Sippi
and allyall know thats saying a lot[80]

In "I Ask Harlem," the speaker expresses faith in Harlem's viability as a
black community and calls on Harlem to take pride in its blackness:

Harlem you will survive and remain alive & creatively arrive
                    in spite of white renewal or
                    previewed renovations. . . .
You Harlem, I ask you Harlem, to say it loud
HARLEM IS BLACK and I'm proud.[81]

And in "Harlem Poster," he declares his solidarity with the innocence
(or guilt, for that matter) of a black revolutionary whose photograph is
displayed in a "wanted" poster in a Harlem post office.[82] Phrases from
several of the poems in *A Black Pow Wow of Jazz Poems* (1973) inflect
Harlem in the syntax of racial perception. "Gris Gris" speaks of "giving
them / a free trip to Harlem via Watts Happenings on A-Train."[83] "S.C.
[Stokely Carmichael] Threw S.C. [Saint Christopher] into the Railroad
Track" mentions

His Bambara face His Nilotic frame His Ashanti majesty His
                                          Hipness of Harlem
He has thrown the white medal of St. Christopher away
He is now free . . .
He has a gri-gri of his own
a black gri-gri . . .
brought from the black sorcerer . . .
from black Africa by me.[84]

The speaker of "Horny Harrar House Blues" says, "Harlemese black-
cherry / I'm in bed with you."[85] In addition, the poet identifies a pantheon of jazz greats with Harlem in "Jazz Is My Religion":

Like man / Harlem, Harlem U.S.A. used to
be a jazz heaven where most of the jazz ser-
mons were preached but now-a-days due to cha
cha cha and rotten rock'n'roll alotta good
jazzmen have sold their souls but jazz is
still my religion because I know and feel the
message it brings like Reverend Dizzy

Gillespie / Brother Bird and Basie / Uncle
Armstrong / Minister Monk / Deacon Miles Davis /
Rector Rollins / and Max Roach / Priest
Ellington / His Funkness Horace Silver / and
the Great Pope John COLTRANE and Cecil
Taylor They Preach a Sermon That Always
Swings!!   Yeah jazz is my religion.[86]

Older black poets of the preceding generations were also touched by
the new spirit of blackness. A "new" Gwendolyn Brooks left her mainstream publisher for Dudley Randall's Broadside Press in Detroit and
allied herself with Haki Madhubuti (Don L. Lee) and the other young
midwestern black poets who honored her in their collection of poems,
To Gwen with Love: An Anthology Dedicated to Gwendolyn Brooks (1971).
In Washington, Sterling Brown still taught at Howard University, a
principal center, in the South, for the new black poetry. And in New
York, Hughes himself presided over the new black poetry scene until
his death in 1967. In the few years remaining him in the period after the
Harlem riot, Hughes returned to the theme of Harlem as the "landscape
of the dream deferred" with a contemporary poignancy. Although Har-
lem scarcely was mentioned specifically in Hughes's *Ask Your Momma*
(1961),[87] the concept of "THE QUARTER OF THE NEGROES" that uni-
fies the volume was an evident reformulation of the Harlem motif of
Montage. In *The Panther and the Lash* (1967), published the year of
Hughes's death, the Harlem motif was again transformed by its master.
The poem "Harlem," from *Montage,* was reprinted with the title
"Dream Deferred," breaking its titular link with the Harlem motif, but
"Puzzled," from *One-Way Ticket,* was retitled "Harlem." "Junior Addict," a new poem about Harlem in *The Panther and the Lash,* suggests
that Hughes's lifelong practice of renewing the theme of Harlem with
the changing times would have continued had he lived on into his seventies and eighties with the century, because it evokes and comprehends the
holocaust of narcotics visited on young Harlem in the 1950s and 1960s:

The little boy
who sticks a needle in his arm
and seeks an out in other worldly dreams,
who seeks an out in eyes that droop
and ears that close to Harlem screams,
cannot know, of course,
(and has no way to understand)
a sunrise that he cannot see
beginning in some other land –

but destined sure to flood – and soon –
the very room in which he leaves
his needle and his spoon,
the very room in which today the air
is heavy with the drug
of his despair.[88]

In his final volume of poetry, Hughes could still see hope for Harlem (to which the junior addict had blinded himself with the "drug of his despair"), for keeping faith with Harlem and its people had become the axis of Langston Hughes's career.

In the poetry of the Black Arts movement, the Harlem of newspaper headlines and presidential-commission reports often merged ironically with the "inner city" of the spirit. The contemporary euphemism "inner city," used as a positive way of referring to the ghetto or urban slum in the 1960s and 1970s, combined with the idea of black Harlem as an "interior city" in the psychological or spiritual sense that the term also encompassed. The term therefore offered the new black poets a current metaphor saturated with the modalities of the black experience in urban America, through which they could explore the black consciousness they had sifted from the ashes of Harlem. Older poets followed their lead. After the riot of 1964, the reinvigorated Harlem motif was taken – in spite of decades of disillusionment – as a common symbol by three different generations of Afro-American poets, singing together in the original spirit of its initial use as the setting and subjectivity object of a resurgent black patrimony.

Indeed, one of the authentic literary masterpieces about Harlem is Melvin B. Tolson's verse narrative, *Harlem Gallery: Book I, the Curator* (1965).[89] Tolson was a contemporary of the New Negro poets and Hughes's elder by three years, although his major work was not published until after the riot of 1964. With the publication of *Harlem Gallery,* in 1965, Tolson fulfilled a lifelong ambition to compose a work vast enough to encompass the vitality and epic variety of Harlem, a task he had attempted three decades earlier in *A Gallery of Harlem Portraits.* In Tolson's plan, never completed because of his death in 1966, *Harlem Gallery* was conceived to be the first of five books that would encompass the history of black people in America in a comprehensive poem. The unwritten books were to have been *Egypt Land* (Book 2); *the Red Sea* (Book 3); *the Wilderness* (Book 4); and *the Promised Land* (Book 5). That such a work was to have begun, and perhaps ended, with Harlem indicates the central significance Tolson assigned to Harlem in the drama of Afro-America. *Harlem Gallery* is a complete work, nevertheless, and one of the major achievements of Afro–American literature, for, as Tolson himself observed, Harlem is "Negro America, its comedy and tragedy in prismatic epitome."[90]

A critic has commented that Tolson's *Harlem Gallery*, like Hart Crane's "The Bridge," Ezra Pound's "Cantos," and, T.S. Eliot's "The Wasteland" and "Four Quartets," combines exploration of inner depths and symbolic landscapes at the point of intersection between self and "a community figured by landscape that has been mythologized through symbolic extension."[91] Composed in twenty-four sections, each identified by a letter of the Greek alphabet, from alpha to omega, in an ode form that Tolson had developed earlier in *Libretto for the Republic of Liberia,* Tolson's *Harlem Gallery* is "a narrative work so fantastically stylized that the mind balks at comparisons," according to Karl Shapiro's introduction to the poem.[92] The principal personae in Tolson's narrative poem are the curator of the Harlem Gallery; an art critic; and three artists (a painter, a writer, and a composer). The two art professionals define the binary poles of Tolson's narrative. The curator – an octoroon, who embodies the thematic question "What is a Negro?" (p. 138) in his ambiguous racial identity – is observer or participant in all the action of the poem, providing the organizing point of view. On the other hand, Dr. Obi Nkomo, an expatriate Zulu and art critic, incorporates an integral African perspective and an easy familiarity with the high culture of the West, bringing a detached, ironic, humane perspective to bear on the course of the narrative. The three artists direct the focus of the narrative to the implications of artistic genius for a people and a culture. "Wise men judge a race by its geniuses" and by its arts and sciences, Tolson had written in a *Washington Tribune* column. "In other words, a people is judged by its brains."[93]

The Harlem environments shaping Tolson's narrative are the Zulu Club and the Harlem Gallery itself. The Zulu Club conforms to a stereotype associated with Harlem since the Renaissance of the 1920s. The "habitués" – Frog Legs Lux and his Indigo Combo; Dipsey Muse; Wafer Waite; Vincent Aveline; Joshua Nitze; Black Diamond; Shadrach Martial Kilroy – constitute an intertextual composite of social interaction ritualized by Harlem narratives of the 1920s, and Snakehips Briskie's "snake act in the Garden of Eden" out-Harlems even the Scarlet Creeper in *Nigger Heaven* at his worst:

> Convulsively, unexampledly,
> Snakehips' body and soul
> began to twist and untwist like a gyrating rawhide –
> began to coil, to writhe

like a prismatic-hued python
in the throes of copulation.
Eyes bright as the light
at Eddystone Rock,
an ebony Penthesilea
grabbed her tiger's eye yellow-brown
beanpole Sir Testiculus of the evening
and gave him an Amazonian hug.
He wilted in her arms
like a limp morning glory.
"The Zulu Club is in the groove," chanted Hideho,

"and the cats, the black cats, are *gone!*"
(p. 66)

The Harlem Gallery, on the other hand, is the location for the interplay of black artist and black bourgeoisie. The Harlem Gallery is sustained by the uneasy synergy of clashing attitudes. The centerpiece of the museum's permanent collection is John Laugart's *Black Bourgeoisie,* a masterwork that teases out the conflicts underlying the uncertain compromise between the curator and the regents of the Harlem Gallery. In the same *Washington Tribune* column vaunting the role of genius, Tolson had taunted the misplaced emphasis of bourgeois display: "A race is not judged by its dollars. Its skyscrapers. Its big business. Its high powered cars. If these things measured racial and national genius, America would lead the world."[94]

The Zulu Club and the Harlem Gallery are the settings and the occasions for discussion, because Tolson elaborates his vision of the culture capital and ghetto of Harlem as much through debate as through event, personality, and setting.[95] The talk in *Harlem Gallery* is principally about race, and the integrity of art is a closely allied second subject that is never entirely separable from the issue of race. Tolson's focus is on the ambiguity of black Harlem and of its image. Harlem is paradoxical in essence, and the Harlem motif in art and culture resonates ambivalently with the tension of its contradictory meanings:

In the black ghetto
the white heather
and the white almond grow,
but the hyacinth
and asphodel blow
in the white metropolis!
O Ceobulus,

> O Thales, Solon, Periander, Bias, Chilo
> O Pittacus,
> unriddle the phoenix riddle of this?
> (p. 155)

In the context of a different discussion, Tolson had said, "An intelligent mind is a mind that thinks in terms of sunshine and shadow. . . . Yes, the intelligent mind places opposite ideas in juxtaposition. Therefore, it is good at epigram and irony. . . . Intelligence sees the underlying identity of things. . . . Caviar and cabbage differ only in the arrangement of electrons."[96] Consequently, Tolson creates a Harlem of the arts that is at the same time factual and fantastic, historical and anachronistic, representative and idiosyncratic, that, in Mariann Russell's words, "represents the people not only as they are but as they [have been and] are to be. The focus of today, surrounded by the peripheral vision of yesterday and tomorrow, acquires the indefinite suggestiveness of the symbol when the work of art itself becomes symbol."[97]

Tolson's use of the motif of black Harlem conformed to its use in the poetry of the Black Arts movement. Tolson's commitment to the evolving theme of black Harlem as a crystallizing focus of the Afro-American and Africana experiences triangulated with the Black Arts movement's concentration on the best-known "inner city" of black America as the physical landscape of a spiritual renewal of the race, locating Harlem once more at the nexus of Afro-American being. Tolson's consolidation of four decades of Harlem chronology in the present-time of *Harlem Gallery* corresponded with the unexpected degree of acceptance and continuity of the received legacy of the Harlem motif that accompanied the stylistic and thematic innovations of the younger poets of the Black Arts movement. Tolson's decades-long obsession with the Harlem he had known in the late 1930s matched the revived contemporary interest in Harlem after the insurrection, and his quest, in his long poem, to create a new poetic language shaped by an authentic black aesthetic produced a masterpiece of the affirmative black literature with a collective racial voice called for by the younger partisans. Tolson's habit of depicting identifiable Harlem personalities *à clef* also resembled the Black Arts movement's frequent choice of Harlem as a legendary setting for black heroes. His daring in molding the Harlem landscape to his purposes anticipated the imaginative Harlem narratives of Charles Wright and Ishmael Reed.

11

Echoes in a Burnt Building

The reaching out for a new sensibility of racial consciousness within the riot-torn landscape of Harlem and the other inner cities of America's urban centers – understood previously as territories of disillusionment and despair, but appreciated after 1964 as scenes for phoenix-like rebirth – touched chords of solidarity beyond nationality and race. The Harlem landscape of the inner city, envisioned by the Black Arts movement, was an evident parallel, for the poets of the recently emerging nations of Africa and the Caribbean, to their own efforts to come to grips with colonial or postcolonial circumstances. At the same time, in the United States, many poets who were not black depicted Harlem in ironic counterpoint to the forces of a misguided or dislocated social order, valuing the angle of observation that the motif offered on the predatory economic and political practices of the United States and its capitalistic cohort nations.

In the late 1960s and early 1970s, non–black authors typically employed Harlem as an illustration of the Western world's predilection for racist forms of oppression. Martin Glass's "Lip Service Poem of Resistance," for example, indicts American capitalism with a litany of victims that includes Harlem:

> There is one fact and one fact only: the Oppressed.
> The Oppressor, in almost every case,
> is American Capitalism.
> In every country in South America, from Caracas to Cape
> Horn,
> in every country in Africa, from Tunis to Port Elizabeth,
> in Panama, Pakistan, Iraq and Martinique,
> in Mississippi, Harlem, Calabria and the Philippines.[1]

On the other hand, Abeylard Pereira Gomes's "O amigo," from *Elegia para John Fitzgerald Kennedy,* cites Harlem to praise the assassinated American president as a man of uncharacteristic kindness, youthful enthusiasm, poetic vision, and deathless ideals, who opened a clearing in the jungle of prejudice:

> E queria
> Iguais fôssem
> Aos brancos de Ohio
> Filadélfia e Oklahoma,
> Os negros
> de Harlem Atlanta e
> Alabama[2]

> *He wanted*
> *To make equal*
> *The whites of Ohio*
> *The Negroes*
> *of Harlem Atlanta and*
> *Alabama*

Both poets cite Harlem, without further explanation, as a patent instance of oppression – Glass in his litany of the victims of the international oppression of American capitalism, and Pereira Gomes in his view of Kennedy as a fallen leader of uncharacteristic compassion, who had offered hope to victimized Americans both black and white. Anne Sandowski's "Poem about Birth" defines the ghetto riots of the 1960s as violence born of the racist oppressors' technology of blood by linking the ghetto uprisings, beginning with the Harlem riot, with an incident in which white soldiers in Mozambique rip open the belly of a pregnant African woman:

> Harlem.
> > They ripped her belly wide
> Watts.
> > Mozambique blood flowed
> Hough.
> > Young infant blood flowed[3]

The soldiers' bloody abortion, equated with the killing of Malcolm X and Martin Luther King, Jr., is reborn in the street violence of America's ghettos. In different ways, all three – Glass, Pereira Gomes, and Sandowski – identify Harlem as a victim of direct oppression, whether in Glass's straightforward accusation of America's oppressive capitalism, in

Pereira Gomes's lament for the loss of a protector of the oppressed, or in Sandowski's vision of a birth of resistance to racial oppression in the riots of the long hot summers.

Harlem's relationship to the larger social order is more complex in the poetic visions of other non-black authors of this period. Diane Di Prima's "Goodbye Nkrumah" bids farewell to the founding father of Ghana's national independence, on the occasion of the coup that topples his regime. The poem views America as a self-destructive nation, moving toward self-immolation because of a misguided and amoral foreign policy, and Nkrumah's downfall is seen as simply one more CIA plot: "When the radio told me there was dancing in the streets, / I knew we had engineered another coup; / Bought off another army." Harlem is an element in "Goodbye Nkrumah," because Di Prima's speaker contrasts the response to the fall of the president of Ghana with the reaction to the murder of Patrice Lumumba, when black radicals and white radicals had demonstrated together in Harlem. Now former black allies reject the support of Di Prima's speaker: "And I wondered / what the boys in the Black Arts Theatre were saying / and sent them my love and my prayers, which they would not / accept. / green poster LUMUMBA LIVES flooded Harlem in those / days"; but the speaker understands that the black partisans have to go it alone: "It's their war, all I can do is wait / is not put detergents in the washing machine, / so the soil will / still be productive / when the Black men, or the Chinese, come to cultivate it."[4] Brazilian Affonso Romano de Sant'Anna's "Empire State Building" reverses the traditional descent into the underworld by locating the infernal nadir of capitalism at the top of the Empire State Building, then still the world's tallest building. For a guide or conveyor, the poet in Manhattan gets a Yellow Cab instead of a Virgil or Charon. In the underworld of Manhattan, Harlem is a side entrance to Hell, an available secret entrance to the underworld of capitalism, although the poet does not have to use it, because the gates of the city stand unguarded:

> O leão, o leopardo, a lôba
> não estavam na entrada da cidade
> embora eu penetrasse pelo Harlem.[5]

> *The lion, the leopard, the wolf*
> *were not at the entrance to the city*
> *which nevertheless I would have penetrated*
> *through Harlem.*

When the image of a descent into the underwold is superceded by The Crucifixion, with the Cross formed by the narrow horizontal strip of

Manhattan and the vertical superlative of the world's tallest building, the poet begins again with Harlem:

> Já que esta ilha é uma cruz,
> vereis do lado esquerdo superior dêste calvário
> o *Harlem*. Aí não vos deveis fixar por demais os olhos
> a menos que sofrais de daltonismos ancestrais.
> Há a *George Washington Bridge*
> por onde do sul vieram os negros
> e os cães ladrando atrás.[6]

> *Now that this island is a cross*
> *you will see on the upper lefthand side of the Calvary*
> *Harlem. You shouldn't rest your eyes there too long*
> *unless you suffer from ancestral colorblindness.*
> *There you have the George Washington Bridge*
> *where the Negroes come from the South*
> *with bloodhounds barking behind.*

Barbara Bellow Watson's "Echoes in a Burnt Building" imagines Harlem after the riots as a burned-out Wonderland in which Alice awakens to find herself become black. She sits astonished, between "fire-demented walls," in a world where "the rats long as ribbons roll about / cackling across their battle and its rout," and as she waits, "amazed, awake among the ash / sitting asplit / untaught," an ironic song evokes details of post-riot Harlem with echoes of classic English verse:

> Alice born black, unwashed among the ash,
> whiter than that sweet snow
> that sleeping hope the sad ones push
> which thou ownedst long ago.
> . . . .
> Money my fame, Harlem my happy name:
> trade is the trick and truth is just the same.[7]

"Echoes in a Burnt Building" was inspired by Watson's experience as a graduate student commuting to Columbia University, looking out at Harlem from the Park Avenue train tracks, walking across 125th Street, and then "dealing with the mandarin world of Columbia." The poem conveys Alice's astonishment by echoing Spenser's *Prothalamion* and Eliot's *Wasteland* (2. 115, 117–19 and 3.183–4), amid the burned out landscape of Harlem:

> Babies born in the pit, sing me one song:
> Sweet Thames, sweet Harlem, roll my sins along,

> comfort me with hailstones, hang my head,
> swing me alive among the dancing dead.

Echoes of Shakespeare's *Othello* (3.3) are heard:

> Whiter than water are thy mistress' lips,
> pale hoarding for a merchandiser's quips.
> Behind their boards far mandarins shall fake
> syrups of sight to medicine thee awake.

Watson's Harlem is also textured with more general references to Renaissance conventions of courtly love ("Whiter than water are thy mistress' lips"); Christian cosmology ("What was that pit?"); and the diction of Mother Goose ("that Black lamb whom the white sheep still herd / where only blood can wash and law's a word"). This Harlem is conceptualized as a Lewis Carroll-ish, through-the-looking-glass world. Watson's high-literary resonances evoke an unsettlingly ironic reflection of Western culture in the riot-torn landscape of Harlem, where Black Alice "sits hypnotic stiff among the charred / garbage and bricks, the doors and windows barred, / the flag of heaven furled." The poem concludes with a glimpse into a burned-out building, where boys ("brown sticks / smiling behind the pales of eight and six") are seen extending themselves on the green felt of a pool table, the only vista of "green fields" in the barren, unyielding landscape of Harlem. Unlike other non-black poets in this period, who employed the motif of black Harlem as a reference in the service of some larger theme, Watson takes Harlem as her main subject in this poem. Nevertheless, her use of Harlem as an oblique and ironic illumination of a disoriented, and even demented, civilization – here symbolized by the singular counterpoint of the high-literary tradition of Europe to the post-riot condition of Harlem – resembles the use of black Harlem as an animadversion of a social order gone amiss characteristic of Glass, Pereira Gomes, Sandowski, Di Prima, and Romano de Sant'Anna after the Harlem riot of 1964.

The view of some non-blacks, established in the heyday of the Harlem vogue, of Harlem as a territory of exotic and erotic Negro allure never vanished completely, even in poetry of the third phase of the Harlem motif. After the ghetto uprising of 1964, the Brazilian Ariel Marques still employed Harlem as a provocatively sensuous image of night, in a poem whose principal innovation to the Latin American *negrismo* tradition consists of dedicating the theme, conventionally reserved for *la mulatta,* to a full-blooded Negro woman:

> Em pouco a noite despejou seu Harlem
>
> pelas ocidentais ruas da cidade,

e a negra que eu vira em meio à multidão,
na noite se fundiu, sem nenhum alarde.[8]

A little later the night decanted its Harlem

through the western streets of the city,
and the Black woman I was looking at in the middle of the
crowd,
merged into the night, without ostentation.

And the Japanese Hajime Kijima's two poems about Harlem, in the text accompanying Ruiko Yoshida's photographs in *Harlem: Black Angels,* continue to view Harlem, as did Yvan Goll, Federico García Lorca, and others, as an enclave of humane warmth, authentic emotion, and jazz in the dehumanizing, technological frigidity of Manhattan's urbanized landscape. The title of the collaborative volume repeats the notion of "black angels" sentimentalized two generations earlier in "Píntame angelitos negros" (Paint for me little black angels), by the Venezuelan Andrés Eloy Blanco: "Harlem is the town / Where black angels keep on flapping their wings."[9] "For Ruiko and Her Pictures" celebrates Yoshida's warmth and artistry, which made Harlem's humanity manifest to Kijima in the "giant labyrinth" of "cold Manhattan island" and restored his own humanity in New York, where "distrust inhabits tall buildings, / No place where senses aren't locked in." Yoshida's photographs took Kijima past Manhattan's locks and keys:

> You led me, clutching your camera,
> To churches in Harlem, to midnight jazz bars.
> You took photos, each photo a soft breath
> Your lens groped through the labyrinth, the dark.[10]

Her images of a little Afro-Japanese boy growing up in Harlem in the decade after the riot of 1964 suggest that any ironic echo of Van Vechten's *Nigger Heaven* in the title *Harlem: Black Angels* was probably not intended.

In the same period, black poets throughout the African diaspora were developing a consciousness of the fundamental unity of the Africana experience. The motif of black Harlem, which many Africana poets outside the United States associated with the Civil Rights movement, as well as with the ghetto uprisings of the 1960s across America, was seen as a shared emblem of the common aims and actualities of black life. Harlem, to them, became a symbol of the destiny of Africana peoples to arise renewed, in spite of the unrelenting cultural, social, and political interposition by the European West. Like their Afro-American counterparts, the Africana poets who employed the Harlem motif in its third phase echoed usages established during the period of the Black Awakening and the Dream Deferred, but now the usage patterns of the earlier phases were redirected toward an anticipated resurgence of black spirit throughout the diaspora, with Harlem serving as a microcosmic instance. Cameroonian Valère Epée, according to Antoine de Paduoe Chonang, presents Harlem as "un paradis artificiel: Harlem ou 'Jazzonie.' "[11] Epée's Harlem is a city of refuge and a dreamscape of jazz and blues:

> Harlem!
> Harlem aux yeux rêveurs
> Au sourire épaté en forme d'un grand coeur
> Où Sonny Boy au moins respire en homme libre
> Libre de marchander ses bras pour quelques cents
> > De troquer son coeur lourd contre une heure d'amour
> > De s'en aller ensuite aux cabarets poser
> > Sur les lèvres tendues de toutes les trompettes
> > > les éclats de ses joies
> > > le sanglot de sa honte

> *Harlem!*
> *Harlem of the dreamy eyes*
> *Of the flabbergasted smile of a great heart*
> *Where Sonny Boy at least breathes like a free man*
> *Free to bargain his arms for a few hundreds*
> > *To barter his heavy heart for one hour of love*
> > *To go away afterward to the cabarets to pose*
> > *On the tense lips of all the trumpets*
> > > *The bursts of laughter of his joy*
> > > *The sob of his shame*[12]

Other poets reemployed the dream-deferred motif of black Harlem as an icon of black suffering, calling for a black response. In "I Share the Pain," South African James Matthews identifies the oppression of apartheid with the common Africana suffering endured in Harlem and other black towns of the diaspora:

> I share the pain of my black brother
> and a mother in a Harlem ghetto
> with that of a soul brother in Notting Hill
> as I am moved from the land I own
> because of the colour of my skin.[13]

The poem ends, however, on a note more typical of the period after 1964 by expressing the belief that the race's very suffering will, in the end, become the source of its liberation:

> Now our pain unites us
> into burning brands of rage
> that will melt our fetters
> and sear the flesh of the mockers
> of our blackness and our heritage.[14]

In "Poema universal," Angolan Jofre Rocha writes of the suffering of the riot-torn landscapes of Harlem and Watts as examples of the Negro's universal suffering transformed into revolution:

> No coração de um negro
> a dor é universal.
>
> E a dor dos encurralados
> nos slums de Nova York
> a dor que se faz ódio à solta
> nas ruas de Los Angeles[15]

> *In the heart of a Negro*
> *the pain is universal.*
>
> *The pain of those corralled*
> *in the slums of New York is*
> *the pain which becomes hate on the loose*
> *on the streets of Los Angeles*

Cameroonian Nicolás Pasteur Lappe, in "H . . . comme," focuses directly on Harlem's endurance of oppression but, like Matthews and Rocha, with the anticipation of a black awakening in Harlem:

> H . . . comme ces ghettos infernaux
> où ils vous enferment comme des pestiférés,
> dans une quarantaine éternelle
> sans espoir d'émancipation
> . . . .
>
> H . . . comme ton sommeil hiemal
> dont tu émergeras
> H . . . comme Haschish
> H . . . comme Harlem.[16]

H . . . for those hellish ghettos
where they trap you like plague rats
in an eternal quarantine
with no hope of emancipation.
. . . .

H . . . for the wintry slumber
from which you must awaken
H . . . for Heroin
H . . . for Harlem.

Puerto Rican Juan Romero, in "Harlem," also details the ghetto's misery through a litany of its afflictions and oppressions: "HARLEM: the Soul Center of North America East / HARLEM: where black and brown bodies sing and sway to keep misery away,"[17] but Romero's litany concludes with a prayer for the resurgence of "HARLEM: the Soul Center of North America East," so that blacks generally may prosper and not simply endure: "HARLEM: Harlem, USA, Here's Harlem yesterday, and today / So I say 'Harlem, Harlem, I pray for tomorrow, / that my brothers may live in happiness / and not in sorrow.' "[18] Trinidadian Lennox Raphael, in "Sidewalk Blues," envisions the obscene realities of urban existence both uptown and downtown in New York in ways that recall the oblique Harlem visions of Ray Johnson and Oliver Pitcher, in the second phase of the Harlem motif, but that also anticipate the racial regeneration awaited by Matthews, Rocha, Lappe, and Romero:

> then a cow stepped on a bomb in a supermarket
>   and the civilization became ashes
>   and god came out of the earth
> a stick of pot between his teeth and rubbers on his sex
>   digging the scene
>
> and on the third day he went to the world's fair
>   with abraham lincoln at his side
>
>   holding an umbrella over his sex
>   and waving to the skeletons uptown
>
>   while
>   (downtown)
> the garment district was naked with fear
>   atop
>   the empire state building
>   where
> i now stop.[19]

Trinidadian Edward Brathwaite and Guinean Sikhé Camara's use of the Harlem motif also follows previously established patterns, but in other respects they typify its employment in black poetry outside the United States, after 1964, as a microcosm of resurgent Africanadom. In Brathwaite's *The Arrivants: A New World Trilogy,* three references trace the progression of the Africana faces of black Harlem reflected in this century. In "The Journey," the black presence is traced from the ancient river civilizations of Egypt and Meroë through the diaspora of slavery and colonialism to the streets of New York:

> . . . and then it was New
> York, selling news-
> papers in Brooklyn and Harlem.
> Then Capetown and Rio; remember how we
> took Paris by storm: Sartre, Camus, Picasso and all?[20]
>
> (p. 36)

This first phase identifies Harlem with the dynamic motivating power of a dream:

> Yeah man!
> so went the
> mud hut, hole-
> hatted glorious
>
> dream. Harlem
> was heaven
> and Paris a palace
> for all.
>
> (p. 40)

"The Emigrants," however, associates the unrelenting realities encountered by these dream-seekers with the motif of black Harlem: "The city is so vast / its ears have ceased to know / a simple human sound" (p. 54). In London, the undergrounds are cold from darkness and fear. And "In New York / nights are hot / in Harlem." Finally, in "Jah," titled with the Rastafarian name for the deity, Harlem resounds again with the voice of the African spirit:

> Nairobi's male elephants uncurl
> their trumpets to heaven
> Toot-Toot takes it up
> in Havana
> in Harlem   (p. 162)

Brathwaite includes Harlem as one of several microcosmic locales in the geographic dispersal of the African diaspora, and his use of black Harlem recapitulates the stages of the motif's evolution, concluding with its characteristic employment as a landscape of the resurgent spirit of Africanadom.

Sikhé Camara, in "Mon frère de Harlem," celebrates his black brother in the microcosm of Harlem as the quintessential expression of racial being with whom all blacks everywhere can identify. After detailing the panorama of black history embodied by "Mon frère de Harlem," the poet recognizes his own selfhood reflected in the face of Harlem, recalling Jean Brièrre's "Me revoici Harlem":

> Et c'est pourquoi mon frère de Harlem,
> Mon frère noir,
> Je vois sur ton visage noir
> Les traits de ma race,
> Sur ton visage large
> Comme une surface,
> Sur ta large face épaisse
> Comme un lard,
> En tes lippes lunaires gonflées
> Comme un Signe,
> Dans tes dents blanches blanchies,
> Tes dents vermeilles,
> Je retrouve la marque de mon peuple martyr,
> La beauté de sa virilité
> Dans tes oreilles écloses
> Comme des pétales de fleur
> Tes yeux qui expriment non la rancoeur, l'amour,
> Tes cheveux hirsutes et rebelles,
> Tes cheveux pareils au gazon noir,
> Tu es bien le produit de quatre Siècles d'aventures.[21]

> *And it is because, my Harlem brother,*
> *My black brother,*
> *I see on your black visage*
> *The traits of my race,*
> *On your visage expansive*
> *Like a surface,*
> *On your broad face thick*
> *like a bacon slab,*
> *On your moonlike lower lip stuck out*

like a Sign
On your blanched white teeth,
Your rosy teeth,
I rediscover the mark of my martyred people,
The beauty of its virility
In your ears blossoming
Like flower petals
Your eyes that express not rancor but love,
Your hair shaggy and rebellious,
Your hair like black grass,
You are very much the product of four centuries of
                                                        adventures.

Sikhé Camara's speaker asserts his fraternal solidarity with all of Afro-America in the identity of the black brother in Harlem, the microcosm of black being symbolizing possibility and renewal:

Je suis un homme de Harlem,
Un homme total,
De la grande chaîne douloureuse de l'histoire.
Je veux être de mon monde, de ma societé, ma race.[22]

I am a man of Harlem,
A complete man,
From the sorrowful great chain of history.
I wish to be of my own world, my own society, my own
                                                        race.

In a similar vein, in "Happy New Year, Harlem!", Florette Morand of Guadeloupe utilizes the symbolic overtones implicit in the idea of New Year's Eve in Harlem. As the speaker tries to decide whether to attend the New Year's Eve celebrations on Seventh Avenue in Harlem, its festive excesses are juxtaposed with the idea of genuine beginnings implicit in the holiday:

La 7e avenue, la 7e avenue
L'atteindrai-je
Dans l'orgie des trompettes
L'enlancement des serpentins
La jubilation de cette foule en fête?
Happy new year! . . .
Voici venu de Times Square
Tout Harlem qui déferle
Criant sa joie,

Roulant ses rires,
Avec l'espoir,
Sur la 125e rue.
Happy new year![23]

7th Avenue, 7th Avenue
Will I reach it
In the orgy of trumpets
In the encirclement of serpentines
In the jubilation of that partying crowd?
Happy New Year! . . .
Here is, come from Times Square,
All Harlem which breaks [like a wave]
Screaming its joy,
Rolling its laughter,
With hope,
On 125th Street.
Happy New Year!

The general hints of renewal in "Happy New Year, Harlem!" are sharpened further by ironic associations with January 1 in Afro-American history. January 1 is the date on which the annual Christmas jubilee of American slaves concluded, with the return to the quotidien rigors of slavery — often with a new, temporary master, to whom one could be rented for annual terms beginning traditionally on New Year's Day; but January 1 is also the anniversary of the authentic jubilee of the day on which the terms of the Emancipation Proclamation took legal effect. Both the false jubilee, which renewed slavery annually, and the true jubilee, which ended slavery in the United States, are echoed and evoked in the question concerning "la jubilation de cette foule en fête" (the jubilation of that partying crowd).

For a variety of black poets outside the United States, Harlem's status as the microcosmic landscape of an Africana resurgence continued to rest on Harlem's cultural primacy, its historical leadership, its dreams and aspirations, and its legendary heroes. In "Words Are Also Born," South African Mafika Pascal Gwala reasserts the traditional identification of Harlem as the black Paris:

Since this word's been sown
Afrikaans does not dodge Harlem
— after all blacks need their own Paris
Since this word's been sown
ghetto Blacks dig Woppko Jensma

Since this word's been sown
honky tonk has refused
to remain in America.
And words are also born.[24]

In "Quand les nègres revendiquent," Cameroonian Marcel Mvondo II
depicts Harlem – the microcosmic symbol for black America – as a starting point for the Afro-American crusade for civil rights in the 1960s:

Ils sont partis au petit jour vêtus de courage
Comme Samson privé de lumière
Ils sont partis de Harlem pour Selma et Montgomery
Prêcher la croisade de la liberté a l'Amérique éruptive.[25]

They set out in the early light dressed in courage
Like Samson deprived of light
They left Harlem for Selma and Montgomery
To preach the crusade of liberty to eruptive America.

In "Old Black Woman, Hanging Loose in Time," Trinidadian Wilfred
Cartey salutes the unexpected progress of a dream in Harlem in the figure of an old black woman sitting in the window of a Harlem tenement:

Old Black woman, hanging loose in time
High in a Harlem tenement
You share the window with a dream,
Prune wrinkled face once full, black ripened plum
You gaze upon the leapfrog games of Harlem Prep.
You squint your eyes and watch black
Black children go skip-skipping up
Go running through the cheers and hand-claps
Across the wet-wet shining eyes of mothers
Go skip-skip-skipping up
And of sisters and sister-lovers
Of fathers and of brother-lovers
Who had never dreamt to see these young
Black drop-outs dropping up to stages
And skip-skip-skipping up to platforms for their prizes.[26]

And the legendary Harlem figures of Claude McKay and Malcolm X are
evoked by Jamaicans Bob Stewart and Reginald Wilson, and by Haitian
René Depestre. In "Sonnet for McKay," Bob Stewart links "nigger Harlem" with Morocco and "black Marseilles," as places where his fellow
Jamaican Claude McKay

> . . . found a deep, a dark return of blood
> That bled your pen, set hands to strum and play
> A song of dancing banjohood –
> So far from home, so very long away,
> In a jazz beat, back street African café.[27]

In "For Our American Cousins," Reginald Wilson portrays Harlem's mourning for a fallen Malcolm X as a scene of anagnorisis – a recognition of shared identity, altering irrevocably the barriers of geography and history that separate blacks in the diaspora:

> Then black mothers moaned and wept
> on the curbs of Harlem
> as the crepe-draped catafalque
> that bore his great body
> grumbled by through the mourning streets.
> Then our pain was made manifest
> beyond enduring.
> Though we could not conceive it,
> we knew.
> Though we could not bear it,
> we stood.[28]

In René Depestre's "Malcolm X," the final ode of *Un arc en ciel pour l'occident crétien,* in which seven female deities from the voodoo pantheon transform themselves into seven mortal heroes of black history, the persona of Grande Brigette speaks of Malcolm X as the lamb of Harlem in the black Jerusalem:

> Et il pleure Malcolm X l'agneau de Harlem
> Il remonte en pleurant les rues de son enfance
> Et il remonte encor plus loin dans le passé
> Ses larmes traversent le temps et les pays
> Elles coulent avec les fleuves les plus vieux[29]

> *And he weeps Malcolm X the lamb of Harlem*
> *He walks weeping down the streets of his childhood*
> *And he walks still further down the past*
> *His tears cross over time and countries*
> *They flow with the oldest rivers[30]*

These multifaceted significances for Harlem are subsumed under a single unifying ideal, for Mafika Pascal Gwala, Marcel Mvondo II, Wilfred Cartey, Bob Stewart, Reginald Wilson, and René Depestre all identify

Harlem as a symbolic landscape of the resilient spirit of black peoples everywhere.

South African Keorapetse Kgositsile and Jamaican Lebert Bethune turn repeatedly to the theme of Harlem as the resurgent microcosm of Africanadom. In "For B.B. King and Lucille," Kgositsile presents Harlem as part of the geography of oppression and exploitation expressed in the music of B.B. King:

> Do you remember the slaveship?
> Harlem Accra Johannesburg
> Bagamoyo! Do you remember
> Despair? B.B. is çalling your name
> Brother! Sister, it is sadness and joy
> We are talking about.
> The hemorrhage of a continent,
> Of the brutality of the sea,
>
> Of men forced to show teeth
> Without laughter. Of sleepless
> Nights when you turn the light
> Off and shudder again
> Knowing yesterday today tomorrow again.[31]

Kgositsile offers Harlem more typically as an icon of the new Africana assertiveness of his black contemporaries in "Time," which associates Harlem with an inescapable historical destiny:

> This moment
>   like a tyrant strides
>   across sunrise and sunset
>   claiming its own
>   panoramic view
> no matter what the recorded lies
>
> This moment
>   like a tyrant strides
>   across Meadowlands or
>   Harlem streets painting
>   tomorrows against today's
>   fading moments of public hide and weep.[32]

"Epitaph" anticipates the bloody downfall of the racist oppressors:

> We were rolling the coffin of imperialism
>   to the colonial graveyard

> And millions of black people were dancing
> > by the graveside
> I was walking down bloodstained streets
> > of Sophiatown and Harlem
> And the beast gave me a rabid missionary grin
> Don't you know he tried to buy my conscience
> > with bloodstained bills
> And adolescent fascist nuns carried their prophylactic
> > supplies to the Congo!
> I was listening to the wind
> > And a voice thundered,
>
> "Damned are they that ransacked the world!"
> > And black children laughed and danced
> > To the rhythms of a new promise.[33]

"The Awakening" depicts Harlem as the scene of blacks' irreversible arousal from the sleep of three centuries of domination by the West:

> Amidst sit-ins, kneel-ins, sleep-ins and mass mis-education
> Brother Malcolm's voice penetrated alienated bloodcells
> Teaching Black manhood in Harlem USA
> Endorsing "Bandung,"
> Retrieving Black balls cowering in glib Uncle Tomism
> Forcing me to grow up ten feet tall and Black
> My crotch too high
> For the pedestal of Greco-Roman Anglo-Saxon
> adolescent Fascist myth.
>
> Now I see everything against a Black background
> As Black and proud as Melba
> Breaking the blood-dripping icons of Western congenital
> > chicanery
> Enthralling me like the cataract of a cosmic orgasm.[34]

Similarly, in Lebert Bethune's "Harlem Freeze Frame," the voice of Harlem exalts a gaudy but undeniable fact of black survivability to startle and confound the racists with the impotence of their oppressions:

> On the corner – 116th and Lenox,
> > all in brown down to his kickers,
> > and leaning on a post like some gaudy warrior
> spear planted, patient eyes searching the veldt

This gleaming wrinkled blunthead old sweet-daddy
    smiles a grim smile
    as he hears a voice of Harlem scream

        "WE ARE SUPPOSED TO BE DEAD BUT
        WE AINT"

and his slow strut moves him on again.[35]

In Bethune's "Apollo at the Apollo," the static complacency of the West, embodied by a statue in Harlem's Apollo Theatre of the most civilized of the Hellenic deities, is confounded by the energizing dynamism of the Harlem show crowd:

With his deep frightless eyes
His white deltoids
His pure marble fig-leaf
That frozen pose for the camera
His hairless plòtted thighs – Apollo
Could never recognize himself
Or
At the heart of the gushing laughter
Dare to risk a word about his real connections
No
Here with Screaming Jay Hawkins and
The Wild Man from Borneo
The Raylettes

Martha and the Vandellas
Not to mention those two hot Mommas
Lil and Ella Mae – one black one yellow –
Who waggle between the acts
Like real live jelly from the roll
That kinda god
Would have to trade his fig for meat
That kinda god would have to trade his pose for motion
That kinda god
Would have to lose his timelessness
"TONIGHT! LIVE! at THE APOLLO"[36]

Harlem after the riots was understood to represent the reinvigoration of the spirit to resist the forces of racist oppression. The motif of black Harlem, established internationally by previous generations of poets, was employed once more by non-black poets for the angle of observation it offered on issues of the moment, and by black poets outside the

United States as a shared motif of the common vicissitudes and aspirations of the black experience throughout the African diaspora. Whereas non-black poets cited Harlem as an instance of the capitalist West's inclination toward racist forms of oppression, Africana poets outside the United States turned repeatedly to black Harlem as a microcosmic symbol of the destinies of all Africana peoples to arise, renewed in spirit, certain of ultimate victory in the struggle against the unrelenting opposition of the racism of the West. Inspired by the Black Arts movement's renewed spirit of nation building within the riot-torn landscapes of Harlem and the other inner city ghettos of America, non-black poets listed Harlem in their indictment of racism, and Africana poets outside the United States employed Harlem, in the motif's third phase, with a sense of Africana solidarity in the global racial struggle with the Eurocentric West.

12

Mumbo Jumbo

After the riot of 1964, writers of fiction continued to employ black Harlem as a psychologically and socially realistic setting for narratives, as had authors in the 1940s and 1950s, for like earlier realists, most novelists – particularly black novelists – continued to assume "that man is a social being who ought not to be separated from the social and historical context, no matter how alienating and discontinuous, in which he finds his significance and develops his potential as an individual."[1] Achieving the illusion of fully developed human experience remained the overriding aesthetic impulse in the majority of Harlem narratives in the 1960s and 1970s. In such novels, Harlem was depicted as a landscape of discrimination, exploitation, and despair, reflecting the nadir to which Harlem's deterioration had plummeted during the decade, and figuration was limited by verisimilitude. In a range of works, narrativity corresponded to the recognizable and credible actuality of the Harlem setting.

Double Dunk, Barry Beckham's fictionalized retelling of the life of Harlem basketball star Earl ("the Goat") Manigault, is "a cautionary tale about the deleterious effects of ghetto existence."[2] The protagonist of George Cain's *Blueschild Baby,*[3] also named George Cain, returns from prison to wander "the corridors of bedlam" of hard-core drug use in Harlem and finally to harrow hell, in three days of drug withdrawal. Louise Meriwether's *Daddy Was a Number Runner*[4] is a funky, textured memoir about growing up black in Harlem, which proceeds to a single conclusive epithet: " 'Shit.' The word hung between us in the silence. Then I sighed and repeated it. 'Shit' " (p. 188). Shane Stevens's *Go Down Dead*[5] is a first-person narrative, written in a version of juvenile street argot. The book begins with the statement "One thing about living here in Harlem you know it cant get no worse" (p. 1) and concludes with a clear echo of Duke, in *The Cool World:* "I is going sit right here till they come for me and then I going light this fire stick and they going be one less stinking building in this stinking motherfucking Harlem. Yeah" (p. 181). Even the novels for young audiences that were given Harlem settings by Rosa Guy, Walter Dean Myers, and Mary Elizabeth Vroman present their juvenile protagonists discovering themselves and their potential in the harsh reality of ghetto Harlem. Some dimension of the underlying rage that exploded on the streets during the Harlem uprising of 1964 is presented in each of these works, but the riot itself – the major theme of Black Arts' poetry – is largely absent from the fiction of the period. John A. Williams is one of the few naturalistic novelists of this period to incorporate it, even implicitly, into his storytelling and to deal with its possibilities. *The Man Who Cried I Am* (1967), set in the pause between the peaceful, inspirational civil-rights March on Washington, in August of 1963, and the assassination of President Kennedy later in the year, provides a rare fictional illumination, if not explanation, of the summers of rage that began with the 1964 Harlem riot. Still, the sensibility of the Black Arts movement influenced the writing of fiction, as well as poetry, and in the aftermath of the Harlem uprising several storytellers, like the poets, seemed liberated to experiment with black Harlem as the setting and subjectivity object of a reassertive black patrimony.

The Harlem settings of Henry Dumas's short stories "Harlem" and "The Voice" present a naturalistic surface but are figural narratives, like so many of Dumas's other prose pieces, contrived beyond conventional restraints of the illusion of verisimilar human experience, to emphasize anagogic levels of signification. "The Voice" dramatizes the mourning of the three young members of a Harlem singing group over the death of the fourth and most talented member of the quartet and elaborates the development of their grief and confusion to a point of resolution and clarity. The story begins with the boys "just kicking around down there, me, Willie, Blake, trying not to think about Spencer, but knowing all the time that we were lost without him, knowing that we would never sing the same again, knowing that something had died within us as a group"[6] (p. 161), and modulates to a unified conclusion with the boys singing a song that the dead boy had composed:

> We sang from our souls, and before long everybody was standing round listening. Spencer's mother was trying not to cry. And then all of a sudden Blake caught a note, and we all heard it and we came to his aid. We got to feeling good, and the people backed us up with some hand clapping. Spence should have been there then, because we were all singing and making one voice. (p. 175)

The drama of "The Voice" develops by playing Blake's compulsion to let it all out, "even though it was scaring the hell out of us" (p. 169), against the unexpressed and unarticulated feelings of Willie and the narrator, who "believed in something but didn't know how to say what it was. Blake believed in something and was saying it" (p. 172). The episode turns, though, on the statements of three men of God: an observant Jew, a priest, and a minister. The Jewish man and the priest answer Blake's blasphemous anger with pithy, anagogic affirmations of faith that remind us of Dumas's penchant for parables and fables. First, the Jewish man deals with the issue of the existence of God:

> "Look, *Reverend*," [Blake] said, "these guys here are my friends, see, and havent seen God, but they believe in Him. You're a preacher so I guess you *seen* him?"
>
> Slowly put surely the man breathed and said, "Yes." . . .
>
> "What do you mean," I asked the man.
>
> But he didn't answer. Instead he started walking down the hill. He unleashed the dog and it began to range all around. Suddenly Blake turned around and asked, "Where?"
>
> And the man said, "Here." He pointed with his arm, sweeping the whole landscape.
>
> Blake broke into a fierce laugh. He bent over and groaned his guts out. (p. 168)

Next, the priest answers for Blake the issue of God's race and skin color:

> All of a sudden [Blake] turned on the priest and asked, "Okay tell me what color is God?"
>
> "I once saw a painter," the priest said, "after he had labored weeks on a painting. It was a painting of a summer sunset over a lake. There was a house where a man sat playing a guitar. When I looked at the painter's hands I saw all the colors I saw on the painting. . . ."
>
> Blake didnt say anything. He stuffed his hands in his pockets and drifted up the street. We couldnt tell from his back if he was laughing or not. (p. 171)

These two explanations are apparently enough to satisfy Blake and to justify the final resolution, for alert readers, but a third hieratic figure, the minister, appears, to explain: "Dont worry about the confusions of religion and the babel of tongues. They're all man-made. God has one religion and he's always on time" (p. 174).

Dumas's narrative procedure is virtually identical in the existing sections of his unfinished novel *The Map of Harlem*. Harold Kane, Dumas's speaker in this narrative, like the unnamed narrator of "The Voice," is a keen observer, but an Islamic man of God, Elder Dawud, is the priestly spokesman. In a very different context and idiom, Dawud's extended reading of the Harlem setting corresponds to the old Jewish man's and to the priest's briefer interpretations. Dawud's point is that to know blacks, one must know how to read Harlem, just as in "The Voice," to know of God's existence one has only to look at the landscape, or to know the truth about the color of the painter one need only view the painting: "The black man in this country has got to learn one thing: how to use the key to his soul, for the soul of the black man is an unexplored region. . . . Who has the map of Harlem? Listen, Harlem has it. Harlem has it. And I speak in the name of One who wants Harlem to keep it" (pp. 29–30). The turbulence of drums and thunder is breaking out all around Harlem as Dawud preaches, and as the people converge – "moblike, pursuing the wind with anything they could get their hands on" – in Harlem Square, Dawud is pushed off the scene. Nevertheless, Harold Kane has internalized Dawud's call to read the map of Harlem: "Soon he turned his head and headed uptown, walking close to the wall and looking in at the shops and stores of Harlem, as if he were watching reflections that moved to and fro in the glass, fading and fleeing like ghosts" (p. 30). Dumas's Harlem pieces are inventive, didactic prose constructs that resist conventional critical labels, for the apparent naturalistic setting, like the variety of multiplicity of short forms, is redirected by a figural method that coincides only incidentally with a naturalistic purpose.

The most innovative feature of Harlem narratives by Afro-American writers in this period is the unprecedented fabulation of the famous black community as a comic setting of enormous plasticity, beyond conventional notions of time and history, physical reality, and human psychology. Chester Himes's description of identifiable Harlem locales is, for the most part, accurate, in *A Rage in Harlem*,[7] which initiated a series of Harlem thrillers published in the 1960s, featuring Coffin Ed Johnson and Grave Digger Jones, who play only relatively minor roles in this first outing. The aesthetic thrust of Himes's geography of Harlem is to project a satiric landscape of pure rage. Himes's people are implausible human grotesques, careening through improbably articulated obstacles of plot, in flight from impossible demons or in pursuit of bizarre goals. A core of authentic anger roils constantly just under the surface of the narrative, ready to burst forth expressively and excoriatingly in extraordinary passages like the following, in which a dying character rages in an aria of blood:

> Jodie reached down with a violent motion, clutched him over the face with the palm of his left hand, put his right knee in

Goldy's back between the shoulder blades, jerked Goldy's head back against the pressure of the knee, and cut Goldy's taut black throat from ear to ear, straight down to the bone.

Goldy's scream mingled with the scream of the locomotive as the train thundered past overhead, shaking the entire tenement city. Shaking the sleeping black people in their lice-ridden beds. Shaking the ancient bones and the aching muscles and the t.b. lungs and the uneasy foetuses of unwed girls. Shaking plaster from the ceilings, mortar from between the bricks of the building walls. Shaking the rats between the walls, the cockroaches crawling over kitchen sinks and leftover food; shaking the sleeping flies hibernating in lumps like bees behind the casings of the windows. Shaking the fat, blood-filled bedbugs crawling over black skin. Shaking the fleas, making them hop. Shaking the sleeping dogs in their filthy pallets, the sleeping cats, the clogged toilets, loosening the filth.

Hank jumped aside just in time.

The blood spurted from Goldy's throat in a shower, spraying the black street, the front fender and front wheel of the hearse. It gleamed for an instant with a luminous red sheen on the black pavement. It dulled the next instant, turning dark, fading into deep purple. The first gushing stream slackened to a slow pumping fountain as the heart pumped out its last beats. The flesh of the wide bloody wound turned back like bleeding lips, frothing blood.

The sweet sickish perfume of fresh blood came up from the crap-smelling street, mingled with the foul tenement smell of Harlem. (pp. 105–6)

Himes skirts the edge of revulsion with the virtuosity of his storytelling and the comic temper of his rage, relying on Harlem's standing as a narrow frame of utter flexibility, where anything that is violent and vicious can happen and only fools survive. At one point, Jackson, the picaresque innocent, who emerges from the slaughter with his delusions entirely intact, drives his hearse as far south as East Ninety-fifth Street, skirting what the narration defines as the southern border of Harlem, only to turn north again and remain within the imaginative frame. The only moment outside of Harlem takes place at the end of the novel in a downtown office building, as a young assistant district attorney, "his blond crew-cut hair shining with cleanliness" (p. 149), attempts the Augean task of "the unfolding of the saga" (p. 150) for legal disposition.

The most striking fabulations of black Harlem in the 1960s and 1970s were *The Wig* (1966), by Charles Wright, and *Mumbo Jumbo* (1972), by

Ishmael Reed. In Charles Wright's novel, some fundamental but unde-
fined social transformation has occurred to the setting (1966),[8] but the
change is taken so for granted by Lester Jefferson, the protagonist and
narrator, that he seems unaware of a need to explain or acknowledge it.
Although Lester's determination to find the solution to all his problems
in an economy-sized jar of some race-altering cosmetic – here, something called Silky Smooth Hair Relaxer – is a timeless topic for satire in
Afro-American culture, the opening paragraph explicitly locates the time
frame of his narrative in the late 1960s: "It was hard to smile; everyone
seemed to jet toward the goal of The Great Society, while I remained in
the outhouse, penniless, without 'connections.'" Yet *The Wig* is replete
with puzzling, fragmentary asides about Harlem, mentioned in passing
in Lester's campy, overwrought, and solipsistic prose style, out of which
the reader is left to reconstruct a sense of the Harlem setting. The people
in Lester's building characterize Harlem in traditional ways, although
their extreme personae give the terms a bizarre twist. Nonnie Swift, a
florid, pregnant, part-time whore, laments that her son will be born into
the "unchained slavery" of Harlem (p. 10). Miss Sandra Hanover, neé
Alvin Brown, from Brooklyn, is a transvestite with an even more florid
personal style than Nonnie. Sandra's psychiatrists do an ironic turn on
the flight north by diagnosing him (her?) as a homosexual from the
South, come to liberal Harlem and New York, where "it's all right to
go in drag" (p. 18). Lester's asides suggest contradictory chronological
directions. Some statements recall the Harlem of the 1920s: "The bitter
saliva puddles of the poor are covered with sperm, dropped by the slum-
ming whites and their dark friends who wallow in the nightclubs that
go to the early morning. These are people who can afford the daytime
fear of the city" (pp. 27–8). Other unexplained details provoke a sense
of some future distopia: "125th Street with its residential parts, its quaint
stinking alleys is a sea of music, Georgian chants, German lieder, Italian
arias, Elizabethan ballads. Arabic lullabies, lusty hillbilly tunes. Negro
music is banned except for propaganda purposes" (p. 29). On a job inter-
view, Lester is encouraged to take a six-week course "in the art of being
human, the art of being white" (p. 39), and he remembers the case of
the Negro model whose murder was classified as a justifiable homicide
because he had displayed a rosebud in place of his penis at a Greenwich
Village happening.

At one point, Lester allows as to how "the cops are our friends" (p.
31). People have to run along "the right side of Eighth Avenue" through
an honor guard of twelve policemen per block, and, in this context right
seems to be the opposite of wrong, rather than of left (p. 30–2). To a
grateful mother who needs something with which to discipline her

youngest, who does not want to attend a segregated school, one helpful policeman offers his nightstick and apologizes for not having his cattle prod with him. Lester's friend Little Jimmie Wishbone, the former movie star, says, "It jest don't seem like Harlem any more" (p. 30), and Mr. Sunflower Ashely-Smithe, the "thoroughbred American Negro" head of Paradise Records, refers ambiguously to "the changeover" (p. 64). The world outside of Harlem also seems strangely transformed. At Fifth Avenue and Eighty-Second Street, diseased dogs howl discontentedly, and the unemployed form a "sad sea" in front of the apartment buildings. The pelts of enormous sewer rats are highly prized. The death toll of some ongoing war of attrition, reported daily in the *New York Times,* is being monitored by a self-abasing black servant in the ninetieth-floor penthouse of "the last stronghold of concentrated capitalists" (p. 72). On the one occasion when Lester makes a formal pronouncement about Harlem, he says, "Harlem, the very name a part of New World History, is a ghetto nuovo on the Hudson; it reeks with frustration and an ounce of job," but he adds, "[T]he heart of Harlem – 125th Street;" has "grandeur, if you know how to look at it" (p. 27).

The emphasis of Lester's narration tends toward the self-serving comparison or the put-down. His irresponsibility as a narrator is transparent, but the authenticity of his desperation begins to cut through the campy prose style and become more credible, and more intense, as his tale progresses. When, finally, his golden silky smooth locks begin to pay off for Lester, success makes him absurdly invisible. The job at which he prospers provides a demeaning and anonymous kind of celebrity, for he becomes notorious, crawling around the sidewalks of New York City on his hands and knees in a chicken suit, singing a jingle for a fried-chicken franchise. With his new status Lester manages to seduce "the Deb," "café Society's darling" (p. 125), but she recognizes the Negro beneath the ersatz locks and dumps him. Looking at the sky from his window, Lester wants to shout: "But I didn't mean anything! All I wanted was to be happy. I didn't know to want to be happy was a crime, *a sin*" (p. 128). He recalls how, on his sixteenth birthday, a mysterious Mr. Fishback had told him, "Lester Jefferson . . . you're almost a man. It's time you learned something. The Harlem skyline is the outline of your life. There is very little to discover looking at the pavement. . . . You're on your own for now. *My presence won't be required until . . .*" (p. 129). Later, after the one moment of happiness in the entire narrative, when Lester has spent one night of ecstasy with a young lady he does not know, the mysterious Mr. Fishback reappears, tells Lester that the Deb has been killed in a car accident, and takes the now-despairing protagonist to view her body at a mortuary under the Triboro Bridge. There

Fishback shaves off the Wig; then he orders Lester to strip naked and think about something arousing. Lester's narrative ends with him smiling as a mortician's steel instrument is stuck into his erection, and saying, "I'm beginning to feel better already" (p. 145). Only then can a reader be certain that the historically grounded but wildly implausible narrative of *The Wig* has been the flow of life flashing before the eyes of someone who is already dead or dying and that the Harlem of the narrative is a telling but unmediated reflection of the moribund narrator's existential state of mind.

Ishmael Reed's *Mumbo Jumbo*[9] identifies the cultural dynamics of the Harlem Renaissance with the struggle for control of a sacred text going back to the beginnings of time and civilization in Africa. *Mumbo Jumbo's* point of departure is the outbreak of Jes Grew, a "psychic epidemic" of African cultural modalities, which erupts in New Orleans (p. 5). As a result, white people are beginning to do the turkey-trot on their lunch hours, and white kids dance belly to belly, bunny hugging doing the black bottom and the funky butt. "ON WALL STREET SAXOPHONES MAKE A STRONG RALLY WHILE VIOLINS ARE DOWN. EVEN THE SAP IN THE TREES MOVES NASTY" (pp. 105–6). An italicized paragraph in the narrative pronounces, in an omniscient and partisan voice, that Jes Grew is not a plague but an antiplague. Plagues, arising from the bad air of decomposing animals and the wrath of God, waste the body away; Jes Grew, on the other hand, crackling with life, ebullience, and ecstasy; enlivens the host; clears the air with the smell of roses and perfumes; and delights the gods. Authorities, nonetheless, fear that "if this Jes Grew becomes pandemic it will mean the end of Civilization As We Know It" (p. 4).

Jes Grew breaks out in the spiritual landscape of Reed's HooDoo aesthetic, New Orleans, but its incipient force inclines toward Harlem, where odd but resonant events are being played out mysteriously. At an ersatz rent party called a Chitterling Switch in Harlem, presidential candidate Warren G. Harding makes a little speech before heading down into the basement to "scarf" some soul food. On the corner of Market Street and Broad, in the financial district, two robber barons are caught in the crossfire of a failed attempt to assassinate a black numbers banker, who was investing his proceeds. In Chinatown, four conspirators – representative descendants of the races of the four inhabited continents of the earth, who first met in an Art History class at City College – have formed a revolutionary gang called Mu'tafikah. Their goal is to liberate masterpieces of non-Western art from museums (Centers of Art Detention), so that the gods can return, to create a spiritual hurricane that will sweep away the debris of two thousand years. A headline in the *New*

York Sun only adds to the sense of the world spun off its axis: "VooDoo General Surrounds Marines at Port-au-Prince" (p. 22). Only PaPa La-Bas, *Mumbo Jumbo*'s protagonist, is able to see through the confusion to the heart of the matter: *"Jes Grew is seeking its words. Its text. For what good is a liturgy without a text?"* (p. 6). PaPa LaBas's insight is underestimated, though, and his discoveries ignored, even as he begins to close in on the truth about the Jes Grew outbreak.

PaPa LaBas is a "noonday HooDoo, fugitive hermit, obeahman, bota-nist, animal impersonator, 2 headed man, You-Name-It" (p. 45) – a fig-ure of mysterious ancestry, said to be descended either from the JuJu of Arno or the Moor of Summerland. In Harlem, LaBas functions as a " 'so-called' astrodetective" (p. 64), with headquarters in Mumbo Jumbo Kathedral, where he teases meaning and understanding out of vestiges of African spiritual procedures that he manages to uncover. In spite of the accuracy of his predictions of the birth of Jes Grew, made by means of knockings at a numerology convention, PaPa LaBas's methods, sum-marized as "the Work," are under challenge and in disrepute. LaBas's constant running on about Jes Grew "seeking its text" has alienated his leading disciple Berbelang, who abandons his mentor and joins the Mu'tafikah. A white disciple, Charlotte, has also defected from Mumbo Jumbo Kathedral and is exploiting PaPa LaBas's *Blue Back: A Speller* as a source of authentic-sounding materials for the special effects in her va-riety act. Even Earline, who has remained with PaPa LaBas, is disgrun-tled, ignoring steps in his spiritual protocols and tasking him with inco-herence. "Why must you mix poetry and concrete events?", she complains (p. 26).

PaPa LaBas's forensic solution of a modern crime – the murder of one Abdul Sufi Hamid, in Harlem – becomes the cosmic resolution of an ancient sacrilege. In investigating the murder, PaPa LaBas discovers the existence of an ancient struggle between two secret societies, whose at-tention has been focused, in modern times, on Jazz Age Harlem in the 1920s. The Book of Thoth – a sacred text giving definitive form to the agricultural dances of the divine Egyptian prince Osiris – has found its way to Harlem and is attracting the force of the Jes Grew. Osiris was murdered by his brother Set, who wanted to copy his brother's success, but the manuscript was given to their sister Isis, from whom it was sto-len later by monotheistic conspirators, who sought to restore repressive values, in the spirit of Set. At the foundation of the aesthetic order of Western civilization, LaBas learns, is an ancient secret society known as the Atonist Path. This society suppressed the Book of Thoth, after its rediscovery during the Crusades. Because of schisms within the Atonist Path, the manuscript was brought to America, in the 1890s, by Hinckle

Von Vampton – in reality, the immortal leader of a despised wing of the Atonist Path. Von Vampton divided and dispersed the text into fourteen parts, in a ritual reenactment of the murder and dismemberment of Osiris, who is embodied in the text. With the emergence of Jes Grew, Von Vampton has been rehabilitated by the Atonist Path and appointed to be the Great White Host, with plenipotentiary powers to find and destroy the sacred text, because, "You see there are all kinds of Atonists. Politically they can be 'Left,' 'Right,' 'Middle,' but they are all together on the sacredness of Western Civilization and its mission. They merely disagree on the means of sustaining it" (p. 136).

The other side is also concentrating on Harlem. A mysterious ship tied up at a West Side pier turns out to be the traveling headquarters of Benoit Battraville, a Haitian aristocrat and the leader of the cosmic opponents of the Atonists in the ancient struggle. Battraville is in the United States attempting to capture the Great White Host and hand him over to the *loas,* the Dahomean gods of Haitian voodoo, as an offering to induce them to end the American occupation of Haiti. As he consults with La-Bas to identify the Great White Host, Battraville confirms Papa's theories.

The contemporary crime in *Mumbo Jumbo* is the murder of Abdul Hamid Sufi. Hamid, a young Harlem intellectual and editor, "out there in the street watching what was once a beautiful community become a slum hole" (p. 32), before his death had been engaged in translating an anthology written in hieroglyphics. When Papa LaBas realizes that the anthology Hamid was translating was the reassembled manuscript of the Book of Thoth, LaBas deduces that Von Vampton murdered the editor, in an abortive attempt to recover the sacred text. At the climax of the novel, when Von Vampton, at a soiree at Madame Lewaro's, attempts to introduce one of his associates (in blackface) as the definitive "breakthrough" poet of the Harlem Renaissance, Papa LaBas lays out his solution to the murder: "If you must know, it all began 1000s of years ago in Egypt, according to a high up member of the Haitian aristocracy" (p. 160). Papa LaBas seizes Von Vampton and his Talking Android, turning them over to the tender mercies of Battraville and the Haitian *loas,* but Jes Grew wanes as quickly as it waxed, and the text's ornate container turns out to be empty. Papa LaBas is puzzled until he receives a letter that Hamid had mailed to him before his murder. In a misguided moment of self-censorship, Hamid had decided to burn the Book of Thoth because he considered it obscene, and, with the destruction of its sacred text, the Jes Grew pandemic recedes.

Ishmael Reed's Harlem, in *Mumbo Jumbo,* is basically the Harlem Renaissance setting of myth and legend, with its meaning re-made with

quick wit and a strong dose of anachronistic elements from ancient African and modern Afro-American history and culture. The cast of characters includes parodies of a range of easily identifiable personalities of the
1920s. Buddy Jackson – number banker, patron of the race, and Masonic
grand master – recalls numbers king Caspar Holstein in all three respects.
Schiltz, Jackson's nemesis, is Dutch Schultz, Holstein's white adversary
in organized crime. Hinckle Von Vampton, the villain of the piece, who
educates himself in Afro-American literature and passes himself off as a
Negrophile, is a caricature of Carl Van Vechten. Nathan Brown, a Harlem poet who rejects Von Vampton's invitation to write for a little magazine called the *Benign Monster* ("I am teaching Harlem youngsters so
that they won't be influenced by people like you" [p. 117]) is evidently
Countee Cullen. Major Young, another black poet who rejects Van
Vampton's importuning, brings Langston Hughes to mind. The hostess
of the Chitterling Switch is named Madame Lewaro, the acronym de-
vised by Enrico Caruso for the suburban villa of Madam C. J. Walker.
Mumbo Jumbo's narrative voice characterizes the 1920s as a drag race for
the champion *gros-ben-àge* of the times, occurring before a "crowd of
society idlers you would find at 1 of those blue ribbon dog shows"
(p. 21).

Reed's parody of a detective novel plays a brilliant redefining riff on
the high civilization of the West, locating the origins of its religion, history, and aspirations to civilization in the frustrated envy felt by an untal-
ented but murderous sibling for his more gifted and acclaimed African
brother, and, as Reed's signifying detective makes his solution of a contemporary murder in Harlem the resolution of an ancient cosmic viola-
tion, the motif of black Harlem takes on new dimensions of resonance.
Mumbo Jumbo ends in the 1970s, with Papa LaBas smiling, as he drives
back to Harlem after giving a lecture on the Harlem Renaissance to a
university class "that knew what he was talking about":

> People in the 60s said they couldn't follow him. . . . What's
> your point? they asked him in Seattle whose central point, the
> Space Needle, is invisible from time to time. What are you driv-
> ing at? they would say in Detroit in the 1950s. In the 1940s he
> haunted the stacks of a ghost library. In the 30's he sought to
> recover his losses like everybody else. In the 20s they knew. And
> the 20s were back again. (p. 218)

In the third phase, in the 1960s and 1970s, the literary rendering of
black Harlem returned to the original impulses of the Harlem motif in
the 1920s. The adjustments of a middle phase had been made to the black
enclave's deterioration from culture capital to racial ghetto, and a sense

of possibility was energized again by an awareness of Harlem's significance in a larger drama of racial and cultural striving. Perspectives had
broadened considerably, however, over the decades. Where Alain Locke
had proclaimed the birth of a New Negro psychology in the promising
emergence of black Harlem, the poets of the Black Arts movement were
seeking an inner city of the spirit in the ashes of a riot. Where Locke had
discerned a new America in the birth of a New Negro psychology in
Harlem, Charles Wright and Ishmael Reed, certainly – but Chester
Himes and Henry Dumas also – sanctioned in their narratives alternative
cosmologies of being and meaning, in an unprecedented fabulation of
black Harlem as a setting of enormous plasticity.

Epilogue:
Black Harlem and the Literary Imagination

      Black Harlem in literature is an original twentieth-century *topos,* a modern motif created by African-American writers inspired by the fervor of the racial transformation of the Manhattan neighborhood north of Central Park and reinterpreted over the decades by writers of different races. Although the literary trope of black Harlem is indisputably a creation of the discourse of African-American literature in the United States, the coherence and continuity of the usage of the trope has evolved within the broader cultural frame of the modern Africana literatures written by authors of African racial or cultural descent in Spanish, French, and Portuguese as well as in English. From one international generation of black writers to the next, the motif has remained the avatar of an ethos of spiritual, cultural, and political renewal of peoples of African descent in the various linguistic zones of the diaspora. Additionally, the trope of black Harlem illustrates significant resonances and interrelationships with literatures outside the Africana discourse, for many writers of European and Asian as well as African descent have found the idea of Harlem to be relevant to their preoccupations and employed the figure of black Harlem in significant ways. Novels set in Harlem, with very few exceptions, have been written in English and published in the United States by authors of the different races who are American citizens or longtime residents, but poetry about Harlem has ranged widely across national and linguistic frontiers.[1] Neither borrowed from Western sources nor inherited from African or Africana traditions and verbal modes, the literary figure of black Harlem has crossed frontiers of language, nationality, and culture to become what a philosopher of literature has termed "an intimate immensity, a sacred space with the oneiric dimensions of an ancestral forest,"[2] but here associated, by memory and imagination, with a corner of a modern city.

From its earliest and most rudimentary literary formulation, black Harlem has been a metonymic projection into the dimension of meaning articulated in the vocabulary of place. Over time, the struggle for signification in the recurrent imaging of black Harlem has made the motif a kind of cultural text for continual retelling and exegesis, a palimpsest or scriptural field for literary figuration on which a significant portion of the imagining of three modern generations of writers has been drawn. The literary motif has evolved in a series of engagements with interpretation: dialogues of a sort – sometimes sustained, at other times sporadic – involving individual authors with the popular reading and literary legacy of the motif itself, as well as with the fact and the history of Harlem. Consequently, the motif's relationship to the actual locale has been oblique and complicated over the decades, but the correspondence, however elusive, has been persistent, and Harlem's incremental development by the literary imagination can be seen, for the purposes of literary historiography, as an important synapse of historical, social, and cultural forces.

Beginning with the Black Awakening of the 1920s, the mutating virtuality of the Harlem motif has offered an unexpected and revealing point of contact among many disparate modern currents. In the first phase, the Harlem of literature was typically a domain of seers, attuned to intimations of cultural possibility. Harlem was hailed as a mythic landscape, in which the African inheritance was being reclaimed for the diaspora; the neighborhood's racial transformation was identified with a reborn consciousness, seeking a philosophy of racial selfhood in order to defy the hegemony of so-called universal standards, whose ethnocentric norms denied the worth of the African patrimony. This mythic view of Harlem was affirmed by the New Negro writers of the United States and was taken by the Afro-Hispanic poets of the Greater Antilles, the indigenist writers of Haiti, and the *negrismo* poets of French West Africa and the Caribbean as a portent of the primacy of their own perceptions over the former preeminence of European culture. Black Harlem's initial image as a culture capital of African values in exile resonated ironically with its alternative formulation by a daring and disillusioned international assortment of young writers of the same age, who were not black but for whom Jazz Age Harlem, embodied by the image of the cabaret, was a unique focus. Facing a crisis of confidence in their own cultural patrimony, such writers as William Rose Benét, Maxwell Bodenheim, Federico García Lorca, Yvan Goll, Yonezo Hiroyama, Fannie Hurst, Alfred Kreymborg, Salvatore Quasimodo, and Carl Van Vechten celebrated Harlem for the exuberance of its primal joy as a conveniently urban heart of darkness, a ready setting of profound otherness close at hand, without seeming to sense the paradox in expecting that so alien a place could offer such facile meanings. The commercial vogue, in turn, led many of the New Negro poets and short-story writers to cultivate the interest in Harlem images in longer works of fiction. Too many of the New Negro novelists, influenced by the commercial demand for what was in effect a generic Harlem novel, focused thematically on dis-spiriting topics of passing, intraracial color prejudice and class division; concentrated stylistically on the atavistic and exotic local color of the Harlem cabarets; and turned away from the manifold approach many of them had begun to define earlier in poetry and short fiction, which per-ceived in the figure of Harlem both the potential of an immanent self-hood and the ironies and actualities of black life.

The second phase of the literary motif of black Harlem was in the nature of a period of adjustment. Unlike traditional myth, which is usu-ally generated in a once or future time at considerable distance from the actuality of experience and observation, the literary motif of black Har-lem was undergoing mythification in historical and sociological time, in defiance of the existential actualities of an obscured and oppressive past and an uncertain present. The initial promise of the black culture capital of the 1920s threatened to be overwhelmed by the emerging ghetto of the 1930s and 1940s, for Harlem was becoming sufficiently wretched to undermine the idea of the liberated racial refuge it had come to symbol-ize. Major alterations in the master text of Harlem necessitated revision, but a reinterpretation in keeping with the motif's original exegetical im-pulse, as well as with the facts, was not easily developed. The naturalistic techniques of the new generation of novelists spoke in fiction to Har-lem's decline. In *The Street,* Ann Petry observed Harlem keenly as a source of limitation and control, rather than of aspiration of hope; in *Invisible Man,* Ralph Ellison transformed Harlem into a complex analog for the self that the unnamed narrator begins to discover in the chaos of possibility of New York; and in *Go Tell It on the Mountain,* James Bald-win employed Harlem as a secular ground, in which the narrative voice can be rooted with social, chronological, and psychological exactness in time, place, and history, even as the novel explores the mystical and rhetorical fancies of the fundamentalist black church; but working with Harlem's deterioration in other genres posed a formidable problem. Po-ets, in particular, seemed demoralized and avoided the topic of Harlem. Only Langston Hughes, among the New Negro writers, continued to write creative literature about Harlem after its voguish heyday had passed. Perhaps his Harlem – rooted in the resilient ethos of jazz and blues, unlike the culturally deracinated Harlems of his contemporaries – was better able to respond to disheartening alteration. Hughes's *Montage of a Dream Deferred* (1951) restored a credible sense of possibility and offered a new key to the lyric use of the Harlem motif, for Hughes synthesized the facts of racial oppression in America with the faith of black Americans through the contemporary jazz modes of boogie-woogie and bebop in the unifying and comprehensive symbolic locus of Harlem. With his renewed vision of Harlem as the symbol of the continuing denial of a historical faith, Langston Hughes not only reclaimed the *topos,* as he had defined its terms a generation earlier, but also reasserted its challenge, by rhyming "What happens to a dream deferred" with the tag "Good morning, daddy, Ain't you heard?", pointing the way for the coming literary generation. Enabled by Hughes's reinterpretation, a younger generation of Afro-American poets – including Calvin C. Hernton, Ray Johnson, Oliver Pitcher, Walt DeLegall, William Browne, and Amiri Baraka – turned to the evolving theme of Harlem, even as the drama of racial struggle in the United States focused on the nonviolent Civil Rights movement in the South. Outside the United States, other black poets, particularly the Afro-Portuguese revolutionaries of the generation of the liberation struggles, heard the voice of Harlem in the global call for an Africana consciousness, and a generation of Afro-Portuguese poets, including Noemia de Sousa, José Craveirinha, Agostinho Neto, and Francisco José Tenreiro, took Harlem as an emblem of civil injustice corresponding to their own colonial situations as their countries struggled for political autonomy. At the same time, a disaffected new literary generation of white bohemians, seeking to escape the rigidity of bourgeois conformity and complacency, recognized mocking contrasts and ironic coincidences between themselves and the plight of blacks in Harlem and flipped the meaning of the neighborhood north of Central Park from an earlier significance of primitive joy to one of preternatural suffering. Paradoxically, this suffering made the declining New York ghetto an effective spiritual buffer zone, where white bohemians of the Beat Generation – notably Allen Ginsberg – took cultural and psychological haven, precisely when Harlem had ceased to be a city of refuge for blacks.

A turbulent third phase in the evolution of the literary motif was initiated by the Harlem riot of July 18 to July 21, 1964. Such riots, generally ignored as a subject for poetry after the violence of 1919 and 1943, were interpreted as events of mythic dimension, textual revisions "written" into the physical text of Harlem by the populace in the long, hot summers of the 1960s. Because it rioted first and brought its special resonance as an Africana motif to the issue of the burning ghettos, writers turned to Harlem most often as a primary symbol of the contemporary black condition, although almost every urban center in America faced its own riot-torn landscape by 1968. The reading of the Harlem riot differed markedly between black and non-black writers. Writers who were not black employed black Harlem after the riots for its oblique perspective on the grasping, racist, self-destructive tendencies of a misguided social order, but a third generation of black authors seasoned the cultural and sociopolitical concerns of the preceding two by figuring the Harlem uprising as the emblem of a new racial sensibility. While the newly independent nations of Africa and the Caribbean struggled with the creation of postcolonial identities, the Black Arts movement sought an aesthetic for nation building within the riot-torn inner city of Harlem. In this third phase, after 1964, the Africana use of Harlem resembled its initial formulation but with a bitter difference. The Black Arts movement's idea of Harlem as an interior landscape merged not with a vision of a culture capital but with the contemporary euphemism for a racial slum. Charles Cobb, Conyus, Victor Hernandez Cruz, Henry Dumas, David Henderson, Gayl Jones, Etheridge Knight, Audre Lorde, Haki Madhubuti (Don L. Lee), Larry Neal, Gil Scott-Heron, Ntozake Shange, Quincey Troupe, and many other young writers of a new generation identified Harlem as the "inner city" of the black spirit, in the "soul land" of America. A celebratory reworking of the ontology of black Harlem became a feature of the innovative Harlem narratives of Ishmael Reed's *Mumbo Jumbo* and Charles Wright's *The Wig*. Black writers outside the United States recognized the motif of eruptive Harlem, nation building within the riot-torn ghetto, as an Africana microcosm symbolizing a resurgent spirit throughout the African diaspora, and post-riot Harlem was deployed as a shared motif of black life's common tragedies and potentialities by Lebert Bethune, René Depestre, Laminé Diakhaté, Jean Louis Dongmo, Valère Epée, Keorapetse Kgositsile, Nicolás Pasteur Lappe, Lennox Raphael, and Juan Romero. Black writers generally began to sense the fundamental unity of the Africana experience, and several generations of blacks began writing together about Harlem, an unanticipated glory after the holocausts of slavery and segregation.

With the approach of the 1990s, the great migration north to urban centers, which created black Harlem, has begun to reverse as a growing number of blacks return to their southern roots,[3] and black Harlem stands poised for a substantial alteration in its residential, as well as its racial, character. Block after block of housing stands empty, some of it just abandoned to decay, but much of it sealed for later exploitation, and several ambitious commercial initiatives are on the verge of implementation. Rivals to black Harlem's preeminence as a popular image of racial being are only to be expected as the turn of another century creates new racial legends in fresher landscapes with more appealing resonances. Yet writers continue to be engaged by the idea of black Harlem, and the motif continues to be shaped as much by its legacy of earlier exegesis as by what may happen next. Tom Wolfe's *Bonfire of the Vanities*, for example, portrays Manhattan's social idols mired in the lurid otherness of Harlem and the South Bronx, while Grace Edwards-Yearwood's first novel, *In the Shadow of the Peacock,* tells the story of a woman whose life is shaped by her birth during the Harlem riot of 1943.

What is to be said, then, of the Harlem that the writers have made? The question uncovers a coherence and continuity that cuts across national and linguistic divisions within the modern literatures of the black world. The concerted extension of the motif also strengthens a growing scholarly awareness of an Africana literary tradition, composed in the European languages but deriving its identity and authority from distinctive forms, practices, and achievements of the African diaspora. The Harlem motif is grounded in traditional figurative uses, within the African diaspora, of legendary places, whether real or imaginary: the briar-patch, in African-American folk tales; Egypt and the Promised Land, in the diction of the spirituals; Guinea, in the cosmology of Haitian voodoo; and Babylon and Ethiopia, in the imagery of contemporary Rastafarians. These spiritual spaces in which black peoples have vested their spirit and history throughout the African diaspora are the cultural precedents for the literary use of black Harlem by black writers. The popular reading of Harlem's creation at the beginning of the twentieth century was informed by these precedents. In the course of its elaboration, the motif of black Harlem acquired the status of an Africana literary kind, becoming a generic motif, faithful to a traditional black use of legendary landscapes, synthesizing the historical concerns and cultural modalities of the Africana experience in a modern, urban form. Afro-America's psychic investment in the idea of Harlem has been matched by few other symbolic places, and its extraordinary aesthetic and spiritual authority continues to be acknowledged by black writers around the world, honoring much that was lost and celebrating much that has survived.

To assert the Harlem motif's specific roots in the Africana use of symbolic places is not to deny the broad influence, on the motif, of the "poetry of place" in Western literature, dating back to Virgil's *Georgics,* in which the city is characterized by moral as well as physical attributes.[4] Major Western poets have limned personal and imaginative landscapes of their respective cities: London, in Michael Drayton's *Poly-Olbion* (Part 1, 1612; Part 2, 1622), William Cowper's *The Task* (1785), and William Wordsworth's *Prelude* (Book 7, "Residence in London," 1799–1805, 1850); Paris, in Charles Baudelaire's *Fleur du mal* (1855); and Manhattan, in Walt Whitman's *Leaves of Grass* (1857). Images of Europe's influential urban centers of modernity have been reflected in the idea of the black culture capital of Harlem, and *The Soul of the City: An Urban Anthology* (1923), a compilation of "city" poems by one hundred thirty-five British and American writers, from John Milton to T. S. Eliot, placed special emphasis on the issue of the city in poetry at a formative moment in the genesis of the motif of black Harlem as a literary kind.

Harlem's duality as a perceived symbol of racial desire, as well as a sign of the desire's denial, may even correspond in its way to what a critic has termed "a mythic doubleness and a contradictory bounty" in Shakespeare's cities.[5] On the one hand, Harlem's spiritual geography has elaborated a universe of desire so deeply rooted in the modern sensibility that its cosmos of values would not be denied by the mere fact of decay and deterioration in New York's celebrated ghetto. On the other hand, the observable reality of Harlem has been intrinsic to the motif's power and relevance, because its authority was rooted in the initial popular reading of the fact of Harlem's rapid transformation into a black community, and outstanding developments in the physical text of Harlem had to be accommodated by the exercise of interpretation. Between these complementary and contradictory impulses, the mediation of individual literary imagining has arched wide in the evolution of the form and meaning of the literary motif in this century. The imaging of black Harlem has resonated differently in the usage of authors of the different races, however, because figuration of black Harlem has evolved, in a parallel but bifurcated progression, from the dual visions of the black and non-black authors of the 1920s. For Africana writers, the Harlem motif has been inseparable from the idea of re-making racial being and challenging accepted views of the Negro race in the history, culture, and mythology of the West, in the tradition of Claude McKay's *Home to Harlem*. Three generations of poets and novelists of African descent have employed the Harlem motif consistently as the emblem of an ethos of racial renewal – with emphasis on cultural affirmation, after Harlem's spectacular emergence; on disillusion and dispossession, throughout the period of Harlem's decline; and on a resurgent sensibility, after the nadir of the 1964 riot. Before the term "ghetto" began to be applied to it during the depression years, Harlem was imaged as the legendary capital of the race, in contrast to other Negro sections, known as "darktowns," "bronzevilles," and other more or less derogatory labels. The inherent tension between the terms has remained the motif's essential challenge, as the legendary culture capital degenerated into the "montage of a dream deferred" and struggled to be reborn as the "inner city" of the Black Arts. Unless one distinguishes between the literary motif of black Harlem and its close counterpart, the literary motif of the black ghetto, one may fail to recognize how persistently Africana writers have struggled to continue to incorporate a self-created ontology of blackness in their imaging of Harlem, even when such a formulation was placed in crisis by Harlem's deterioration. Although the term "Harlem" has undeniably often seemed to express a dimension of the ghetto – maybe even the ultimate black ghetto – "black ghetto" and "black Harlem" have been conflicting ideas, at least for most Africana writers.

Harlem's fate was less critical, however, to its literary use by writers who were not black. Either as a ghetto or a culture capital, Harlem provided a contrasting ethos and aesthetic to their own cultural milieu, which could be deployed as a striking instance of "otherness," whenever the writer needed to place his or her own situation in stark relief. With some exceptions – notably Federico García Lorca – writers who are not black have clung to Van Vechten's emphasis, in *Nigger Heaven,* on the fundamental human otherness of black life, focusing on Harlem as a fundamentally alien landscape but one readily employable as a metaphor of exotic texture for issues of the moment in Western culture. Because their Harlems were conceived initially as landscapes of fundamental human otherness, albeit in the heart of the great modern metropolis, authors who were not black have tended to weave the motif of black Harlem intermittently into the cultural and mythological fabric of the West, when it served the ethos of the time: as an occasional signifier of primitivism, in the 1920s; of bourgeois alienation, in the 1940s and 1950s; and of radical political idealism in the 1960s.

The dual development of the Harlem motif suggests, therefore, that the parallel ideational impulses that initially attracted the attention of writers of different races have remained the integral focuses of their respective literary uses of it, even as they responded individually to the actual urban setting or to its imaginative rendering by others. With the Harlem motif, as with many another literary structure, the evolving formulation of figurative terms within the discourse carries a force that can shape or distort subsequent imaging by the individual author. This is not to ascribe greater understanding or misguided motives to one group of writers or the other with respect to Harlem, or to argue the influence of determinative racial forces. The variegated uses of the motif of black Harlem reinforce the conviction that works that respond to social, historical, and cultural forces are wrought by the free and deliberate exercise of choice, imagination, and perception and are not to be regarded as mere reflections of social forces that could not be otherwise. Federico García Lorca was not confined by the discourse of non-black writers, which tended generally to reduce Harlem to an artifact of otherness; Langston Hughes was able to revitalize the motif during its moment of crisis in the discourse of African-American poetry by the aptness of his individual reformulation. The evolutionary patterns of the literary idea of black Harlem have been wrought incrementally by the free imaginative exercise of individual writers in a process of repetition, revision, and reinterpretation that one major theoretician of African-American literary criticism characterizes as "signifying"[6] and the matrix of "ceaseless input and output," and that another defines as "blues."[7] The bifurcated character of the literary usage of black Harlem exemplifies dualistic and multi-layered patterns of cultural diffusion across divisions of long standing, suggesting that when modern writers – especially black and white American authors – employ virtually the same literary symbology, iconography, and motifs, they signify differently, from divergent universes of discourse, in the pursuit of divergent cultural programmes.

The trope of Harlem is a single literary figure embodying two distinct, and largely contrary, ideas of the nature, meaning, and potential of black cultural being, which have emerged and developed in a shared form that still continues to be read and revised divergently in their respective universes of discourse. Writers, both black and white, employing the figure of black Harlem reflect a complex intermingling of literary currents, for the history of the evolution of the literary figure of black Harlem traces paths of convergence on a specific motif by individual writers from broadly diverging universes of discourse. Traditional African-American and Western literary use of symbolic landscapes converge in the literary motif of black Harlem, but even as the races are beginning to come together in increasing numbers and a greater variety of ways in the national agora, black writers continue to create in quite differentiated, though no longer entirely separated, psychic and mythological spaces in American culture, and writers who are not black still seem to feel they are conjuring with some alien ontology when they pipe an African-American cultural element out of the channel of its discourse. In the mutually shared literary commonplace of black Harlem, two distinct and relatively antagonistic universes of discourse converge across the great American cultural divide of race. The divergent convergence of three generations of literary imagining on a single trope in such a large body of texts is a rare opportunity in the ongoing search for theoretical approaches to elucidate the continuities of African-American and Africana discourse and illuminate the involvement of these traditions with the discourse of the West.

Appendix 1
A Checklist of Black Harlem in Poetry

Ackerman, Avotcja. "God." In *Thoughts*. New York: n.p., 1971, unpaginated.

Allen, Bob. "Musical Vietnams." In *The Writing on the Wall,* ed. Walter Lowenfels. Garden City, N.Y.: Doubleday, 1969, p. 40.

Anderson, S. E. "A New Dance." In *The New Black Poetry,* ed. Clarence Major. New York: International Publishers, 1969, pp. 23–4.

Angelou, Maya. "Harlem Hopscotch." In *Just Give Me a Cool Drink of Water 'fore I Diiie*. New York: Random House, 1971, p. 48.

Baraka, Amiri / LeRoi Jones. "Return of the Native." In *Selected Poetry of Amiri Baraka / LeRoi Jones*. New York: Morrow, 1979, p. 101.

Benford, Lawrence. "The Beginning of a Long Poem on Why I Burned the City." In *The New Black Poetry,* ed. Clarence Major. New York: International Publishers, 1969, pp. 26–7.

Benson, Oscar Jerome. "This Is Harlem." Vertical File, Schomburg Center for Research in Black Culture.

Bethune, Lebert. "Apollo at the Apollo." In *A Juju of My Own*. N.p.: An Afro-American Production, 1965, p. 45.

"Harlem Freeze Frame." In *A Juju of My Own*. N.p.: An Afro-American Production, 1965, p. 13.

Blanding, Don. "Blue Belle Blues: Harlem." In "Point-Black: Poems on The Negro, 1633–1970," typescript, ed. Al Cartusciello. Schomburg Center for Research in Black Culture, p. 303.

Bodenheim, Maxwell. "Pronounced Fantasy." In *The Selected Poems (1914–1944)*. New York: Beechhurst Press, 1946, pp. 63–4.

"Renunciation." In *Light in the Valley*. New York: Harbinger House, 1942, pp. 18–19.

Bradley, Juanita. "Untitled." In *Stuff: A Collection of Poems, Visions, and Imaginative Happenings from Young Writers in Schools – Open and*

Closed, ed. Herbert Kohl and Victor Hernandez Cruz. New York: World Publishing, 1970, p. 73.

Brathwaite, Edward. *The Arrivants: A New World Trilogy.* London: Oxford University Press, 1973.

"The Emigrants," pp. 51–58.

"Jah," pp. 162–4.

"The Journeys," pp. 35–40.

Brièrre, Jean F. *Black Soul.* Havana, Cuba: Editorial Lex, 1947.

"Harlem." *Haïti-Journal* (Edition Spéciale de Noel) (1945), 51.

"Lumumba" (fragment). *Poesía negra de América,* ed. José Luis Gonzalez and Monica Mansour. Mexico City: Ediciones Era, 1976, pp. 383–5.

"Me revoici, Harlem." In *Anthologie de la nouvelle poésie nègre et malgache de langue française,* ed. Léopold Sédar Senghor. Paris: PUF, 1948, pp. 122–3.

Brown, Sterling A. "Harlem Street Walkers." In *Southern Road.* New York: Harcourt Brace, 1932, p. 112.

"Maumee Ruth." In *Southern Road.* New York: Harcourt Brace, 1932, pp. 10–11.

"Mecca." In *Southern Road.* New York: Harcourt Brace, 1932, p. 109.

Browne, William. "Harlem Sounds: Hallelujah Corner." In *Beyond the Blues,* ed. Rosey Eva Pool. Lympne Hythe, Kent: Hand & Flower Press, 1962, pp. 65–6.

"Saturday Night in Harlem." In *Beyond the Blues,* ed. Rosey Eva Pool. Lympne Hythe, Kent: Hand & Flower Press, 1962, pp. 66–7.

Camara, Sikhé. "Mon frère de Harlem." In *Poèmes de combat et de verité.* Paris: Oswald, 1967, pp. 76–80.

Camille, Roussan. "Nedje." In *Assaut à la nuit.* Port-au-Prince, Haiti: Imprimerie de la Etat, 1940, pp. 43–6.

Cartey, Wilfred. "Old Black Woman, Hanging Loose in Time." In *Red Rain.* New York: Emerson Hall, 1977, p. 4.

Césaire, Aimé. *Cahier d'un retour au pays natal.* Paris: Présence Africaine, 1956.

Cobb, Charles. "Mekonsippi #1." In *Furrows.* Tougaloo, Miss.: Flute Publications, 1967, p. 50.

Conyus. "He's Doing Natural Life." In *Natural Process,* eds. Ted Wilentz and Tom Weatherly. New York: Hill & Wang, 1970, pp. 4–5.

"i rode with geronimo." In *New Black Voices,* ed. Abraham Chapman. New York: New American Library, 1972, pp. 228–30.

Corso, Gregory. "Writ on the Steps of Puerto Rican Harlem." In *Penguin Poets #5: Gregory Corso, Lawrence Ferlinghetti, Allen Ginsberg.* Hammondsworth: Penguin Books, 1963, pp. 34–5.

Cortez, Jayne. "For the Poets." In *Mouth on Paper*. New York: Bola Press, 1977, pp. 6–7.

"Nighttrains." In *Mouth on Paper*. New York: Bola Press, 1977, pp. 42–3.

"So Many Feathers." In *Mouth on Paper*. New York: Bola Press, 1977, pp. 18–20.

Craveirinha, José. "Africa." *Présence Africaine*, 57 (1966), 472–3.

Cruz, Victor Hernandez. "Urban Dream." In *The New Black Poetry*, ed. Clarence Major. New York: International Publishers, 1969, pp. 46–7.

Cullen, Countee. "From the Dark Tower." In *Copper Sun*. New York: Harper & Bros., 1927, p. 3.

"Harlem Wine." In *Color*. New York: Harper Bros., 1927, p. 13.

da Cruz, Viriato. "Mamã negra." In *Antologia da poesia de expressão portugûesa*, ed. Mário de Andrade. Paris: Oswald, 1958.

Dadié, Bernard B. "Christmas." In *Hommes de tous les continents*. Paris: Présence Africaine, n.d., pp. 62–4.

"Harlem." In *Hommes de tous les continents*. Paris: Présence Africaine, n.d., pp. 55–6.

"Jour sur Harlem." In *Hommes de tous les continents*. Paris: Présence Africaine, n.d., p. 57.

del Cabral, Manuel. "Una carta para Franklin." In *Segunda antología tierra*. Madrid: n.p., pp. 119–22.

"Lo blanco regresa." In *Segunda antología tierra*. Madrid: n.p., n.d., pp. 178–83.

"Viejo chino de Brooklyn." In *Antología tierra: 1939–1949*. Madrid: Ediciones cultura hispánica, 1949, pp. 121–2.

DeLegall, Walt. "Elegy for a Lady." In *Beyond the Blues*, ed. Rosey Eva Pool. Lympne Hythe, Kent: Hand & Flower Press, 1962, pp. 88–90.

Depestre, René. "Malcolm X." *Présence Africaine*, 57. (1966), 212–13.

Deutsch, Babette. "Voices on Riverside." In *The Collected Poems*. Garden City, N.Y.: Doubleday, 1969, p. 169.

Diakhaté, Laminé. "Sur le tombeau de John Kennedy." *Présence Africaine*, 57, (1966), 110–17.

Di Prima, Diane. "Goodbye Nkrumah." In *Revolution Letters Etc*. San Francisco: City Lights Books, 1971, pp. 64–5.

Dongmo, Jean-Louis. "Le tambour parlant." *Présence Africaine*, 60 (1966), 120–1.

Dragonette, Ree. "From *Shrovetide*." In *New American Review #5*. New York: New American Library, 1971, pp. 169–73.

Duckett, Alfred. "Mother's Day in Harlem." In *Glowchild and Other Poems*, ed. Ruby Dee. New York: Third Press, 1972, p. 68.

Raps. Chicago: Nelson–Hall, 1973.
"I Hear Harlem," pp. 5–10.
"Saturday Night Uptown," p. 57.
"What Harlem Is to Me," pp. 61–5.
"What's Your Excuse," p. 53.
"White Is the Color," p. 27.
"Send Me a Letter." In *Glowchild and Other Poems,* ed. Ruby Dee. New York: Third Press, 1972, pp. 65–6.

Dumas, Henry. *Poetry for My People,* eds. Hale Chatfield and Eugene Redmond. Carbondale: Southern Illinois University Press, 1970.
"Harlem Gulp," pp. 41–2.
"Ikef 16: Guts," p. 155.
"Mosaic Harlem," pp. 80–1.

Eastman, Max. "Jilted in Harlem." In "Point-Black: Poems on the Negro, 1633–1970," typescript, ed. Al Cartusciello. Schomburg Center for Research in Black Culture, p. 357.

Eastmond, Claude T. "The Subway." In *Light and Shadows*. Boston: Christopher Publishing, 1934, pp. 59–60.

Ebon. "Viet Nam Cotillion / or Debutante Ball in the Pentagon / The Statue of Liberty has her / Back / To Harlem." In *Revolution: A Poem*. Chicago: Third World Press, 1968, p. 16.

Edwards, Joyce. "Psychedelic Dream." In *Stuff: A Collection of Poems, Visions and Imaginative Happenings from Young Writers in Schools – Open and Closed,* ed. Herbert Kohl and Victor Hernandez Cruz. New York: World Publishing, 1970, pp. 89–90.

Emanuel, James. "Animal Trick." In *Panther Man*. Detroit: Broadside Press, 1970, pp. 12–13.
"For 'Mr. Dudley,' a Black Spy." In *Panther Man*. Detroit: Broadside Press, 1970, p. 14.
"A Harlem Romance." In *A Black Man Abroad: The Toulouse Poems*. Detroit: Lotus Poems, 1978, p. 57.
"Stop Light in Harlem." In *The Treehouse, and Other Poems*. Detroit: Broadside Press, 1968, p. 12.
"To Harlem: A Note on Langston Hughes." In *Panther Man*. Detroit: Broadside Press, 1970, p. 21.

Engle, Paul. "The Last Whiskey Cup." In "Point-Black: Poems on the Negro, 1633–1970," typescript, ed. Al Cartusciello. Schomburg Center for Research in Black Culture, p. 304.

Epée, Valère. *Transatlantic Blues*. In *La poésie camerounaise moderne*. Yaoundé: Université de Yaoundé, 1974, pp. 136–40.

Evans, Mari. "Langston." In *Black Out Loud,* ed. Arnold Adoff. New York: Dell, 1970, p. 49.

"Vive Noir!" In *I Am a Black Woman*. New York: Morrow, 1970, pp. 70–3.

Fabio, Sarah Webster. "Tribute to Duke." In *Understanding the New Black Poetry*, ed. Stephen Henderson. New York: Morrow [Quill Paperbacks], 1973, pp. 243–6.

Farris, John. "W. 102nd St." *Journal of Black Poetry*, 1, (1969), 75.

Feeney, Leonard." "Obsequies in Ebony." In "Point-Black: Poems on the Negro, 1633–1970," typescript, ed. Al Cartusciello. Schomburg Center for Research in Black Culture, p. 304.

Fidel Chavez, Marco. "Mi corazón permanece en la penumbra." In *Black Poetry of the Americas*, ed. Hortensia Ruiz del Vizo. Miami: Editorial Universal, 1972, pp. 106–7.

Field, Edward. "From *Ode to Fidel Castro*." In *Poets of Today*, ed. Walter Lowenfels. New York: International Publishers, 1964, pp. 51–2.

Fields, Julia. "Harlem in January." *Umbra*, (1967–8), 53.

Figueroa, José-Angel. "East 110th Street." In *East 110th Street*. Detroit: Broadside Press, 1973, pp. 24–30.

Florit, Eugenio. "Los poetas solos de Manhattan." In *Ultima poesía cubana*, ed. Orlando Rodriguez Sardiñas. Madrid: Hispanova, 1973, pp. 67–8.

Gamble, Christopher. "Untitled." In *Stuff: A Collection of Poems, Visions and Imaginative Happenings from Young Writers in Schools – Open and Closed*, eds. Herbert Kohl and Victor Hernandez Cruz. New York: World Publishing, 1970, pp. 106–7.

García Lorca, Federico. "Norma y paraíso de los negros." In *El poeta en Nueva York*. New York: Grove Press, 1955, pp. 16–17.

"El rey de Harlem." In *El Poeta en Nueva York*. New York: Grove Press, 1955, pp. 18–25.

Ginsberg, Allen. *Collected Poems: 1947–1980*. New York: Harper & Row, 1984.

"Howl, " pp. 126–33.

"I Am a Victim of the Telephone," p. 344.

"Kaddish," pp. 209–24.

"The Lion for Real," pp. 174–5.

"Many Loves," pp. 156–8.

"Morning," pp. 337–8.

"My Sad Self," pp. 201–2.

"Psalm IV," p. 238.

"Sea Battle of Salamis Took Place off Perama," p. 288.

"Sunflower Sutra," pp. 138–9.

"Today," pp. 345–7.

"Vision 1948," p. 8.

"Who," p. 595.

Giovanni, Nikki. "The Laws of Motion (for Harlem Magic)." In *The Women and the Men*. New York: Morrow, 1975, unpaginated.

"The New Yorkers." In *Cotton Candy on a Rainy Afternoon*. New York: Morrow, 1978, pp. 29–31.

"Walking down Park." In *Re:Creation*. Detroit: Broadside Press, 1970, pp. 21–2.

Glass, Martin. "From *Lip Service: Poem of the Guilty*." In *Campfires of Resistance: Poetry from the Movement,* ed. Todd Gitlin. Indianapolis: Bobbs-Merrill, 1971, pp. 73–4.

Goll, Yvan. "Harlem River." In *Elégie de Lackawanna*. Paris: Edition Saint-German-des-Pres, 1973, pp. 38–9.

"Jean sans terre à son frère noir." In *Yvan Goll*. Paris: Editions Seghers, 1956, pp. 129–30.

Gregory, Carole. "Ghetto Lovesong-Migration." In *The New Black Poetry,* ed. Clarence Major. New York: International Publishers, 1969, pp. 56–7.

Grimes, Nikki. "Untitled." *Poems*. Harlem: n.p., 1970, unpaginated.

Guillén, Nicolás. "Un negro canta en Nueva York." In *Man Making Words,* ed. Robert Marquez and David Arthur McMurray. Amherst: University of Massachusetts Press, 1972, pp. 64–7.

"Pequeña oda a un negro boxeador cubano." In *Man Making Words,* ed. Robert Marquez and David Arthur McMurray. Amherst: University of Massachusetts Press, 1972, pp. 52–5.

Gwala, Mafika Pascal. "Getting off the Ride." In *Jol'iinkomo*. London: Donker, 1977, pp. 60–8.

Hamilton, Bobb. "Brother Harlem Bedford Watts Tells Mr. Charlie Where Its at." In *You Better Believe It: Black Verse in England,* ed. Paul Breman. Baltimore: Penguin Books, 1973, pp. 233–8.

"Poem to a Nigger Cop." In *Black Fire,* ed. LeRoi Jones and Larry Neal. New York: Morrow, 1968, p. 452.

Hand, Q. R. "Come One, Come All." In *Anthology of Our Black Selves*. Newark: Jihad Publications, 1966, pp. 25–6.

"LBJ's Nightmare." In *Anthology of Our Black Selves*. Newark: Jihad Publications, 1966, pp. 26–31.

Harding, Phillip M. "Banjo – 135th Street." In *Harlem Interiors*. Teaneck, N.J.: Blockprint Press, n.d., unpaginated.

"Blues Singer-Smalls." In *Harlem Interiors*. Teaneck, N.J.: Blockprint Press, n.d., unpaginated.

"Danceman – Lenox Ave." In *Harlem Interiors*. Teaneck, N.J.: Blockprint Press, n.d., unpaginated.

Harris, Bill. "Griot de la Grand." *Black Scholar,* 12 (1981), 55.

Haynes, Albert E., Jr. "Eclipse." In *Black Fire,* ed. LeRoi Jones and Larry Neal. New York: Morrow, 1968, pp. 406–9.

Henderson, David. "Neon Diaspora." In *Black Fire,* eds. LeRoi Jones and Larry Neal. New York: Morrow, 1968, pp. 230–2.

De Mayor of Harlem. New York: Dutton, 1970.

"Bopping," pp. 16–17.

"By Day Harlem Blue Sky," p. 43.

"Do Nothing Till You Hear from Me," pp. 56–7.

"Egyptian Book of the Dead," pp. 112–17.

"Elvis Jones Gretch – Freak (Coltrane at the Half-Note)," pp. 52–5.

"Harlem Anthropology," p. 128.

"Harlem Xmas," p. 59.

"Jocko for Music and Dance," p. 58.

"Keep on Pushing (Harlem Riots / Summer / 1964)," pp. 31–6.

"The Last Set Saga of Blue Bobby Bland," pp. 41–2.

"Marcus Garvey Parade," pp. 39–40.

"Pope Arrives in New York City / Broadway Hustlers Go Wild," pp. 22–4.

"Psychedelic Firemen," pp. 27–30.

"Reverend King / Elijah Too / El Malik / MLK," pp. 107–10.

"Saga of the Audubon Murder," p. 26.

"Sketches of Harlem," p. 44.

"So We Went to Harlem," pp. 18–21.

"Sprinkle Goofer Dust," p. 25.

"They Look This Way and Walk That Way / As Tribal as They Can be under the Law," p. 42.

"Walk with the Mayor of Harlem," pp. 13–15.

"Yarmuul Speaks of the Riots," p. 38.

"They Are Killing All the Young Men." In *For Malcolm,* eds. Dudley Randall and Margaret Burroughs. Detroit: Broadside Press, 1967, pp. 46–54.

Hernton, Calvin C. "Jitterbugging in the Streets." In *Black Fire,* ed. LeRoi Jones and Larry Neal. New York: Morrow, 1968, pp. 205–9.

"Young Negro Poet." In *Sixes and Sevens,* ed. Paul Breman. London: Breman, 1962, p. 21.

Hill, Elton (Abu-Ishak). "Theme Brown Girl." In *The New Black Poetry,* ed. Clarence Major. New York: International Publishers, 1969, pp. 71–2.

Hines, Alfred. "Harlem Harem." *American Aphrodite,* 12 (1953), 69–72.

Hirayama, Yonezo. "A Yellow Man Looks at a Black World within a White World." *Aoyama Bunaku,* 46 (1936), unpaginated.

Horne, Theodore. "Malcolm Exsiccated." In *For Malcolm,* ed. Dudley

Randall and Margaret Burroughs. Detroit: Broadside Press, 1967, p. 67.

Huerta, Efraín. "Harlem negro." In *Poesía negra de América,* ed. José Luis Gonzalez and Monica Mansour. Mexico City: Ediciones Era, 1976, p. 127.

Hughes, Langston. *Ask Your Momma.* New York: Knopf, 1961.
"Ask Your Momma," pp. 60–5.
"Horn of Plenty," pp. 40–6.
"Ode to Dinah," pp. 24–32.
Dear Lovely Death. Amenia, N.Y.: Troutbeck Press, 1931.
"Aesthete in Harlem," unpaginated.
Fields of Wonder. New York: Knopf, 1947.
"Dimout in Harlem," pp. 95–6.
"Harlem Dance Hall," p. 94.
"Stars," p. 101.
"Trumpet Player: 52nd Street," pp. 91–3.
Good Morning Revolution: Uncollected Writings of Social Protest, ed. Faith Berry. New York: Hill, 1973.
"Advertisement for the Waldorf-Astoria," pp. 19–22.
"Air Raid over Harlem," pp. 28–32.
"The Same," pp. 9–10.
Montage of a Dream Deferred. New York: Holt, 1951.
"College Formal: Renaissance Casino," p. 41.
"Comment on Curb," p. 74.
"Dive," p. 33.
"Good Morning," pp. 71–2.
"Harlem," p. 71.
"High to Low," pp. 43–4.
"Island," p. 75.
"Juke Box Love Song," p. 10.
"Likewise," pp. 66–7.
"Movies," p. 15.
"Neighbor," p. 63.
"Night Funeral in Harlem," pp. 59–61.
"Not a Movie," p. 16.
"125th Street," p. 33.
"Passing," p. 57.
"Projection," p. 26.
"Same in Blues," pp. 72–3.
"Shame on You," p. 50.
"Theme for English B," pp. 39–40.
One-Way Ticket. New York: Knopf, 1949.

"The Ballad of Margie Polite," pp. 75–6.
"Could Be," p. 100.
"Deceased," p. 116.
"Negro Servant," p. 70.
"Puzzled," pp. 71–2.
"Visitors to the Black Belt," pp. 65–6.
The Panther and the Lash: Poems of Our Time. New York: Knopf, 1967.
"Junior Addict," pp. 13–14.
"Lenox Avenue Bar," p. 10.
":Prime," p. 4.
Selected Poems. New York: Knopf, 1959.
"Consider Me," pp. 286–7.
"In Explanation of Our Times," pp. 281–3.
Shakespeare in Harlem. New York: Knopf, 1942.
"Death in Harlem," p. 57.
"Harlem Sweeties," pp. 18–19.
"Midnight Chippie's Lament," pp. 105–6.
"Reverie on the Harlem River," p. 123.
"Shakespeare in Harlem," p. 111.
The Weary Blues. New York: Knopf, 1926.
"Blues Fantasy," pp. 37–8.
"Cabaret," p. 29.
"The Cat and the Saxophone," p. 27.
"Disillusion," p. 104.
"Harlem Night Club," p. 32.
"Harlem Night Song," p. 62.
"Jazzonia," p. 25.
"Lenox Avenue: Midnight," p. 39.
"Negro Dancers," p. 26.
"Nude Young Dancer," p. 33.
"Song of a Banjo Man," p. 36.
"Summer Night," p. 103.
"To a Black Dancer at the Little Savoy," p. 35.
"To a Little Lover-Lass, Dead," p. 31.
"To Midnight Nan at Leroy's," p. 30.
"The Weary Blues," pp. 23–4.
"Young Prostitute," p. 34.
"Young Singer," p. 28.
Iliev, Ilho. "Janus of Many Faces." In "Point-Black: Poems on the Negro, 1633–1970," ed. Al Cartusciello. Typescript. Schomburg Center for Research in Black Culture, p. 314A.

Inada, Lawson Fusao. "Plucking out a Rhythm." In *Before the War*. New York: Morrow, 1971, pp. 13–14.

Jackson, Mae. "(To Someone I Met on 125th Street, 1966)." In *Can I Poet with You*. New York: Black Dialogue Publishers, 1969, p. 9.

Jamal, Ali Bey Hassan (Joseph Kitt). "Tempting." In *Poems from Attica*. Detroit: Broadside Press, 1974, p. 23.

Jarvis, José Antonio. "Harlem Comedy." In *Bamboula Dance and Other Poems*. St. Thomas, Virgin Islands: Art Shop, 1935, p. 9.

"Harlem Tragedy." In *Bamboula Dance and Other Poems*. St. Thomas, Virgin Islands Art Shop, 1935, p. 10.

Joans, Ted. "Duke's Advice." In *A Black Pow-Wow of Jazz Poems*. London: Calder & Boyars, 1973, p. 47.

"Ego-sippi." In *A Black Manifesto*. London: Calder & Boyars, 1971, p. 58.

"Freedom." In *All of Ted Joans and No More*. New York: Excelsior Publishing, 1961, p. 52.

"Gris-Gris." In *A Black Pow-Wow of Jazz Poems*. London: Calder & Boyars, 1973, pp. 14–18.

"Hallelujah, I Love Jazz So." *Présence Africaine*, 72 (1966), 115–16.

"Harlem Poems." *Journal of Black Poetry*, 1 (1969), 45–6.

"Harlem Poster." In *A Black Manifesto*. London: Calder & Boyars, 1971, p. 82.

"Harlem to Picasso." In *Afrodisia*. New York: Hill & Wang, 1970, p. 61.

"Horny Harrar House Blues." In *A Black Pow-Wow of Jazz Poems*. London: Calder & Boyars, 1973, p. 26.

"I Ask Harlem." In *A Black Manifesto*. London: Calder & Boyars, 1971, p. 65.

"I Love a Big Bird." In *All of Ted Joans and No More*. New York: Excelsior Publishing, 1961, p. 72.

"Jazz Is My Religion." In *A Black Pow-Wow of Jazz Poems*. London: Calder & Boyars, 1973, p. 146.

"New Names." In *A Black Pow-Wow of Jazz Poems*. London: Calder & Boyars, 1973, p. 76.

"Passed on Blues: Homage to a Poet." In *A Black Pow-Wow of Jazz Poems*. London: Calder & Boyars, 1973, pp. 123–5.

"Promised Land." In *A Black Pow-Wow of Jazz Poems*. London: Calder & Boyars, 1973, p. 87.

"S.C. Threw S.C. into the Railroad Yard." In *A Black Pow-Wow of Jazz Poems*. London: Calder & Boyars, 1973, p. 23.

"Soul Brother Seymour." In *All of Ted Joans and No More*. New York: Excelsior Press, 1961, p. 31.

"That Was the World of Langston Hughes." *Présence Africaine,* 57 (1966), 57–8.

"True Blues for a Dues Payer." In *A Black Pow-Wow of Jazz Poems.* London; Calder & Boyars, 1973, p. 107.

"Way Down Yonder." In *Afrodisia.* New York: Hill & Wang, 1970, p. 25.

"Wild West Savages." In *Afrodisia.* New York: Hill & Wang, 1970, pp. 22–3.

Johnson, Alicia Loy. "Black Lotus / A Prayer." In *The New Black Poetry,* ed. Clarence Major. New York: International Publishers, 1969, pp. 74–6.

"The Long March." In *Nine Black Poets,* ed. R. Baird Schuman. Durham, N.C.: Moore Publishing, 1968, pp. 150–5.

"On May 21, for a Dedication." In *Présence Africaine,* 66 (1968), 124–5.

Johnson, Fenton. "Harlem: Black City." In *Songs of the Soil.* New York: Trachtenberg, 1916, p. 6.

Johnson, Helene. "Bottled." In *Caroling Dusk: An Anthology of Verse by Negro Poets,* ed. Countee Cullen. New York: Harper, 1927, pp. 221–33.

"Poem." In *Caroling Dusk: An Anthology of Verse by Negro Poets,* ed. Countee Cullen. New York: Harper, 1927, pp. 218–19.

"Sonnet to a Negro in Harlem." In *The Book of American Negro Poetry,* ed. James Weldon Johnson. New York: Harcourt Brace & World, 1922, p. 281.

Johnson, Ray. "Walking East on 125th Street (Spring 1959)." In *Black Fire,* ed. LeRoi Jones and Larry Neal. New York: Morrow, 1968, pp. 418–19.

Johnston, Percy. "In Memoriam: Prez." In *Burning Spear.* Washington, D.C.: Jupiter Hammon Press, 1963, p. 40.

Jones, Gayl. "Tripart." In *Soulscript: Afro-American Poetry,* ed. June Jordan. Garden City, N.Y.: Doubleday [Zenith Books], 1970, p. 13.

Jordan, June. "All the World Moved." In *The New Black Poetry,* ed. Clarence Major. New York: International Publishers, 1969, pp. 89–90.

"Poem against the State? (of Things): 1975." In *Things That I Do in the Dark.* New York: Random House, 1977, p. 123.

"Poem for my Family." In *Some Changes.* New York: Dutton, 1971, pp. 54–6.

Kaufman, Bob. "Lorca." In *Ancient Rain: Poems, 1956–1978.* New York: New Directions, 1981, p. 4.

"Walking Parker Home." In *Giant Talk: An Anthology of Third World Writings,* ed. Quincey Troupe and Rainer Schulte. New York: Random House, 1975, pp. 256–7.

Kemp, Arnold. "A Black Cop's Communion." In *We Speak as Liberators,* ed. Arnold Kemp. Dodd, Mead, 1970, p. 83.

Kerouac, Jack. "166th Chorus." In *Mexico City Blues (242 Choruses).* New York: Grove Press, 1959, p. 166.

Kgositsile, Keorapetse. "The Awakening." In *Black Fire,* eds. LeRoi Jones and Larry Neal. New York: Morrow, 1968, pp. 226–7.

"Epitaph." In *My Name Is Afrika.* New York: Doubleday, 1971, p. 60.

"For B.B. King and Lucille." In *The Present Is a Dangerous Place to Live.* Chicago: Third World Press, 1974, p. 31.

"Time." In *My Name Is Afrika.* New York: Doubleday, 1971, p. 46.

Khali, Basile. "Negroes' Music." *Présence Africaine,* 57 (1966), 81–82.

Kilgore, James C. *A Black Centennial.* East St. Louis, Ill.: Black River Writers Press, 1975, unpaginated.

"Signs of Ohio, December, 1970." In *A Time of Black Devotion.* Ashland, Ohio: Ashland Poetry Press, pp. 40–2.

"A Time of Black Devotion." In *A Time of Black Devotion.* Ashland, Ohio: Ashland Poetry Press, pp. 21–4.

Kijima, Hajime. "For Ruiko and Her pictures." In *Harlem: Black Angels.* Photographs by Ruiko Yoshida. Tokyo: Kodansha, 1974, p. 108.

"Untitled." In *Harlem: Black Angels.* Photographs by Ruiko Yoshida. Tokyo: Kodansha, 1974, pp. 95–6.

Knight, Etheridge. "The Bones of My Father." In *Belly Song.* Detroit: Broadside Press, 1973, pp. 55–6.

"Dark Prophecy: I Sing of Shine." In *Belly Song.* Detroit: Broadside Press, 1973, pp. 25–6.

"This Poem." In *Belly Song.* Detroit: Broadside Press, 1973, p. 44.

"This Poem Is for." In *Belly Song.* Detroit: Broadside Press, 1973, p. 58.

Kreymborg, Alfred. "Crossing the Color Line." In *The New Yorker Book of Verse,* ed. Alfred Kreymborg. New York: Harcourt Brace, 1935, p. 283.

"Harlem." In *Scarlet & Mellow.* New York: Boni & Liveright, 1926, p. 68.

Kurtz, Aaron. "From *Behold the Sea.*" In *Poets of Today: A New American Anthology,* ed. Walter Lowenfels. New York: International Publishers, 1964, pp. 77–9.

Lappe, Nicolàs Pasteur. "H . . . Comme." *Présence Africaine,* 112 (1979), 112.

Lara Filho, Ernesto. "Sinceridade." In *Seripípi na gaiola*. Luanda: ABC, 1970, p. 20.

Lateef, Daoud. "White Man on Lenox Avenue." In *The Young Black Poets of Brooklyn,* ed. Yusef Iman. [Brooklyn]: n.p., 1971, p. 19.

Levy, Ferdinand. "House-Rent Party (Harlem Saturday Night)." In *Flashes from the Dark*. Dublin: Sign of the Three Candles, 1941, pp. 44–5.

Liberthson, Leo. "Summer in Harlem." In "Point-Black: Poems on the Negro, 1633–1970." ed. Al Cartusciello. Typescript. Schomburg Center for Research in Black Culture, p. 384.

Loftis, N. J. *Black Anima*. New York: Liveright, 1973.
  "Black Anima," pp. 93–110.
  "Changes: Two," pp. 7–10.
  "Changes: Nine," pp. 34–9.
  "Fourteen," pp. 58–9.

Lopes, Nei. "O samba ubíquo." In "Feira livre," an unpublished collection of poems quoted in David Brookshaw, *Race and Color in Brazilian Literature*. Metuchen, N.J.: Scarecrow Press, 1986, p. 232.

Lorde, Audre. "Dear Toni Instead of a Letter Of Congratulation upon Your Book and Your Daughter Whom You Say You Are Raising to be a Correct Little Sister." In *From a Land Where Other People Live*. Detroit: Broadside Press, 1973, pp. 40–2.
  "Digging." In *The Black Unicorn*. New York: Norton, 1978, pp. 56–7.
  "Equinox." In *From a Land Where Other People Live*. Detroit: Broadside Press, 1973, pp. 11–12.
  New York Head Shop and Museum. Detroit: Broadside Press, 1971.
  "Monkey Man," p. 34.
  "New York City 1970," pp. 1–2.
  "A Sewer Plant Grows in Harlem," p. 9.
  "To Desi as Joe as Smoky the Lover of 115th Street." In *Celebrations: An Anthology of Black American Poetry,* ed. Arnold Adoff. Chicago: Follett Publishing, 1977, pp. 100–1.

Luciano, Felipe. "Hot Blood / Bad Blood." In *Black Spirits,* ed. Woodie King. New York: Random House, 1980, pp. 124–5.

MacLeod, Norman. "Night out of Harlem." In *Negro,* ed. Nancy Cunard. 1934; rpt., New York: Ungar, 1970, p. 268.

McKay, Claude. "Harlem Dancer." In *Selected Poems*. New York: Harcourt Brace & World, 1953, p. 61.
  "Harlem Shadows." In *Selected Poems*. New York: Harcourt Brace & World, 1953, p. 60.

"The Tropics in New York." In *Selected Poems*. New York: Harcourt Brace & World, 1953, p. 31.

McRae, John T. "Untitled." In *Ghetto '68,* ed. Sol Battle. New York: Panther House, 1968, p. 8.

Madgett, Naomi Long. "Her Story." In *The Poetry of Black America: Anthology of the Twentieth Century,* ed. Arnold Adoff. New York: Harper & Row, 1973, p. 183.

Madhubuti, Haki (Don L. Lee). "Marlayna." Cited in Annette Oliver Shand, "The Relevance of Don L. Lee as a Contemporary Poet." *Black World,* 21 (1972), 47.

"Nigerian Unity or Little Niggers Killing Little Niggers." In *Directionscope*. Detroit: Broadside Press, 1971, pp. 109–15.

"To be Quicker / for Black Political Prisoners / on the inside & outside – Real." In *Directionscope*. Detroit: Broadside Press, 1971, pp. 202–3.

"We Walk the Way of the New World." In *Directionscope*. Detroit: Broadside Press, 1971, pp. 188–91.

Major, Clarence. "American Setup." In *In a Time of Revolution,* ed. Walter Lowenfels. New York: Random House, 1969, pp. 85–8.

"Instant Revolution." In *Black Spirits,* ed. Woodie King. New York: Random House, 1972, pp. 128–30.

Marques, Ariel. "Ode a uma negra." In *Poesia viva*. Rio de Janeiro: Editora Civilização Brasileira, 1968, p. 69.

Martin, Herbert Woodward. "New York the Nine Million." In *Face the Whirlwind,* ed. Ronnie M. Lane. Grand Rapids, Mich.: Pilot Press, 1973, pp. 36–8.

Martin, Lucia. "The Drum." In *Stuff: A Collection of Poems, Visions and Imaginative Happenings from Young Writers in Schools – Open and Closed,* ed. Herbert Kohl and Victor Hernandez Cruz. New York: World Publishing, 1970, pp. 76–7.

Mason, Mason Jordan. "Last Impression of New York." In *Poetry of the Negro,* ed. Langston Hughes and Arna Bontemps. New York: Doubleday, 1970, pp. 521–2.

Matthews, James. "I Share the Pain." In *If You Want to Know Me,* ed. Peggy L. Halsey, Gail Morlan, and Melba Smith. New York: Friendship Press, 1976, p. 26.

Mbiri, Antar S. K. *A Song out of Harlem*. Clifton, N.J.: Humana Vox Publications, 1980.

"Charles Street," pp. 21–7.

"In Spain, in Harlem: It is the night of the horses," pp. 13–17.

"Lost Heroes," pp. 30–1.

"Rivers," pp. 3–4.

"Second (Minuet in Duet) Movement: African Twist, Latin Boogaloo then Shingaling," pp. 71–2.

"Song out of Harlem," pp. 28–9.

"Third (Passacaglias Blues) Movement: City of Sores," p. 73.

"Window Woman," pp. 10–11.

Mbiti, John. "New York Skyscrapers." In *Présence Africaine,* 57 (1966), 342.

Mendez Herrera, José. "Blak [*sic*] Belt." In *Lira negra,* ed. José Sanz y Diaz. Madrid: Colección Crisol, 1945.

Micheline, Jack. "O'Harlem." In *Third Rail #1* (1961), 1–4.

Miles, Josephine. "Government Injunction: Restraining Harlem Cosmetic Co." In *Poetry of the Negro,* ed. Langston Hughes and Arna Bontemps. New York: Doubleday, 1970, p. 554.

Moerman, Ernst. "Louis Armstrong," trans. Samuel Beckett. In *Negro,* ed. Nancy Cunard. 1934; rpt., New York: Ungar, 1970, p. 185.

Morand, Florette. "Happy New Year, Harlem!" In *Les poètes de la Guadeloupe.* Paris: Grassin, 1978, pp. 203–4.

Mshairi, Tauhid. "Spiritual Unity." *Journal of Black Poetry,* 1 (1968), 77–9.

Mungin, Horace. "Harlem." In *Now See Here, Homes.* New York: Brother's Distributing, 1969, pp. 3–4.

"To Wilkin's NAACP." In *Now See Here, Homes.* New York: Brother's Distributing, 1969, p. 2.

Murray, Jim. "You Are What You Do." In *three hundred sixty degrees of blackness comin at you,* ed. Sonia Sanchez. New York: 5X Publishing, 1971, pp. 77–8.

Murray, Pauli. "Harlem Riot, 1943." In *The Poetry of Black America: Anthology of the Twentieth Century,* ed. Arnold Adoff. New York: Harper & Row, 1973, p. 109.

Mvondo, Marcel, II. "Quand les nègres revendiquent . . ." In *Les voix de poètes camerounais.* Yaoundé: Editions APEC, 1965, pp. 45–6.

Neal, Larry. "The Baroness and the Black Musician." In *Black Fire,* ed. LeRoi Jones and Larry Neal. New York: Morrow, 1968, p. 309.

"Can I Tell You This Story, or Will You Send Me through All Kinds of Changes." In *Hoodoo Hollerin' Bebop Ghosts.* Washington, D.C.: Howard University Press, 1968, pp. 58–62.

"Cross Riff." In *Hoodoo Hollerin' Bebop Ghosts.* Washington, D.C.: Howard University Press, 1968, p. 58.

"Ghost Poem #1." In *Hoodoo Hollerin' Bebop Ghosts.* Washington, D.C.: Howard University Press, 1968, pp. 7–8.

"Harlem Gallery: From the Inside." In *Hoodoo Hollerin' Bebop Ghosts.* Washington, D.C.: Howard University Press, 1968, pp. 24–5.

"Malcolm X – An Autobiography." In *Hoodoo Hollerin' Bebop Ghosts.* Washington, D.C.: Howard University Press, 1968, pp. 8–10.

"The Summer after Malcolm." In *Hoodoo Hollerin' Bebop Ghosts.* Washington, D.C.: Howard University Press, 1968, pp. 70–1.

Neto, Agostinho. "Aspiração." In *Antologia da poesia negra de expressão portuguêsa,* ed. Mário de Andrade. Paris: Oswald, 1958, pp. 43–4.

"Voz de sangue." In *Antologia temática de poesia africana,* ed. Mário de Andrade. Lisbon: de Costa, 1979, p. 147.

Niger, Paul. "Nuit sur les bords de la Mekrou." In *Initiation.* Paris: Edition Seghers, 1954, pp. 35–45.

Nunes, Cassiano. "Harlem's Blues." In *Antologia dos poetas da Brasilia,* ed. Joanyr de Oliveira. Brasilia: Editora de Brasilia, 1971, p. 38.

Ortiz, Adalberto. "Casi color." In *Tierra, son y tambor: Cantares negros y mulatos.* Introduction by Joaquin Gallegos Lara. Mexico, D.F.: Ediciones la Cigarra, 1945, pp. 55–6.

Oyarzun, Luis. "La canción de Harlem." In *Lira negra,* ed. José Sanz y Diaz. Madrid: Colección Crisol, 1945, pp. 137–9.

Patterson, Raymond R. "At That Moment." In *26 Ways of Looking at a Black Man.* New York: Award Books, 1969, p. 31.

"Emma, 1925." Unpublished typescript, 1981, in my possession.

"Have You Got the Time." In *26 Ways of Looking at a Black Man.* New York: Award Books, 1969, p. 11.

"New York, New York: A Shell Game." In *26 Ways of Looking at a Black Man.* New York: Award Books, 1969, pp. 19–20.

"Pope Paul Visits Harlem, A.D. 1965." In *26 Ways of Looking at a Black Man.* New York: Award Books, 1969, p. 25.

"Riot Rimes, U.S.A." In *26 Ways of Looking at a Black Man.* New York: Award Books, 1969, pp. 99–183.

Pedroso, Regino. "Hermano negro." In *Poesía afroantillana y negrista,* ed. Jorge Luis Morales. Rio Piedras: Editorial Universitaria, Universidad de Puerto Rico, 1976, pp. 181–3.

Penny, Rob. "Be Cool, Baby." In *The Poetry of Black America: Anthology of the Twentieth Century,* ed. Arnold Adoff. New York: Harper & Row, 1973, pp. 390–1.

Pereira, Gomes Abeylard. "O amigo." In *Elegy for John Fitzgerald Kennedy.* Rio de Janeiro: Liveraria São José, 1967, pp. 41–3.

Perkins, Eugene. "The Heart of the Black Ghetto." In *Black Arts: An Anthology of Black Creativity,* ed. Ahmed Alhamisi and Harun Kofi Wangara. Detroit: Black Arts Publications, 1969.

"To Make a Poet Black." In *Black Is Beautiful*. Chicago: Free Black Press, 1968, p. 30.

Pitcher, Oliver. "Harlem: Sidewalk Icons." In *Beyond the Blues,* ed. Rosey Eva Pool. Lympne Hythe, Kent: Hand & Flower Press, 1962, pp. 160–1.

Plotkin, David George. "Centaurs in a Harlem Cabaret." In "Point-Black: Poems on the Negro, 1633–1970," ed. Al Cartusciello. Typescript. Schomburg Center for Research in Black Culture., p. 274.

Powell, Luray R. "Harlem," *Amsterdam News,* November 8, 1980, p. 17.

Prime, Cynthia Judy. "The Politician's Tale." In *The Sour and the Sweet*. New York: William-Frederick Press, 1972, pp. 2–5.

Quasimodo, Salvatore. "La chiesa dei negri ad Harlem." In *To Give and to Have,* trans. Edith Farnsworth. Chicago: Regnery, 1969, pp. 158–9.

Ragland, J. Farley. "A Harlem Interlude." In *Rhymes of Our Times*. New York: Malliet, 1946, pp. 108–9.

"Manhattan Sketches." In *Rhymes of Our Times*. New York: Malliet, 1946, p. 58.

Ramirez, Froilan J. "University on the Corner of Lenox Avenue (U.C.L.A)." In *three hundred sixty degrees of blackness comin at you,* ed. Sonia Sanchez. New York: 5X Publishing, 1971, p. 60.

Randall, Dorothy. "Lovesong to the Workshop." In *three hundred sixty degrees of blackness comin at you,* ed. Sonia Sanchez. New York: 5X Publishing, 1971, p. 39.

Randall, James. "In Memory of Martin Luther King." In *Face the Whirlwind,* ed. Ronnie M. Lane. Grand Rapids, Mich.: Pilot Press, 1973, pp. 54–5.

"Uptown: 112th St." In *Cities and Other Disasters*. Detroit: Broadside Press, 1973, p. 10.

Randall, Jon C. "Indigoes." In *Indigoes*. Detroit: Broadside Press, 1975, p. 8.

Raphael, Lennox. "Sidewalk Blues." In *In a Time of Revolution,* ed. Walter Lowenfels. New York: Random House, 1969, pp. 108–11.

Reddy, T. J. "Music Makers in the Dark." *Less Than a Score, but a Point*. New York: Random House, 1974, pp. 79–81.

Redmond, Eugene. "barbequed cong: OR we laid MY LAI low." *Black Scholar,* 1 (1970), 53.

"Parapoetics." In *Understanding the New Black Poetry,* ed. Stephen Henderson. New York: Morrow [Quill Paperbacks], 1973, pp. 371–2.

Reed, Clarence. "Harlem '67." In *Black Fire,* ed. LeRoi Jones and Larry Neal. New York: Morrow, 1969, pp. 404–5.

"In a Harlem Store Front Church." In *Black Fire,* ed. LeRoi Jones and Larry Neal. New York: Morrow, 1968, p. 403.

Reed, Tom. "Confused." In *Some Soulful Words.* N.p.: Venue Press, 1970, unpaginated.

Reedburg, Robert. "Epitaph for a Man." In *Today's Negro Voices,* ed. Beatrice Murphy. New York: Messner, 1970, pp. 104–7.

Rhodes, Ronald H. T. "I Got Harlem." In *three hundred and sixty degrees of blackness comin at you,* ed. Sonia Sanchez. New York: 5X Publishing, 1971, p. 10.

Rivers, Conrad Kent. "Africa." In *The Still Voice of Harlem.* London: Breman, 1968, p. 6.

"All Things Black and Beautiful." In *Understanding the New Black Poetry,* ed. Stephen Henderson. New York: Morrow [Quill Paperbacks], 1973, pp. 257–60.

"A Mourning Letter from Paris." In *The Still Voice of Harlem.* London: Breman, 1968, p. 9.

"A Mourning Letter from Paris [variant]." In *The Wright Poems,* ed. Ronald L. Fair. London: Breman, 1972, p. 18.

"Night Letter from Paris." In *The Wright Poems,* ed. Ronald L. Fair. London: Breman, 1972, p. 16.

"Postscript." In *The Wright Poems,* ed. Ronald L. Fair. London: Breman, 1972, p. 11.

"The Still Voice of Harlem." In *The Still Voice of Harlem.* London: Breman, 1968, p. 3.

"The Train Runs Late to Harlem." In *I Am the Darker Brother,* ed. Arnold Adoff. New York: Macmillan [Collier Books], 1968, p. 89.

Rocha, Jofre. "Poema universal." In *Assim se´fez madrugada.* Lisbon: Ediçoes 70, 1977, p. 44.

Rodgers, Carolyn M. "Broadway Uptown." In *The Heart as Ever Green.* New York: Doubleday, 1978, p. 40.

Romano de Sant' Anna, Affonso. "Empire State Building." In *Poesia viva.* Rio de Janeiro: Editora Civilização Brasileira, 1968, pp. 36–42.

Romero, Juan. "Harlem." *Présence Africaine,* 61 (1967), 138–40.

Romney, Hugh. "Altar Piece." In *Beat Coast East,* ed. Stanley Fisher. New York: Excelsior Press, 1960, pp. 53–4.

Rosenbaum, Nathan. "Harlem Cabaret." In "Point-Black: Poems on the Negro, 1633–1970," ed. Al Cartusciello. Typescript. Schomburg Center for Research in Black Culture, pp. 410–13.

Rossardi, Orlando. "A Langston Hughes." In *Ultima poesía cubana,* ed. Orlando Rodriguez Sardiñas. Madrid: Hispanova, 1973, pp. 420–2.

Roumain, Jacques. "Langston Hughes," *Haïti-Journal,* October 20, 1931.

Rukeyser, Muriel. "Ballad of Orange and Grape." In *Breaking Open.* New York: Random House, 1973, pp. 45–7.

Sandowski, Anne. "Poem about Birth." In *Speak Easy, Speak Free*. New York: International Publishers, 1977, pp. 24–6.

Scott, Johnie. "The American Dream." In *The New Black Poetry*, ed. Clarence Major. New York: International Publishers, 1969, pp. 115–19.

"India." In *From the Ashes: Voices of Watts*, ed. Budd Schulberg. New York: New American Library, 1967, p. 117.

Scott-Heron, Gil. "harlem: the guided tour." In *Small Talk at 125th Street and Lenox*. New York: World Publishing, 1970, pp. 24–5.

"paint it black." In *Small Talk at 125th Street and Lenox*. New York: World Publishing, 1970, p. 9.

"riot." In *Small Talk at 125th Street and Lenox*. New York: World Publishing, 1970, pp. 42–3.

"small talk at 125th and lenox." In *Small Talk at 125th Street and Lenox*. New York: World Publishing, 1970, p. 7.

Senghor, Léopold Sédar. "A New York." In *Ethiopiques*. Paris: Editions du Seuil, 1956.

Shange, Ntozake. "Lady in Blue." In *for colored girls who have considered suicide / when the rainbow is enuf* . . . New York: Macmillan, 1977, pp. 36–9.

Smith, Welton. *Penetration*. San Francisco: Journal of Black Poetry Press, 1971.

"Malcolm," pp. 2–3.

"New York; New York," p. 19.

"Phat," p. 20.

Sousa, Noemia de. "Deixa passar o meu povo." In *Antologia da poesia negra de expressão portuguêsa*, ed. Mário de Andrade. Paris: Oswald, 1958, pp. 92–3.

Spriggs, Edward S. "Every Face Is AFROMANISM Surviving." In *Black Fire*, ed. LeRoi Jones and Larry Neal. New York: Morrow, 1968, p. 341.

"For Brother Malcolm." In *For Malcolm*, ed. Dudley Randall and Margaret Burroughs. Detroit: Broadside Press, 1967, p. 73.

Stewart, Bob. "Sonnet for McKay." In *Savacou*, 14–15 (1979–80), 112.

Stowers, J. Anthony. "Dakar." In *The Aliens*. San Francisco: White Rabbit Press, 1967, unpaginated.

Taylor, Tommie Nell. "Buffalo Soldier." In *Love: From Black Women to Black Men*, ed. Frances Johnson Barnes. Hicksville, N.Y.: Exposition Press, 1977, pp. 69–70.

Tenreiro, Francisco José. "Coração em Africa." In *Antologia da poesia de expressão portuguêsa*, ed. Mário de Andrade. Paris: Oswald, 1958, pp. 33–5.

"Fragmento de Blues." In *Obra poética de Francisco José Tenreiro*. Lisbon: Editora Pax, 1967, p. 91.

"Negro de todo o mundo." In *Antologia temática de poesia africana,* ed. Mário de Andrade. Lisbon: De Costa, 1979, pp. 140–3.

Tirolien, Guy. "Satchmo." In *Balles d'or*. Paris: Présence Africaine, 1961, pp. 63–6.

Tiwoni, Habib. "Wavelengths Away." In *Islands of My Mind*. New York: Casha Publications, 1975, p. 39.

Tolson, Melvin B. "African China." In *Kaleidoscope: Poems by American Negroes,* ed. Robert Hayden. New York: Harcourt Brace & World, 1967, pp. 58–62.

A Gallery of Harlem Portraits. Columbia, Mo.: University of Missouri Press, 1979.

"Abraham Dumas," p. 10.

"African China," p. 8.

"Alexander Calverton," p. 181.

"August Lence," pp. 83–4.

"Aunt Hagar," p. 172.

"Aunt Hilda," p. 224.

"Aunt Martha," p. 179.

"Aunt Tommiezene," pp. 13–14.

"Babe Quest," pp. 23–4.

"Bella Scarritt," pp. 201–2.

"Benjamin Rosenbaum," p. 208.

"Ben Shockley," p. 227.

"Biffo Lightfoote," p. 20.

"Big Bessie," pp. 129–35.

"Big Fred Railer," pp. 110–11.

"The Biggest Fool in Harlem," pp. 65–6.

"Big Jim Casey," pp. 189–90.

"Big Shot Lacy," p. 163.

"Black Moses," p. 116.

"Black Zuleika," p. 22.

"Bowyer Bragg," pp. 150–1.

"Carrie Green," p. 69.

"Cato Snoddy," p. 237.

"Chef Sam Logan," p. 92.

"Chittling Sue," p. 33.

"Crip MacKay," pp. 145–6.

"Daddy Oldfield," pp. 37–8.

"Damon Akerman," pp. 114–15.

"Dave Zachary," p. 143.

"David Letts," pp. 48–9.
"Deacon Phineas Bloom," pp. 11–12.
"Diamond Canady," p. 7.
"Doc Brockenbury," p. 34.
"Doctor James," pp. 166–7.
"Dr. Cram Mifflin," p. 71.
"Dr. Harvey Whyte," p. 78.
"Duke Huggins," pp. 184–5.
"Editor Crum," pp. 26–7.
"Edna Borland," p. 203.
"Elbert Hartman," pp. 147–8.
"Enloe Penn," pp. 54–5.
"Ezra Crane," p. 188.
"Faith Hanley," pp. 67–8.
"Ferenc Glaspell," p. 94.
"Festus Conrad," p. 149.
"Flora Murdock," p. 108.
"Francis Keats," p. 24.
"Frank Fullilove," p. 205.
"Frederick Judson," pp. 31–2.
"Freemon Hawthorne," p. 196.
"Freida Maynard," p. 191.
"Fritz Rickman," p. 18.
"Gladys Zimmerman," p. 195.
"Gloomy Dean," p. 5.
"Goldie Keats," p. 198.
"Grand Chancellor Knapp Sackville," p. 25.
"Grandma Grady," p. 75.
"Grandma Lonigan," p. 42.
"Guy Gage," p. 222.
"Harlem," pp. 233–4.
"Harlem," pp. 3–4.
"Harold Lincoln," pp. 156–7.
"Hester Pringle," p. 47.
"Hilmar Enick," p. 199.
"The Honorable Eutaw Lamb," p. 176.
"Horace Allyn," p. 70.
"Isidor Lawson," p. 91.
"Ivory Frysinger," pp. 180–1.
"Jack D'Orsay," p. 104.
"Jack Patterson," pp. 127–8.
"Jacob Nollen," p. 39.

"Jake Bunner," p. 63.
"James Killmer," p. 56.
"Jesse Seegar," pp. 141–2.
"Jobyna Dear," pp. 102–3.
"Jonah Emerson," p. 225.
"Joshua Granite," p. 235.
"Joshua Granite," pp. 119–20.
"Juarez Mary," p. 90.
"Judge Crimpton," p. 168.
"Lady Hope," p. 21.
"Laughing Jim," p. 197.
"Laura Yost," p. 95.
"Lena Lovelace," p. 80.
"Lionel Bushman," pp. 215–16.
"Little Nellie Patmore," p. 173.
"Lovie Long," p. 52.
"Madame Alpha Devine," p. 121.
"Maizelle Millay," p. 109.
"Mammy Tyler," pp. 58–9.
"Margaret Levy," p. 38.
"Marzimmu Heffner," p. 236.
"Marzimmu Heffner," pp. 193–4.
"Michael Ramsey," pp. 218–19.
"Miss Emile Housman," p. 175.
"Miss Eulaline Briffault," p. 6.
"Miss Felicia Babcock," pp. 40–1.
"Miss Hilda Angoff," p. 223.
"Mother Vibbard," p. 174.
"Mrs. Edith Parker," pp. 122–3.
"Mrs. Ernest Quirk," p. 74.
"Mrs. Gertrude Beamish," p. 99.
"Mrs. Josephine Wise," p. 105.
"Mrs. Marcella Loften," p. 170.
"Nana Swancy," p. 206.
"Napoleon Hannibal Speare," p. 50.
"Nig Grinde," pp. 9–10.
"Noble Fetchit," p. 57.
"Nottley the Embalmer," p. 169.
"Nutty Al Moon," pp. 154–5.
"Officer John Cushwa," p. 124.
"Okay Katie," p. 73.
"Old Man Salem," p. 77.

"Old Man Starks," p. 226.
"Old Pettigrew," p. 87.
"Pat Frost," pp. 51–2.
"Pearl Tripplett," p. 64.
"Peg Leg Snelson," p. 30.
"Percy Longfellow," p. 164.
"Poker Face Duncan," pp. 35–6.
"Polly Trotter," p. 118.
"Pops Foote," p. 228.
"Prince Banmurji," p. 60.
"Ralph Farrell," pp. 136–8.
"Ray Rosenfeld," pp. 158–9.
"Reverend Isaiah Cloud," pp. 186–7.
"Reverend Thomas Brazeale," pp. 15–16.
"Rhoda Stacpoole," p. 49.
"Richard Birch," p. 171.
"Richmond Hoover," p. 76.
"Sadie Mulberry," p. 19.
"Samuel Gutterman," p. 93.
"Sara Ashton," p. 36.
"Senola Hurse," p. 16.
"Sergeant Tiffin," pp. 81–2.
"Sidney Sippel," pp. 97–8.
"Silent Sam," pp. 182–3.
"Simon Southorn," pp. 177–8.
"Sister Slemp," pp. 43–4.
"Slick Gunnar," p. 204.
"Sootie Joe," p. 17.
"Sparky Zigsmith," p. 53.
"Stanley de Weerd," p. 217.
"Sterling the Artist," p. 165.
"Steve Wordsworth," pp. 125–6.
"Stillicho Spikes," pp. 28–9.
"The Stranger," pp. 112–13.
"Sylvia Wiggins," pp. 213–14.
"Ted Carson," pp. 220–1.
"Tito Crouch," pp. 211–12.
"Tubby Laughton," p. 144.
"Uncle Gropper," pp. 117–18.
"Uncle Lash," pp. 207–8.
"Uncle Rufus," p. 72.
"Uncle Twitty," p. 200.

"Uncle Walt," pp. 88–9.
"The Underdog," pp. 229–30.
"Uriah Houze," p. 96.
"Vergil Ragsdale," pp. 100–1.
"Victor Garibaldi," p. 79.
"Whirlwind Cotton," pp. 160–2.
"Willie Byrd," pp. 106–7.
"Winged Feet Cooper," pp. 152–3.
"Wu Shang," pp. 209–10.
"Xavier van Loon," pp. 192.
"Zip Lightner," pp. 85–6.
Harlem Gallery: The Curator, Book I. New York: Twayne, 1965.
"Alpha: The Harlem Gallery, an Afric pepper bird," pp. 19–20.
"Beta: O Tempora," pp. 21–5.
"Chi: Despite his caricatures," pp. 145–51.
"Delta: Doubt not," pp. 29–33.
"Epsilon: The idols of the tribe," pp. 34–6.
"Eta: Her neon sign blared two Harlem blocks," pp. 43–53.
"Gamma: The mecca Art is a babel city in the people's Shinar," pp. 26–8.
"Iota: The hour with the red letter stumbles in," pp. 57–63.
"Kappa: Mr. and Mrs. Guy Delaporte III," pp. 64–7.
"Lambda: From the mouth of the Harlem Gallery," pp. 68–70.
"Mu: Hideho Heights," pp. 71–6.
"Nu: Rufino Laughlin," pp. 77–8.
"Omicron: 'Life and Art,' said Dr. Nkomo, 'Beget incestuously,' " pp. 93–7.
"Phi: *Harlem Vignettes* read," pp. 133–44.
"Pi: Omega is not *I Like*," pp. 98–102.
"Rho: New Year's Day," pp. 103–05.
"Sigma: On a red letter day," pp. 106–10.
"Tau: The MS., *Harlem Vignettes*," p. 111.
"Theta: In the *chateau en Espagne* of Vanity," pp. 54–6.
"Upsilon: My Talent was an Uptown whore; my wit a Downtown pimp," pp. 112–32.
"Xi: Hideho Heights," pp. 79–92.
"Zeta: My thoughts tilted at the corners like Nepalese eyes," pp. 37–42.
"John Henry in Harlem." In *Golden Slippers,* ed. Arna Bontemps. New York: Harper Bros., 1941, pp. 38–40.
"Satchmo." In *The Black Poets,* ed. Dudley Randall. New York: Bantam, 1971, pp. 119–20.

Torregian, Sotere. "Poem for the Birthday of Huey P. Newton." In *New Black Voices*. New York: New American Library, 1972, pp. 343–4.

Touré, Askia Muhammad. "Dago Red (Harlem Snow Song)." In *Black Spirits,* ed. Woodie King. New York: Random House, 1972, pp. 223–7.

"Juju." In *Natural Process: An Anthology of New Black Poetry,* ed. Ted Wilentz and Tom Weatherley. New York: Hill & Wang, 1971, pp. 134–8.

Troupe, Quincey. "You Come to Me." In *Embryo*. New York: Barlenmir House, 1972, p. 8.

Wagner, Charles A. "Harlem Cabaret." In *"Point-Black: Poems on the Negro, 1633–1970,"* ed. Al Cartusciello. Typescript. Schomburg Center for Research in Black Culture, p. 288.

Walker, Margaret. "For My People." In *Poetry of the Negro: 1740–1970,* ed. Langston Hughes and Arna Bontemps. New York: Doubleday, 1970, pp. 314–16.

Watson, Barbara Bellow. "Echoes in a Burnt Building." *Kenyon Review,* 27 (1965), 672–3.

Weeks, Ricardo. "Billy the Kid in Harlem." In *Freedom's Soldiers and Other Poems*. New York: Malliet, 1947, pp. 45–6.

"Harlem Junkman." In *Freedom's Soldiers, and Other Poems*. New York: Malliet, 1947, p. 25.

Welburn, Ron. "Monk, the Mau-Mau Man." In *Between a Rock and a Hard Place,* ed. Horace Coleman. Kansas City, Mo.: Bk Mk Press, 1977, pp. 77–8.

Williams, Deborah. "No Title Necessary." In *Night Came Softly,* ed. Nikki Giovanni. N.p.: n.p., 1970, pp. 30–2.

Williamson, Craig. "Untitled, from East Harlem." In *African Wings*. New York: Citadel Press, 1969, pp. 42–3.

Wilson, Reginald. "For Our American Cousins." In *For Malcolm,* ed. Dudley Randall and Margaret Burroughs. Detroit: Broadside Press, pp. 35–6.

Winston, Bessie Brent. "Harlem Girl." In *Alabaster Boxes*. Washington, D.C.: Review & Herald Publishing, 1947, p. 23.

Wright, Jay. "The End of Ethnic Dream." In *Black Fire,* ed. LeRoi Jones and Larry Neal. New York: Morrow, 1968, pp. 365–6.

"An Invitation to Madison County." In *Natural Process: An Anthology of New Black Poetry,* ed. Ted Wilentz and Tom Weatherley. New York: Hill & Wang, 1971, pp. 150–5.

X, Hurley. "Harlem River." *Journal of Black Poetry,* 1 (1969), 24.

X, Marvin. "Harlem Queen." In *Fly to Allah*. Fresno, Calif.: Al Kitab Sudan Press, 1969, pp. 18–19.

Yearwood, Gladstone. "I Am the Soil (A Poem for My Mother)." In *Speak Easy, Speak Free,* ed. Antar S. K. Mberi and Cosmo Pieterse. New York: International Publishers, 1977, pp. 27–9.

Zweig, Paul. "Uptown." In *New York: Poems,* ed. Howard Moss. New York: Avon, 1980, pp. 329–30.

Appendix 2
A Checklist of Black Harlem in Novels

Anderson, Sherwood. *Dark Laughter*. New York: Boni & Liveright, 1925.

Appel, Benjamin. *The Dark Stain*. New York: Dial, 1943.

Arnold, William. *Harlem Woman*. 1952.

Arthur, John. *Dark Metropolis*. Boston: Meador Publishing, 1936.

Baldwin, James. *Another Country*. New York: Dial, 1962.

    Go Tell It on the Mountain. New York: Knopf, 1953.

    Just above My Head. New York: Dial, 1979.

    Tell Me How Long the Train's Been Gone. New York: Dial, 1968.

Barnes, Geoffrey. *Dark Lustre*. New York: King, 1932.

Beckham, Barry. *Double Dunk*. Los Angeles: Holloway House, 1980.

Bodenheim, Maxwell. *Naked on Roller Skates*. New York: Liveright, 1931.

    Ninth Avenue. New York: Boni & Liveright, 1926.

Bontemps, Arna. *Sad-faced Boy*. Boston: Houghton Mifflin, 1937.

Bowyer Campbell, T. *Black Sadie*. Boston: Houghton Mifflin, 1928.

Brown, Eugene. *Trespass*. Garden City, N.Y.: Doubleday, 1952.

Brown, Wenzell. *The Big Rumble: A Novel of Juvenile Delinquency*. New York: Popular Library, 1955.

Cain, George. *Blueschild Baby*. New York: McGraw-Hill, 1971.

Caspary, Vara. *The White Girl*. New York: Sears, 1929.

Childress, Alice. *A Hero Ain't Nothin' but a Sandwich*. New York: Coward, McCann & Geoghegan, 1973.

Conley, Elizabeth G. *The Harlem Go-Getters, and Other Short Stories*. New York: Exposition Press, 1963.

Conrad, Earl. *Rock Bottom*. Garden City, N.Y.: Doubleday, 1952.

Cullen, Countee. *One Way to Heaven*. New York: Harper Bros., 1932.

Diakaté, Laminé. *Chalys d'Harlem: Roman*. Dakar: Nouvelles Editiones Africaines, 1978.

De Jongh, James, and Carles Cleveland. *City Cool: A Ritual of Belonging*. New York: Random House, 1978.

Demby, William. *Love Story Black*. New York: Reed, Cannon & Johnson, 1978.

DeVeaux, Alexis. *Na-ni: A Story and Pictures*. New York: Harper & Row, 1973.

Dodson, Owen. *Boy at the Window*. New York: Farrar, Straus & Young, 1951.

Dortort, David. *The Post of Honor*. New York: McGraw-Hill [Whittlesey House], 1937.

Ellison, Ralph. *Invisible Man*. New York: Random House, 1952.

Ellson, Hal. *Duke*. New York: Scribner's, 1949.

    I'll Fix You. New York: Popular Library, 1956.

    Rock. New York: Ballantine, 1955.

    This Is It. New York: Popular Library, 1956.

Faulkner, William. *Light in August*. New York: Harrison Smith & Robert Haas, 1932.

Fauset, Jessie Redmon. *Plum Bun*. New York: Stokes, 1929.

Ferris, Wally. *Across 110 Street*. New York: Harper & Row, 1970.

Fisher, Rudolph. "City of Refuge." In *The New Negro*. New York: Boni, 1925.

    The Conjure Man Dies. New York: Covici-Friede, 1932.

    The Walls of Jericho. New York: Knopf, 1928.

Fisher, William. *The Waiters*. Cleveland: World Publishing, 1950.

Ford, Charles Henry, and Parker Tyler. *The Young and the Evil*. Paris: Obelisk Press, 1933.

Gary, Romain. *Tulipe*. Paris: Gallimard, 1970.

Guy, Rosa. *Bird at My Window*. Philadelphia: Lippincott, 1966.

    The Disappearance. New York: Delacorte, 1979.

    Edith Jackson. New York: Viking, 1978.

    The Friends. New York: Holt, Rinehart & Winston, 1973.

    A Measure of Time. New York: Holt, Rinehart & Winston, 1983.

    Mirror of Her Own. New York: Delacorte, 1981.

    New Guys around the Block. New York: Delacorte, 1983.

    Ruby. New York: Viking, 1976.

Haskins, Jim. *Diary of a Harlem School Teacher*. New York: Grove, 1969.

Henderson, George Wylie. *Jule*. New York: Creative Age Press, 1946.

Hewlett, John H. *Harlem Story*. New York: Prentice-Hall, 1948.

Hill, Carol. *Jeremiah 8:20*. New York: Random House, 1970.

Himes, Chester. *All Shot up*. New York: Avon, 1960.
  The Big Gold Dream. New York: Avon, 1960.
  Blind Man with a Pistol. New York: Morrow, 1969.
  Cotton Comes to Harlem. New York: Putnam, 1965.
  The Crazy Kill. New York: Avon, 1959.
  The Heat Is On. New York: Putnam, 1966.
  Pinktoes. New York: Putnam, 1965.
  A Rage in Harlem. New York: Avon, 1965.
  The Real Cool Killers. New York: Avon, 1959.
  Run Man Run. New York: Putnam, 1966.
Horwitz, Julius. *The Inhabitants*. Cleveland: World Publishing, 1960.
  The W. A. S. P. New York: Atheneum Publishers, 1967.
Hughes, Langston. *The Best of Simple*. New York: Hill & Wang, 1961.
  Laughing to Keep from Crying. New York: Holt, 1952.
  Simple Speaks His Mind. New York: Simon & Schuster, 1950.
  Simple Stakes a Claim. New York: Rinehart, 1957.
  Simple Takes a Wife. New York: Simon & Schuster, 1953.
  Simple's Uncle Sam. New York: Hill & Wang, 1965.
  Something in Common and Other Stories. New York: Hill & Wang, 1963.
  Tambourines to Glory. New York: Day, 1958.
  The Ways of White Folks. New York: Knopf, 1934.
Hurst, Fannie. *Imitation of Life*. New York: Burt, 1933.
Hurston, Zora Neale. "Book of Harlem." Short story, 7 pp. James Weldon Johnson Collection, Beinecke Library, Yale University.
  "Muttsy." *Opportunity*, 4 (1926), 246–50.
  "Story in Harlem Slang." *American Mercury*, 55 (1942), 84–96.
Joseph, Arthur. *Volcano in Our Midst*. New York: Pageant Press, 1952.
Kaye, Phillip B. [pseud., Alger Adams]. *Taffy*. New York: Crown Publishers, 1950.
Killens, John O. *Cotillion, or One Good Bull Is Half the Herd*. New York: Trident, 1967.
Kirkbride, Ronald de Levington. *Dark Surrender*. New York: Sears Publishing, 1933.
Klass, Sheila. *Come Back on Monday*. New York: Abelard–Schuman, 1960.
Krasner, William. *North of Welfare*. New York: Harper, 1954.
Larsen, Nella. *Passing*. New York: Knopf, 1929.
  Quicksand. New York: Knopf, 1928.
Lipsyte, Robert. *The Contender*. New York: Harper & Row, 1967.
Lowry, Robert. *The Violent Wedding*. Garden City, N.Y.: Doubleday, 1953.
McKay, Claude. *Gingertown*. New York: Harper, 1932.

Home to Harlem. New York: Harper, 1928.

Major, Clarence. *No*. New York: Emerson Hall Publishing, 1973.

Manrique, Manuel. *Island in Harlem*. New York: Day, 1966.

Marshall, Paule. *Brown Girl, Brownstones*. New York: Random House, 1959.

Mayfield, Julian. *The Hit*. New York: Vanguard, 1957.

The Long Night. New York: Vanguard, 1958.

Meriwether, Louise. *Daddy Was a Number Runner*. Englewood Cliffs, N.J.: Prentice-Hall, 1970.

Merton, Thomas. *The Seven Story Mountain*. New York: Harcourt Brace, 1948.

Miller, Charlotte Ruth. *Claudine*. New York: Avon, 1976.

Miller, Floyd. *The Dream Peddlers: A Novel of Spanish Harlem*. New York: Popular Library, 1956.

Miller, Gilmore. *Sweet Man*. New York: Viking, 1930.

Miller, Warren. *The Cool World*. New York: Little, Brown, 1959.

The Siege of Harlem. New York: McGraw-Hill, 1964.

Moon, Bucklin. *The Darker Brother*. Garden City, N.Y.: Doubleday, Doran, 1943.

Without Magnolias. Garden City, N.Y.: Doubleday, 1949.

Myers, Walter Dean. *Fast Sam, Cool Clyde and Stuff*. New York: Viking, 1975.

Niles, Blair. *Strange Brother*. New York: Liveright, 1931.

Offord, Carl. *The Naked Fear*. New York: Ace, 1954.

The White Face. New York: McBride, 1943.

Ornstein, William. *Deep Currents*. Dallas: Story Book Press, 1953.

Peterkin, Julia. *Bright Skin*. Indianapolis: Bobbs-Merrill, 1932.

Petry, Ann. *The Street*. Boston: Houghton Mifflin, 1946.

Pharr, Robert Deane. *The Book of Numbers*. Garden City, N.Y.: Doubleday, 1969.

Giveadamn Brown. Garden City, N.Y.: Doubleday, 1978.

Reed, Ishmael. *Mumbo Jumbo*. Garden City, N.Y.: Doubleday, 1972.

Robinson, John Terry. *White Horse in Harlem*. New York: Pageant Press, 1965.

Roc, John. *Winter Blood*. New York: Trident Press, 1971.

Sales, John. *A Tree Named John*. Chapel Hill: University of North Carolina Press, 1929.

Schuyler, George. *Black No More*. New York: Macaulay, 1931.

Stark, Irwin. *The Invisible Island*. New York: Viking, 1948.

Steptoe, John. *Uptown*. New York: Harper & Row, 1970.

Stevens, Shane. *Go Down Dead*. New York: Morrow, 1966.

Way Uptown in Another World. New York: Putnam, 1971.

Thurman, Wallace. *The Blacker the Berry*. New York: Macaulay, 1929.
  Infants of the Spring. New York: Macaulay, 1932.
Tidyman, Ernest. *Shaft*. New York: Macmillan, 1970.
Tomás, Benito Luciano. *Harlemitta Dreams*. New York: no publisher, 1934.
Toomer, Jean. *Cane*. New York: Boni & Liveright, 1923.
Van Vechten, Carl. *Nigger Heaven*. New York: Knopf, 1926.
Vroman, Mary Elizabeth. *Harlem Summer*. New York: Bantam, 1963.
Wallant, Edward Lewis. *The Pawnbroker*. New York: Harcourt Brace & World, 1961.
White, Walter F. *Fire in the Flint Flight*. New York: Knopf, 1932.
Williams, John A. *The Angry Ones*. New York: Ace, 1960.
  !Click Song. New York: Houghton Mifflin, 1982.
  The Man Who Cried I Am. Boston: Little, Brown, 1967.
  Mothersill and the Foxes. Garden City, N.Y.: Doubleday, 1975.
  Night Song. New York: Farrar, Straus & Cudahy, 1961.
  Songs of Darkness, Songs of Light. Boston: Little, Brown, 1969.
Wood, Clement. *Deep River*. New York: Godwin, 1934.
Wright, Charles Stevenson. *Absolutely Nothing to Get Alarmed about*. New York: Farrar Straus & Giroux, 1973.
  The Messenger. New York: Farrar Straus, 1963.
  The Wig. New York: Farrar Straus & Giroux, 1966.
Wright, Richard. *Native Son*. New York: Harper, 1940.

Notes

Introduction: Vicious Modernism

1   In "Four Shadows of Harlem," *Negro Digest,* 18 (1969), 22–25, Wilfred Cartey examines Harlem's "inner reality encased in the larger, outer reality, Manhattan, the other world," in poems by Langston Hughes, Claude McKay, Léopold Senghor, and Federico García Lorca. In "The Harlem of Langston Hughes's Poetry," *Phylon,* 13 (1952), 276–83, Arthur P. Davis studies the evolving and maturing theme of Harlem in Langston Hughes's poetry. In "The Literature of Harlem," *Freedomways,* 3 (1963), 276–91, Ernest Kaiser surveys works of creative literature with Harlem settings. In *Melvin B. Tolson's Harlem Gallery: A Literary Analysis* (Columbia: University of Missouri Press, 1980), Mariann Russell studies the use of the Harlem motif in Tolson's masterpiece. And in "Symbolic Space, Communal Rituals, and the Surreality of the Urban Ghetto: Harlem in Black Literature from the 1920's to the 1960's," *Callaloo* 11 (1988), 309–45, Günter H. Lenz approaches the liminal reflection of black Harlem in African-American writing in anthropological terms. Only Frances Odum Young's "The Image of Harlem as Reflected in the Works of Major Afro-American Writers, 1920–1922" (Ph.D. diss., University of Maryland, 1983) and my own "Black Harlem in Poetry" (Ph.D. diss., New York University, 1983) have attempted a more comprehensive approach to the topic in recent years.

Chapter 1. The Legendary Capital

1   For additional information about the emergence of black Harlem, the interested reader is referred to several studies to which this summary of the period owes a considerable general debt: Jervis Anderson, *This Was Harlem* (New York: Farrar, Straus & Giroux, 1982); *The Harlem Renaissance: A Historical Dictionary of the Era,* ed. Bruce Kellner (Westport, Conn.: Greenwood Press, 1984); Nathan Huggins, *Harlem Renaissance* (New York: Oxford University Press, 1971); David Levering Lewis, *When Harlem Was in Vogue*

(New York: Knopf, 1981); Gilbert Osofsky, *Harlem: The Making of a Ghetto* (New York: Harper & Row, 1963).

2 Osofsky, *Harlem,* p. 110.

3 Article in the *Harlem Local Reporter,* April 16, 1890, quoted in Osofsky, *Harlem,* p. 80.

4 James Weldon Johnson, *Black Manhattan* (1930; rpt., New York: Atheneum Publishers, 1968), pp. 146–159.

5 Johnson, *Black Manhattan,* p. 156.

6 "The New Negro," in *The New Negro,* ed. Alain Locke (1925; rpt., New York: Atheneum Publishers, 1969), pp. 3–16: p. 16.

7 Theodore G. Vincent, "Foreword," in *Voices of a Black Nation: Political Journalism in the Harlem Renaissance* (San Francisco: Ramparts Press, 1973), p. 20.

8 Osofsky, *Harlem,* pp. 127–49.

9 ASCAP lists well over one hundred fifty songs in which Harlem is either the first or second word of the title. No attempt was made to number songs with indirect but specific allusions to Harlem, such as Duke Ellington's "A-Train."

10 Paul Morand, *New York* (New York: Holt, 1930), pp. 269–270.

11 Huggins, *Harlem Renaissance,* pp. 89–92.

12 Nancy Cunard, "Harlem Reviewed," in *Voices from the Harlem Renaissance,* ed. Nathan Huggins (New York: Oxford University Press, 1976), p. 125.

13 Rudolph Fisher, "The Caucasian Storms Harlem," *American Mercury,* 11 (1927), 398.

14 Arna Bontemps, "The Awakening: A Memoir" in *The Harlem Renaissance Remembered,* ed. Arna Bontemps (New York: Dodd, Mead, 1972), p. 2.

15 Lewis, *When Harlem Was in Vogue,* pp. 119–155.

16 James Weldon Johnson, "Harlem: Culture Capital," in Locke, *New Negro,* p. 301.

17 Arthur A. Schomburg, "The Negro Digs up His Past," in ibid., p. 231.

18 "Worlds of Color," in ibid., p. 412.

19 Locke, "The New Negro," in ibid., p. 7.

20 Ibid., p. 14.

Chapter 2. City of Refuge

1 Alain Locke, "Harlem," *Survey Graphic,* 6 (March 1925), 629.

2 Fenton Johnson, "Harlem, the Black City," in *Songs of the Soil* (New York: Trachtenberg, 1916), p. 6.

3 Claude McKay, *Harlem Shadows* (New York: Harcourt & Brace, 1922).

4 Poems by Claude McKay are quoted from *The Selected Poems of Claude McKay* (New York: Harcourt Brace & World, 1953). Page numbers are given in parentheses in the text.

5 Helene Johnson, "Sonnet to a Negro in Harlem," in *The Book of American Negro Poetry,* ed. James Weldon Johnson (New York: Harcourt Brace & World, 1922), p. 281.

6   Helene Johnson, "Bottled: New York," in *Golden Slippers* (New York: Harper, 1941), pp. 126–8.

7   All quotations from Rudolph Fisher, "City of Refuge," are from *The New Negro,* ed. Alain Locke (1925; rpt., New York: Atheneum Publications, 1969). Page numbers are given in parentheses in the text.

8   Countee Cullen, "Harlem Wine," in "Harlem," *Survey Graphic,* 6 (March 1925), 660.

9   Sterling Brown, "Maumee Ruth," in *Southern Road* (New York: Harcourt & Brace, 1932), pp. 10–11.

10   Brown, "Harlem Street Walkers," in ibid., p. 112.

11   Brown, "Mecca," in ibid., p. 109.

12   All quotations from Hughes's poems are from Langston Hughes, *The Weary Blues* (1926; rpt., New York: Knopf, 1947). Page numbers are given in parentheses in the text.

13   Langston Hughes, *The Weary Blues* (New York: Knopf, 1926).

14   Arnold Rampersad, *The Life of Langston Hughes,* vol. 1: *1902–1941* (New York: Oxford University Press, 1986), p. 16.

15   Langston Hughes, "My Adventures as a Social Poet," *Phylon,* 8 (1947), 206.

16   W. E. B. Du Bois, *The Souls of Black Folks* (1903; rpt., Greenwich, Conn.: Fawcett, 1961), pp. 15–22.

17   Ibid., p. 17.

18   Ibid., pp. 16–17.

19   Martha Cobb, *Harlem, Haiti, and Havana* (Washington, D.C.: Three Continents Press, 1979), p. 50.

20   Langston Hughes, *Dear Lovely Death* (Amenia, N.Y.: Troutbeck Press), unpaginated.

21   Quotations are from Claude McKay, *Home to Harlem* (1928; rpt. Chatham, N.J.: Chatham Bookseller, 1973), and Carl Van Vechten, *Nigger Heaven* (New York: Knopf, 1926). Page numbers are given in parentheses in the text.

22   W. E. B. Du Bois, "The Browsing Reader," *Crisis,* 35 (June 1928), 202.

23   Claude McKay, "A Negro to His Critics," *New York Herald Tribune,* Book Section, March 6, 1932.

Chapter 3. Crossing the Color Line

1   T. Bowyer Campbell, *Black Sadie* (Boston: Houghton Mifflin, 1928).

2   Maxwell Bodenheim, *Ninth Avenue* (New York: Boni & Liveright, 1926) and *Naked on Roller Skates* (New York: Liveright, 1931).

3   For a survey of the gay scene of the Harlem Renaissance, see Eric Garber, "T'ain't Nobody's Bizness: Homosexuality in 1920s Harlem," in *Black Men, White Men: A Gay Anthology,* ed. Michael J. Smith (San Francisco: Gay Sunshine Press, 1983), pp. 7–16.

4   Sidney Alexander, "Lenox Avenue," in *The Poetry of the Negro: 1946–1970* (Garden City, N.Y.: Doubleday, 1970), pp. 556–8.

5   Yvan Goll, "Harlem River," in *Elegie de Lackawanna* (Paris: Edition Saint-Germain-des-Pres, 1973), pp. 38–9.

6   All unattributed translations are my own.

7   *Yvan Goll* (Paris: Seghers, 1956), p. 130.

8   Salvatore Quasimodo, *To Give and to Have,* ed. and trans. Edith Farnsworth (Chicago: Regnery, 1969), p. 158.

9   Ibid.

10 William Rose Benét, "Harlem," in *Harlem and Other Poems* (London: Methuen, Ltd., 1935), pp. 14–15.

11 Alfred Kreymborg, "Crossing the Color Line," in *The New Yorker Book of Verse* (New York: Harcourt Brace, 1935), p. 283.

12 Alfred Kreymborg, *Scarlet & Mellow* (New York: Boni & Liveright, 1926), p. 68.

13 Max Eastman, "Point-Black: Poems on the Negro, 1633–1970," typescript, ed. Al Cartusciello, Schomburg Center for Research in Black Culture, p. 357.

14 Yonezo Hiroyama, " A Yellow Man Looks at a Black World within a White World," *Aoyama Bunaku,* 46 (December 1936). This translation is the author's, in typescript at the Schomburg Center for Research in Black Culture, unpaginated.

15 Federico García Lorca, "El rey de Harlem," in *El poeta en Nueva York,* ed. Angel del Río (New York: Grove, 1955), p. 20.

16 Del Río, Ibid., p. xxxii.

17 Notably Richard L. Predmore, *Lorca's New York Poetry* (Durham, N.C.: Duke University Press, 1980).

18 Federico García Lorca is one the few non-black poets – perhaps the only one – whose use of Harlem would be echoed by black poets. Lorca's employment of Harlem in "El rey de Harlem" in *El poeta en Nueva York* is honored by Bob Kaufman, in "Lorca" in *The Ancient Rain: Poems 1956–1978* (New York: New Directions, 1981), p. 4:

> Spit olive pits at my Lorca
> Give Harlem's king one spoon,
> At four in the never noon.
> Scoop out the croaker eyes
>   of rose-flavored Gypsies
> Singing Garcia,
> In lost Spain's
> Darkened noon.

Similar praise is given by N. J. Loftis, in *Black Anima* (New York: Liveright, 1973), p. 36:

> Is it you, Federico Garcia,
> ⸱walking these mean streets
>   where a skyful
>   of visionary birds

strike at you
along the corners of fear
You who taught us to sing
the poet among his people
   the multitude
   with its king
beautiful, graceful, Garcia
your sex transfixed into a flower's.

19 Walter White, *Flight* (New York: Knopf, 1926). Page numbers for quotations are given in parentheses in the text.

20 Jessie Fauset, *Plum Bun* (New York: Stokes, 1929). Page numbers for quotations are given in parentheses in the text.

21 Nella Larsen, *Quicksand and Passing* (rpt.; New Brunswick, N.J.: Rutgers University Press, 1986). Page numbers for quotations are given in parentheses in the text.

22 George S. Schuyler, *Black No More* (1931; rpt., New York: Macmillan, 1971). Page numbers for quotations are given in parentheses in the text.

23 George S. Schuyler, *Blacker the Berry* (1929; rpt., New York: Macmillan, 1970). Page numbers for quotations are given in parentheses in the text.

24 Rudolph Fisher, *Walls of Jericho* (1928; rpt., New York: Arno Press, 1969). Page numbers for quotations are given in parentheses in the text.

25 Rudolph Fisher, *Conjure Man Dies: A Mystery Tale of the Dark Side of Harlem* (New York: Covici, Friede, 1932). Page numbers for quotations are given in parentheses in the text.

26 Countee Cullen, *One Way to Heaven* (New York: Harper Bros., 1932). Page numbers for quotations are given in parentheses in the text.

27 Wallace Thurman, *Infants of the Spring* (1932; rpt., Carbondale: Southern Illinois University Press, 1979). Page numbers for quotations are given in parentheses in the text.

28 Three short stories by Zora Neale Hurston with a Harlem setting are listed in Robert E. Hemenway's "Appendix: Checklist of Writings by Zora Neale Hurston," in *Zora Neale Hurston: A Literary Biography* (Urbana: University of Illinois Press), pp. 355–9: "Muttsy," *Opportunity,* 4 (August 1926), 246–50; "Story in Harlem Slang," *American Mercury,* 55 (1942), 84–96; and an unpublished typescript, "Book of Harlem," 7 pages, James Weldon Johnson Collection, Beinecke Library, Yale University. All three are reprinted in *Spunk: The Selected Short Stories of Zora Neale Hurston* (Berkeley: Turtle Island Foundation, 1983).

Chapter 4. *Me revoici, Harlem*

1 Rosa E. Valdes Cruz, *La poesía negroide en América* (New York: Las Americas, 1970), pp. 12–13.

La moda de lo negro en Europa y en los Estados Unidos repercutió en Hispanoamérica e hizo que los artistas y escritores se volvieran hacia ese elemento que no era extraño a ellos. . . . y recreó una poesía que no era nueva, pues se venía cultivando desde la época esclavista, pero ahora con un tratamiento literario moderno.

Unless otherwise attributed, all translations are mine.

2 Richard L. Jackson, *The Black Image in Latin American Literature* (Albuquerque: University of New Mexico Press, 1976), pp. 41–2.

3 Marío de Andrade, "Improviso do mal da America," in *Poesías completas* (São Paulo: Livraria Martins Editora, 1974), p. 203.

4 Adalberto Ortiz, "Casi color," in *Tierra, son, y tambor* (Mexico, D.F.: Ediciones la Cigarra, 1945), pp. 55–6.

5 Regino Pedroso, "Hermano negro," in *Mapa de la poesía negra americana,* ed. Emilio Ballagas (Buenos Aires: Editorial Pleamar, 1946), pp. 145–7.

6 Manuel del Cabral, "Poesía negra," *Revista dominicana de cultura,* 1, no. 2, pp. 223–4.

el único acontecimiento literario hasta ahora en America Latina (salvo, desde luego, el caso individual de Ruben [Darío]) que ha manifestado una personalidad inconfundible dentro de nuestra literatura. . . .

Primero, lo racial, con su expresión, su folklore, su color, su movimiento. Segundo, lo mágico, lo imaginativo, lo mítico, lo ritual, lo religioso, lo sobrenatural, etc. Y tercero lo vital, lo humano, lo social, lo universal. . . . [L]a primera [etapa], la animal o elemental, y la segunda, la cerebral o abstracta. Pero creo que es en la tercera etapa donde la poesía negra asciende y toma estatura de poesía universal y eterna. . . . Porque es en esta etapa en donde realmente se encuentra en carne viva con el hombre.

7 Manuel del Cabral, "Viejo chino de Brooklyn," in *Antología tierra: 1930–1949* (Madrid: Ediciones Cultura Hispanica, 1949), p. 122.

8 Manuel del Cabral, "Una carta para Franklin," in *Segunda antología tierra: 1950–1951* (Madrid: [n.p., n.d.]), p. 121.

9 Del Cabral, "Lo blanco regresa," in ibid., p. 179.

10 *Nicolás Guillén: Prosa de prisa,* vol. 2 (Havana: Editorial Arte y Literatura, 1975), p. 6.

Insensiblemente, nos vamos separando de muchos sectores donde debiéramos estar unidos; y a medida que el tiempo transcurra, esa división será ya tan profunda que no habrá campo para el abrazo final. Ese será el día en que cada población cubana – a toda se llega – tenga su "barrio negro," como en nuestros vecinos del Norte. Y ése es el camino que todos, tanto los que son del color de Martí como los que tenemos la misma piel que Maceo, debemos evitar.

Ese, es el camino de Harlem.

11 All quotations from Guillén's poems are from *Man-Making Words,* ed. and trans. Robert Marquez and David Arthur McMurray (Amherst: University

of Massachusetts Press, 1970). Page numbers for quotations are given in the text in parentheses.

12 "Pequeña oda a un boxeador cubano," in *Nicolás Guillén: Obra poética, 1920–1972*, 2 vols, vol. 1 (Havana: Editorial de Arte y Literatura, 1974), p. 487.

13 Noami Garret, *The Renaissance of Haitian Poetry* (Paris: Présence Africaine, 1963), p. 64.

14 Ibid., p. 61.

15 Ibid., pp. 73–85.

16 Etienne Léro, "Misère d'une poésie," in *Légitime Défense*, p. 12, quoted in Lilyan Késteloot, *Black Writers in French*, trans. Ellen Conroy Kennedy (Philadelphia: Temple University Press, 1974), p. 56: "Le vent qui monte de l'Amérique noire aura vite fait, espérons-le, de nettoyer nos Antilles des fruits avortés d'une culture caduque." It should be noted that "Misère d'une poésie" and *Légitime Défense* derive their titles from Andre Breton's *Misère de la poésie* (Paris: Editions Surrèalistes, 1932) and *Défense légitime* (Paris: Editions Surrèalistes, 1926), respectively.

17 Translation of Sartre's essay by S. W. Allen, "Black Orpheus," *Présence Africaine*, 10–11 (1951), 224. For the original French, see Jean Paul Sartre, "Orphée noir," in *Anthologie de la nouvelle poésie nègre et malgache de langue française*, ed. Léopold Senghor (Paris: PUF, 1969), p. xv:

> Le noir qui appelle ses frères de couleur à prendre conscience d'eux-mêmes va tenter de leur présenter l'image exemplaire de leur négritude et se retourna sur son âme pour l'y saisir. Il se veut phare et miroir à la fois; le premier révolutionnaire sera l'annonciateur de l'âme noire, le héraut qui arrachera de soi la négritude pour la tendre au monde, à demi prophète, à demi partisan, bref un poète au sens précis de mot "vates."

18 Allen, "Black Orpheus," p. 231; Sartre, "Orphée noir," pp. xxiii–xxiv:

> une négritude objective qui s'exprime par les moeurs, les arts, les chants et les danses des populations africaines. Le poète se prescrira pour exercice spirituel de se laisser fasciner par les rythmes primitifs, de couler sa pensée dans les formes traditionnelles de la poésie noire.

19 Allen, "Black Orpheus," p. 232; Sartre, "Orphée noir," p. xxv:

> Il faut plonger sous la croûte superficielle de la réalité, du sens commun, de la raison raisonnante pour toucher au fond de l'âme et réveiller les puissances immémoriales du désir. Du désir qui fait de l'homme un refus de tout et un amour de tout; du désir, négation radicale des lois naturelles et du possible, appel au miracle; du désir qui par sa folle énergie cosmique replonge l'homme au sein bouillonnant de la Nature et l'élevè en même temps au-dessus de la Nature par l'affirmation de son Droit à l'insatisfaction.

20   Allen, "Black Orpheus," p. 240; Sartre, "Orphée noir," p. xxxv:

> Peut-être faut-il, pour comprendre cette unité indissoluble de la souf-france, de l'éros et de la joie, avoir vu les Noirs de Harlem danser fréné-tiquement au rythme de ces "blues" qui sont les airs les plus douloureux du monde. C'est le rythme, en effet qui cimente ces multiples aspects de l'âme noire.

21   Hughes, *Weary Blues* (New York: Knopf, 1926), p. 29.
22   Ibid., p. 37.
23   Ibid., p. 39.
24   Aimé Césaire, *Cahier d'un retour au pays natal* (Paris: Présence Africaine, 1968), p. 120.
25   Ibid., p. 36.
26   Paul Niger, *Initiation* (Paris: Seghers, 1955), p. 44.
27   Roussan Camille, *Assaut à la nuit* (Port-au-Prince: Imprimerie de la Etat, 1940), p. 44.
28   Guy Tirolien, "Satchmo," in *Balle d'or* (Paris: Présence Africaine, 1961), p. 65.
29   Ibid., p. 66.
30   Jacques Roumain, "Langston Hughes," *Haïti-Journal*, October 20, 1931, quoted in Carolyn Fowler, *A Knot in the Thread: The Life and Works of Jacques Roumain* (Washington, D.C.: Howard University Press, 1980), p. 137.
31   Ibid.
32   Jean Brièrre, "Harlem," in *Haïti-Journal, Edition spéciale* (1945), p. 63, quoted in Garret, *Renaissance,* p. 154.
33   Jean Brièrre, "Me revoici, Harlem," in *Anthologie de la nouvelle poésie nègre et malgache de langue française,* ed. Léopold Senghor (Paris: PUF, 1969), p. 123.
34   Garret, *Renaissance,* p. 156.
35   Léopold Senghor, "A New York," in *Ethiopiques* (Paris: Editions du Seuil, 1956), in *Voices of Negritude,* ed. Edward A. Jones (Valley Forge, Pa.: Judson Press, 1971), p. 32.
36   Ibid.
37   All collected posthumously in Langston Hughes, *Good Morning Revolution,* ed. Faith Berry (New York: Lawrence Hill, 1973), pp. 9–11, 19–22 and 28–32.

Chapter 5. The Emerging Ghetto

1   For additional information about the decline of black Harlem in the 1930s and 1940s, the interested reader is referred to Dominic J. Capeci, *The Harlem Riot of 1943* (Philadelphia: Temple University Press, 1977); Mark Naison, *Communists in Harlem during the Depression* (Urbana: University of Illinois Press, 1983); and Roi Ottley, *New World A-Coming* (1943; rpt., New York: Arno Press and the New York Times, 1968), in addition to the works by

Jervis Anderson, David Levering Lewis, and Gilbert Osofsky acknowledged in Chapter 1 (note 1).

2   Cited in Capeci, *Harlem Riot*, p. 33.

3   *The Complete Report of Major La Guardia's Commission on the Harlem Riot of March 19, 1935* (1935; rpt., New York: Arno Press and the New York Times, 1969), p. 8.

4   Ibid., p. 7.

5   Capeci, *Harlem Riot*, p. 34.

6   Anderson, *This Was Harlem*, pp. 242–4.

7   Peter M. Bergman and Mort N. Bergman, *The Chronological History of the Negro in America* (New York: New American Library, 1969), p. 439.

8   Ottley, *New World A-Coming*, p. 151.

9   Ibid., pp. 168–78.

10   Capeci, *Harlem Riot*, pp. 19–20.

11   Anderson, *This Was Harlem*, p. 272.

12   Romare Beardon, quoted in Anderson, *This Was Harlem*, p. 273.

13   See Jeff Richardson Donaldson, "Generation '306' – Harlem, New York," Ph.D. diss., Northwestern University, 1974.

14   James Weldon Johnson, "Foreword," *Challenge*, 1 (March 1934), 2.

15   Countee Cullen to Dorothy West, quoted by West in "Dear Reader" column, *Challenge*, 1 (1934), 39.

16   Dorothy West, editorial, *Challenge*, 1 (1934), 29.

17   Alain Locke, "Spiritual Truancy," *New Challenge*, 1 (1937), 81–3.

18   Ibid., p. 3.

19   James Baldwin, quoted in J. Milton Yinger, *A Minority Group in American Society* (New York, 1965), as cited by Richard M. Dalfiume, "The 'Forgotten Years' of the Negro Revolution," in *The Negro in Depression and War: Prelude to Revolution, 1930–1945,* ed. Bernard Sternsher (Chicago: Quadrangle Books, 1969), p. 299.

20   A. Phillip Randolph, "Why Should We March?", *Survey Graphic* 31 (1942), 488–9.

21   James Baldwin, *Notes of a Native Son* (New York: Dial, 1963), pp. 88–90.

22   *The Autobiography of Malcolm X* (New York: Grove, 1966), p. 70.

23   Ibid., p. 76.

24   Ibid., p. 75.

25   Ottley, *New World A-Coming*, pp. 1–2.

Chapter 6. Go Tell It on the Mountain

1   David Dortort, *The Post of Honor* (New York: McGraw-Hill, 1949).

2   Carl Offord, *The White Face* (New York: McBride, 1943).

3   Bucklin Moon, *Without Magnolias* (Garden City, N.Y.: Doubleday, 1949).

4   Phillip B. Kaye [pseud. for Alger Adams], *Taffy* (New York: Crown, 1950).

5   Warren Miller, *The Cool World* (1959; rpt., New York: Fawcett, 1969).

6   Julian Mayfield, *The Long Night* (New York: Vanguard, 1958).

7   Julian Mayfield, *The Hit* (New York: Vanguard, 1957), pp. 109–10.

8   Ann Petry, *The Street* (1943; rpt., Boston: Beacon, 1985). Page numbers for quotations are given in parentheses in the text.

9   Ralph Ellison, *Invisible Man* (1952; rpt., New York: Random House, 1972). Page numbers for quotations are given in parentheses in the text.

10   James Baldwin, *Go Tell It on the Mountain* (1953; rpt., New York: Dell, 1984. Page numbers for quotations are given in parentheses in the text.

11   The only secondary character privileged briefly with this order of expression is the teacher, Miss Rinner, whose explicit racism makes her views about Harlem suspect.

Chapter 7. Montage of a Dream Deferred

1   Melvin B. Tolson, *A Gallery of Harlem Portraits,* ed. Robert M. Farnsworth (Columbia: University of Missouri Press, 1979).

2   Page numbers for quotations from Langston Hughes's *Shakespeare in Harlem* (New York: Knopf, 1942) are given in parentheses in the text.

3   Page numbers for quotations from Langston Hughes's *Fields of Wonder* (New York: Knopf, 1947) are given in parentheses in the text.

4   Page numbers for quotations from Langston Hughes's *One-Way Ticket* (New York: Knopf, 1949) are given in parentheses in the text.

5   Langston Hughes, "Prefatory Note," in *Montage of a Dream Deferred* (New York: Holt, 1951).

6   Richard K. Barksdale, *The Poet and His Critics* (Chicago: American Library Association, 1977), p. 95.

7   Onwucheckwa Jemie, *Langston Hughes: An Introduction to the Poetry* (New York: Columbia University Press, 1976), p. 78.

8   Ibid., p. 64.

9   Ibid., pp. 64–5.

10   Page numbers for quotations from Langston Hughes's *Montage of Dream Deferred* (1951), quoted from *Selected Poems of Langston Hughes* (New York: Knopf, 1959), are given in parentheses in the text. The volume will often be referred to as *Montage* in subsequent references.

11   James A. Emanuel, *Langston Hughes* (New York: Twayne 1967), p. 181.

12   In some sense this poem may indeed be autobiographical, as Jemie proposes, but the college, which is often taken to be Columbia, where Hughes was an undergraduate briefly, by the evidence is City College. The student's route walking to the YMCA is the shortest path on foot to CCNY, in all its particulars. From Columbia University, the first street after the park would have to be Morningside Avenue, not St. Nicholas.

13   Calvin C. Hernton, "Young Negro Poets," in *Sixes and Sevens: An Anthology of New Poetry,* ed. Paul Breman (London: Breman, 1962), p. 21.

14   Rosey Eva Pool, ed., *Beyond the Blues: New Poetry by American Negroes* (Lymphe Hythe, Kent: Hand & Flower Press, 1962).

15   Paul Breman, ed., *Sixes and Sevens: An Anthology of New Poetry* (London: Breman, 1962).

16 Walt DeLegall, ed., *Burning Spear: An Anthology of Afro-Saxon Poetry* (Washington, D.C.: Hammon Press, 1963).

17 Ray Johnson, "Walking East on 125th Street," in *Black Fire: An Anthology of Afro-American Writing,* ed. LeRoi Jones and Larry Neal (New York: Morrow, 1968), pp. 418–19.

18 William Browne, "Harlem Sounds: Hallelujah Corner," in *Beyond the Blues,* p. 65.

19 All quotations from "Return of the Native" are from *Selected Poetry of Amiri Baraka / LeRoi Jones* (New York: Morrow, 1979), p. 101.

20 Amiri Baraka / LeRoi Jones, "City of Harlem," in *Home: Social Essays* (New York: Morrow, 1966), pp. 92–3.

21 Amiri Baraka / LeRoi Jones, letter to the editor, "Correspondence," *Partisan Review,* 25 (1958), 473.

22 Jones, "Home," pp. 87–8.

Chapter 8. *Negro de todo o mundo*

1 Marco Fidel Chavez, "Mi corazón permanence en penumbra," in *Black Poetry of the Americas,* ed. Hortensia Ruiz del Vizo (Miami: Ediciones Universal, 1972), p. 104.

2 Irene Zapata Arias, "Negro, no mueras por las calles," in ibid., p. 106.

3 Bernard Dadié, *Patron de New York* (Paris: Présence Africaine, 1964), p. 61.

> Dans ce pays d'alvéoles éclairés, de coulées de lumierès endiguées, Harlem essaie vainement d'y faire entrer un peu de vie, un peu de tam-tam. Chaque soir les fenêtres qui s'éclairent paraissent être des regards bravant les ténèbres quotidiennes. . . . Les Nègres dans leurs îles font signe au navire América qui passe au large. La nation les observe, les étudie et n'ouvre ses porte qu'à bon escient.

4 Bernard Dadié, "Jour sur Harlem," in *Homme de tous les continents* (Paris: Présence Africaine, n.d.), p. 57.

5 Ibid., pp. 55–6.

6 Ibid., p. 56.

7 Dadié, "Christmas," in ibid., pp. 63–4.

8 Tchicaya U'Tam'si, "Le contempteur," in *Arc musical précédé de Epitome* (Paris: Oswald, 1970), p. 64.

9 Richard A. Preto-Rodas, *Negritude as a Theme in the Poetry of the Portuguese-speaking World* (Gainesville: University of Florida Press, 1970), p. 34.

10 José Craveirinha, "Africa," in "Nova soma de poesia do mundo negro," *Présence Africaine* (1966), 57, 473.

11 Francisco José Tenreiro, "Fragmento de blues," in *Obra poética de Francisco José Tenreiro* (Lisbon: Editora Pax, 1967), p. 91.

12 Tenreiro, "Negro de todo o mundo," in *O canto armado: Antologia temática de poesia africana,* ed. Mário de Andrade (Lisbon: Da costa, 1979), p. 140.

13 Preto-Rodas, *Negritude,* pp. 46–9.

14   Tenreiro, "Negro de todo o mundo," in de Andrade, *O canto armado*, p. 142.

15   Agostinho Neto, "Voz do sangue," in ibid., p. 147.

16   Viriato da Cruz, "Mamã Negra," in ibid., p. 155.

17   Ibid., p. 157.

18   Noemia de Sousa, "Deixa passar o meu povo," in de Andrade, *O canto armado*, p. 153.

19   Ibid., p. 154.

20   I have translated the phrase "e tu, Amigo de doce olhar azul" as "and you, my friend with the sweet blue radiance," since it evidently refers to the glow of the radio dial, described later in the poem as the "ohlo luminoso do radio." This translation avoids far-fetched interpretations of an "idealized blue-eyed friend." See Preto-Rodas, *Negritude*, p. 73.

21   De Sousa, "Deixa passar o meu povo," p. 154.

22   Ernesto Lara Filho, in *Seripípi na gaiola* (1970), reprinted in *No reino de Caliban*, 2 vols., ed. Manuel Ferreira (Lisbon: Seara Nova, 1976), vol. 2, p. 215.

23   Ernesto Lara Filho, "Sinceridade," quoted in Russell G. Hamilton, *Voices from an Empire: A History of Afro-Portuguese Literature* (Minneapolis: University of Minnesota Press, 1975), p. 84.

24   Leo Liberthson, "Summer in Harlem," in "Point Black: Poems on the Negro, 1633–1970," typescript, ed. Al Cartusciello. Schomburg Center for Research in Black Culture, p. 384.

25   Luis Oyarzun, "La canción de Harlem," in *Lira negra*, ed. José Sanz y Diaz (Madrid: Colección Crisol, 1945), p. 138.

26   Aaron Kurtz, from *Behold the Sea*, quoted in *Poets of Today*, ed. Walter Lowenfels (New York: International Publishers, 1964), p. 78.

27   Edward Field, from "Ode to Fidel Castro," quoted in Lowenfels, *Poets of Today*, p. 51.

28   Eugenio Florit, "Los poetas solos de Manhattan," in *Última poesía cubana*, ed. Orlando Sardiñas Rodriquez (Madrid: Hispanova, 1973), pp. 67–8.

29   Efraín Huerta, "Harlem negro," in *Poesía negra de América*, ed. José Luis Gonzalez and Monica Mansour (Mexico City: Ediciones Era, 1976), p. 127.

30   Norman Mailer, *Advertisements for Myself* (London: Deutsch, 1961), p. 285.

31   Ibid.

32   Seymour Krim, "Ask for a White Cadillac," in *Views of a Nearsighted Cannoneer* (New York: Dutton, 1968), pp. 100–2.

33   See Kenneth Rexroth, "The Institutionalization of Revolt, the Domestication of Dissent," in *World Outside the Window: The Selected Essays of Kenneth Rexroth* (New York: New Directions, 1987), pp. 204–5.

34   Jack Micheline, "O'Harlem," *Third Rail*, 1 (1961), 1.

35   Jack Micheline, in *The Bronx and Other Stories* (New York: Hooker Press, 1965), pp. 14–15.

36   Aram Saroyan, *Genesis Angels* (New York: Morrow, 1979), p. 28.

37   Allen Ginsberg, "Howl," in *Howl and Other Poems* (San Francisco: City Lights Books, 1965), p. 16.

38   John Tyrell, *Naked Angels: The Lives and Literature of the Beat Generation* (New York: McGraw-Hill, 1973), p. 89.

39 Allen Ginsberg, "Psalm IV," in *Collected Poetry: 1947–1980* (New York: Harper & Row, 1984), p. 238.
40 Ibid.
41 Tyrell, *Naked Angels,* p. 89.
42 Allen Ginsberg, "Vision: 1948," in *Gates of Wrath* (Bolinas: Grey Fox Press, 1972), p. 7.
43 Ibid.
44 Ginsberg, "Howl," p. 16.
45 Ibid., p. 28.
46 Allen Ginsberg, *Reality Sandwiches: 1953–1960* (San Francisco: City Lights Books, 1963), p. 72.
47 Allen Ginsberg, "The Lion for Real," in *Kaddish and Other Poems* (San Francisco: City Lights Books, 1961), pp. 54–5.
48 Ginsberg, "Howl," p. 13.
49 Allen Ginsberg, "Who," in *Collected Poetry: 1947–1980,* p. 595.
50 Gregory Corso, "Writ on the Steps of Puerto Rican Harlem," in *Penguin Poets #5: Gregory Corso, Lawrence Ferlinghetti, Allen Ginsberg* (Hammondsworth: Penguin Books, 1963), p. 35.
51 Hugh Romney, "Altar Piece," in *Beat Coast East: An Anthology of Rebellion,* ed. Stanley Fisher (New York: Excelsior Press, 1960), p. 53.

Chapter 9. The Inner City

1 Page numbers for quotations from Claude Brown's *Manchild in the Promised Land* (1965; rpt., New York: New American Library, 1966) are given in parentheses in the text.
2 August Meier and Elliot Rudwick, *From Plantation to Ghetto,* 3rd ed. (New York: Hill & Wang, 1976), p. 306.
3 Harlem Youth Opportunities, *Youth in the Ghetto* (New York: Harlem Youth Opportunities Unlimited, 1964), p. 156.
4 Ibid., pp. 120–3.
5 Ibid., pp. 194–5.
6 Malcolm X and Alex Haley, *The Autobiography of Malcolm X* (New York: Grove, 1964), pp. 234–5. Page numbers for quotations are given in parentheses in the text.
7 Ibid., pp. 277–8.
8 John O. Killens, "Prologue," in Fred Halstead, *Harlem Stirs* (New York: Marzani & Munsell, 1966), p. 5.
9 Lester A. Sobel, ed., *Civil Rights, 1960–1966* (New York: Facts on File, 1967), pp. 154–5.
10 Nicholas Pileggi, "A Long Smoldering Summer?", *New York Magazine* (June 21, 1982), 26.
11 *The Report of the National Advisory Commission on Civil Disorders* (New York: Bantam, 1968), p. 1.
12 Tom Wicker, "Introduction," in ibid., p. xi.
13 Peter H. Rossi, "Urban Revolts and the Future of American Cities," in

Cities under Siege: An Anatomy of the Ghetto Riots, 1964–1968, ed. David Boesel and Peter H. Rossi (New York: Basic'Books, 1971), p. 416.

14 *Report of the National Advisory Commission on Civil Disorders,* p. 1.

15 Rossi, "Urban Revolts," pp. 419–20.

16 For example, see *Cities under Siege,* and *Living in Harlem: A Survey of Residents' Attitudes* (n.p: Louis Harris, 1973).

17 Hoyt W. Fuller, "Towards a Black Aesthetic," in *Black Expression: Articles by and about Black Americans in the Creative Arts,* ed. Addison Gayle (New York: Weybright & Talley, 1969), p. 263.

18 Ibid., p. 267.

19 Dudley Randall, "Black Poetry," in Gayle, *Black Expressions,* pp. 111–12.

Chapter 10. Jitterbugging in the Streets

1 Vashti Lewis, "The Black Arts Movement, 1965–1975: A Bibliography," *Minority Voices* (1980), 37.

2 Johnnie Scott, "The American Dream," in *The New Black Poetry,* ed. Clarence Major (New York: International Publishers, 1969), p. 115.

3 Bobb Hamilton, "Brother Harlem Bedford Watts Tells Mr. Charlie where Its at," in ibid., p. 115.

4 Conyus, "i rode with geronimo," in *Dices and Black Bones: Voices of the Seventies,* ed. Adam David Miller (New York: Houghton Mifflin, 1970), pp. 46–7.

5 Lucia Martin, "The Drum," in *Stuff: A Collection of Poems, Visions & Imaginative Happenings from Young Writers in Schools – Opened and Closed,* eds. Herbert Kohl and Victor Hernandez Cruz (New York: World Publishing, 1970), pp. 76–7.

6 Bob Allen, "Musical Vietnams," in *In a Time of Revolution,* ed. Walter Lowenfels (New York: Random House, 1969), p. 40.

7 *Black Fire,* ed. LeRoi Jones and Larry Neal (New York: Morrow, 1968), pp. 208–9.

8 Larry Neal, "Harlem Gallery: From the Inside," in *Hoodoo Hollerin' Bebop Ghosts* (Washington, D.C.: Howard University Press, 1974), pp. 24–5.

9 Bill Harris, "Griot de la Grand," in *Black Scholar* 1 (1981), 55.

10 Sarah Webster Fabio, "Tribute to Duke," in *Understanding the New Black Poetry,* ed. Stephen Henderson (New York: Morrow, 1973), p. 245.

11 Ted Joans, "Dukes Advice," in *A Black Pow Wow of Jazz Poems* (London: Calder & Boyars, 1973), p. 47.

12 Mari Evans, "Langston," in *Black Out Loud,* ed. Arnold Adoff (New York: Dell, 1970), p. 49.

13 *Treehouse and Other Poems* (Detroit: Broadside Press, 1969), p. 21.

14 Conrad Kent Rivers, "For All Things Black and Beautiful," in Henderson, *Understanding the New Black Poetry,* p. 257.

15 Ted Joans, "Promised Land," and "Passed on Blues: Homage to a Poet," in *A Black Pow Wow of Jazz Poems,* pp. 87, 123.

16 Larry Neal, "Malcolm X – An Autobiography," in *Hoodoo Hollerin' Bebop Ghosts,* p. 9.

17 Raymond R. Patterson, "At That Moment," in *26 Ways of Looking at a Black Man* (New York: Award Books, 1969), p. 31.

18 Ricardo Weeks, "Harlem Junkman," in *Freedom's Soldiers and Other Poems* (New York: Malliet, 1947), p. 25.

19 Arnold Kemp, "A Black Cop's Communion," in *We Speak as Liberators: Young Black Poets,* ed. Orde Coombs (New York: Dodd, Mead, 1970), p. 83.

20 June Jordan, "All the World Moved," in *Some Changes* (New York: Dutton, 1971), pp. 54–6.

21 Henry Dumas, "Mosaic Harlem," in *Poetry for My People,* ed. Hale Chatfield and Eugene Redmond (Carbondale: Southern Illinois University Press, 1970), pp. 80–1.

22 Dumas, "Black Gulp," in ibid, p. 41.

23 Albert E. Haynes, Jr., "Eclipse," in Jones and Neal, *Black Fire,* p. 406.

24 Edward S. Spriggs, "For Brother Malcolm," in *For Malcolm,* ed. Dudley Randall and Margaret Burroughs (Detroit: Broadside Press, 1967), p. 73.

25 Haki Madhubuti (Don L. Lee), "To be Quicker / for Black Prisoners / on the inside & outside – Real," in *Directionscope* (Detroit: Broadside Press, 1971), pp. 202–3.

26 Madhubuti, "We Walk the Way of the New World," in ibid., p. 189.

27 Madhubuti, "Marlayna," quoted in Annette Oliver Shand, "The Relevancy of Don L. Lee as a Contemporary Black Poet," *Black World* 21 (1972), 47.

28 Clarence Major, "Harlem '67," in Jones and Neal, *Black Fire,* pp. 404–5.

29 Julia Fields, "Harlem in January," in *Umbra* (1967–8), p. 53.

30 Nikki Giovanni, "Walking down Park," in *Re-Creation* (Detroit: Broadside Press, 1970), p. 22.

31 Habib Tiwoni, "Wavelengths Away," in *Islands of My Mind* (New York: Casha Publications, 1975), p. 39.

32 Ntozake Shange, "Lady in Blue," in *for colored girls who have considered suicide when the rainbow is enuf* (New York: Macmillan, 1977), p. 39.

33 Askia Muhammad Touré, "Dago Red: A Harlem Snow Song," in *Black Spirits: A Festival of New Black Poets in America,* ed. Woodie King (New York: Random House, 1972), p. 223.

34 Audre Lord, "Dear Toni Instead of a Letter of Congratulations upon Your Book and Your Daughter Whom You Say You Are Raising to be a Correct Little Sister," in *From a Land Where Other People Live* (Detroit: Broadside Press, 1973), p. 42.

35 Hurley X, "Harlem River," *Journal of Black Poetry,* 1 (1969), 24.

36 Horace Mungin, "Harlem," in *Now See Here Homes* (New York: Brothers' Distributing, 1969), pp. 3–4.

37 Abu Ishtak (Elton Hill), "Theme Brown Girl," in *The New Black Poetry,* ed. Clarence Major (New York: International Publishers, 1969), pp. 71–2.

38 Gayle Jones, "Tripart," in *Soulscript,* ed. June Jordan (Garden City, N.Y.: Doubleday, 1970), p. 13.

39 José-Angel Figueroa, "East 110th Street," in *East 110th Street* (Detroit: Broadside Press, 1973), p. 25.

40 Maya Angelou, "Harlem Hopscotch," in *Just Give Me a Cool Drink of Water 'fore I Diiie* (New York: Random House, 1971), p. 48.

41 Welton Smith, "phat," in *Penetration* (San Francisco: Journal of Black Poetry Press, 1971), p. 20.

42 Smith, "new york, new york," in ibid., p. 19.

43 Smith, "Malcolm," in ibid., p. 2.

44 Gladstone Yearwood, "I Am the Soil (A Poem for My Mother)," in *Speak Easy, Speak Free,* ed. Antar S. K. Mberi and Cosmo Pieterse (New York: International Publishers, 1977), p. 28.

45 Tauhid Mshairi, "Spiritual Unity," *Journal of Black Poetry,* 1 (1968), 78.

46 Quincey Troupe, "You Came to Me," in *Embryo* (New York: Barlenmir House, 1972), p. 8.

47 Rob Penny, "Be Cool, Baby," in *The Poetry of Black America: Anthology of the Twentieth Century,* ed. Arnold Adoff (New York: Harper & Row, 1973), p. 391.

48 James C. Kilgore, *A Black Centennial* (East St. Louis, Ill.: Black River Writers Press, 1975), unpaginated.

49 Alicia Loy Johnson, "The Long March," in *Nine Black Poets,* ed. Shuman R. Baird (Durham, N.C.: Moore Publishing, 1968), p. 150.

50 Charles Cobb, "Mekonsippi," in *Furrows* (Tougaloo, Miss.: Flute Publications, 1967), p. 50.

51 Eugene Redmond, "barbecued cong: OR we laid MY LAI low," *Black Scholar,* 1 (April 1970), p. 53.

52 Ali Bey Hassan Jama (Joseph Kitt), "Tempting," in *Poems from Attica* (Detroit: Broadside Press, 1974), p. 23.

53 Nikki Grimes, "Untitled," in *Poems* (Harlem: n.p., 1970), unpaginated.

54 Mae Jackson, "(To Someone I Met on 125th Street, 1966)," in *Can I Poet with You* (New York: Black Dialogue Publishers, 1969), p. 9.

55 Bobb Hamilton, "Poem to a Nigger Cop," in Jones and Neal, *Black Fire,* p. 452.

56 Antar S. K. Mberi, *Song out of Harlem* (Clifton, N.J.: Vox Humana, 1980), pp. 3–4, 13–17, 21–7, 71–2, and 28–9.

57 Mberi, "Song Out of Harlem," in ibid., pp. 28–9.

58 Gil Scott-Heron, "Small Talk at 125th and Lenox," in *Small Talk at 125th and Lenox* (New York: World Publishing, 1970), p. 7.

59 Scott-Heron, "Paint It Black" and "Riot," in ibid., pp. 9 and 43–2.

60 Scott-Heron, "Harlem: The Guided Tour," in ibid., p. 25.

61 Conrad Kent Rivers, "Africa," in *The Still Voice of Harlem* (London: Breman, 1968), p. 6.

62 Rivers, "The Still Voice of Harlem," in ibid., p. 9.

63 Ibid., p. 3.

64 All references following are from David Henderson, *De Mayor of Harlem* (New York: Dutton, 1973). Pagination is noted in parentheses.

65 James Emanuel, "For 'Mr. Dudley,' a Black Spy," in *The Treehouse and Other Poems* (Detroit: Broadside Press, 1968), p. 14.

66 Emanuel, "Animal Tricks," in ibid., p. 12.

67 Ibid., p. 13.

68 Emanuel, "Stop Light in Harlem," in ibid., p. 12.

69 Emanuel, "A Harlem Romance," in *A Black Man Abroad: The Toulouse Poems* (Detroit: Lotus Poems, 1978), p. 57.

70 Raymond R. Patterson, "At That Moment," in *26 Ways of Looking at a Black Man* (New York: Award Books, 1967), p. 115.

71 Patterson, "Pope Paul VI Visits Harlem," in ibid., p. 25.

72 Patterson, "New York, New York: A Shell Game," in ibid., p. 20.

73 Patterson's typescript of "Emma, 1925" was presented to me on August 28, 1981 and remains in my possession.

74 Ted Joans, "Soul Brother Seymour," in *All of Ted Joans and No More* (New York: Excelsior Press, 1961), p. 32.

75 Joans, "Freedom," in ibid., p. 52.

76 Joans, "Love a Big Bird," in ibid., p. 72.

77 Joans, "Way Down Yonder," in *Afrodisia* (New York: Hill & Wang, 1970), p. 6.

78 Joans, "Harlem to Picasso," in ibid., p. 61.

79 Joans, "Wild West Savages," in ibid., p. 22.

80 Joans, "Egosippi," in *In a Black Manifesto* (London: Calder & Boyars, 1971), p. 58.

81 Joans, "I Ask Harlem," in ibid., p. 65.

82 Joans, "Harlem Poster," in ibid., p. 82.

83 Joans, "Gris Gris," in *In a Black Pow Wow of Jazz Poems* (London: Calder & Boyars, 1973), p. 15.

84 Joans, "S.C. Threw S.C. into the Railroad Track," in ibid., p. 23.

85 Joans, "Horny Harrar House Blues," in ibid, p. 26.

86 "Jazz Is My Religion," in ibid., p. 146.

87 Langston Hughes, *Ask Your Mama* (New York: Knopf, 1961).

88 Langston Hughes, "Junior Addict," in *The Panther and the Lash: Poems of Our Times* (New York: Knopf, 1967), p. 12.

89 Page number for quotations from Melvin B. Tolson's *Harlem Gallery:* Book I, *The Curator* (1965; rpt., London: Collier-Macmillan, 1969) are given in parentheses in the text.

90 Tolson, quoted in Mariann Russell, *Melvin B. Tolson's Harlem Gallery: A Literary Analysis* (Columbia: University of Missouri Press, 1980), p. 10.

91 Russell, *Tolson's "Harlem Gallery,"* p. 8.

92 Karl Shapiro, "Introduction," in *Harlem Gallery*, pp. 13–14.

93 Tolson, *Washington Tribune* column in *Caviar and Cabbage: Selected Columns of Melvin B. Tolson from the Washington Tribune, 1937–1944*, ed. Robert M. Farnsworth (Columbia: University of Missouri Press), p. 199.

94   Ibid.
95   Russell, *Tolson's "Harlem Gallery,"*, p. 2.
96   Tolson, *Caviar and Cabbage,* pp. 187–9.
97   Tolson, quoted in Russell, *Tolson's "Harlem Gallery,"* p. 68

Chapter 11. Echoes in a Burnt Building

1   Martin Glass, "Lip Service Poem of Resistance," in *Campfires of Resistance: Poetry from the Movement,* ed. Todd Gitlin (Indianapolis: Bobbs–Merrill, 1971), p. 73.
2   Abeylard Pereira Gomes, "O amigo," in *Elegia para John Fitzgerald Kennedy* (Rio de Janeiro: Livraria São José, 1967), p. 42.
3   Anne Sandowski, "Poem about Birth," in *Speak Easy, Speak Free,* ed. Antar S. K. Mberi and Cosmo Pieterse (New York: International Publishers, 1977), pp. 24–5.
4   Diane Di Prima, "Goodbye Nkrumah," in *In a Time of Revolution,* ed. Walter Lowenfels (New York: Random House, 1969), pp. 30–1.
5   Affonso Romano de Sant'Anna, "Empire State Building," in *Poesia viva* (Rio de Janeiro: Editora Civilização Brasileira, 1968), p. 36.
6   Ibid., p. 40.
7   This and subsequent quotations are from Barbara Bellow Watson, "Echoes on a Burnt Building," *Kenyon Review,* 4 (1965), 762–3.
8   Ariel Marques, *Poesia viva,* p. 69.
9   Ruiko Yoshida and Hajime Kijima, *Harlem: Black Angels* (Tokyo: Kodansha, 1974), pp. 95–6.
10   Ibid., p. 108.
11   Antoine de Paduoe Chonang, "La poésie camerounaise moderne," Ph.D. diss., Université de Yaoundé, 1974, p. 138.
12   Valère Epée, *Transatlantic Blues,* as quoted in ibid., p. 138.
13   James Matthews, "I Share the Pain," in *If You Want to Know Me,* ed. Peggy L. Halsey, Gail Morlan, and Melba Smith (New York: Friendship Press, 1976), p. 26.
14   Ibid.
15   Jofre Rocha, "Poema universal," in *Assim se fez madrugada* (Lisbon: Edições 70, 1977), p. 44.
16   Nicolás Pasteur Lappe, "H . . . comme," *Présence Africaine,* 112 (1979), 112.
17   Juan Romero, "Harlem," *Présence Africaine,* 61 (1967), 138.
18   Ibid., p. 140.
19   Lennox Raphael, "Sidewalk Blues," in *In a Time of Revolution,* ed. Walter Lowenfels (New York: Random House, 1969), p. 109.
20   All quotations are from Edward Brathwaite, *The Arrivants: A New World Trilogy* (London: Oxford University Press, 1973). Page numbers are given in the text in parentheses.
21   Sikhé Camara, "Mon frère de Harlem," in *Poèmes de combat et de verité* (Paris: Oswald, 1967), pp. 78–9.

22 Ibid., p. 80.

23 Florette Morand, "Happy New Year, Harlem!" in *Les poètes de la Guadeloupe* (Paris: Jean Grassin Editeur, 1978), p. 203.

24 Mafika Pascal Gwala, "Words Are Also Born," in *Jol'iinkomo* (Johannesburg: Donker, 1977), p. 55.

25 Marcel Mvondo II, "Quand les nègres revendiqvent," in *La voix des poètes camerounais* (Yaoundé: Editions A.P.E.C., 1965), p. 45.

26 Wilfred Cartey, "Old Black Woman, Hanging Loose in Time," in *Red Rain* (New York: Emerson Hall, 1977), p. 4.

27 Bob Stewart, "Sonnet for McKay," in "New Poets from Jamaica: Special Issue," *Savacou*, 5 (June 1971), 112.

28 Reginald Wilson, "For Our American Cousins," in *For Malcolm X*, ed. Dudley Randall and Margaret Burroughs (Detroit: Broadside Press, 1967), p. 36.

29 René Depestre, *Un arc en ciel pour l'occident crétien*, in *Présence Africaíne*, 57 (1966), 212–3.

30 Translation by Marie Collins, in *Black Poets in French*, ed. Marie Collins (New York: Scribner's, 1972), pp. 77–8.

31 Keorapetse Kgositsile, "For B.B. King and Lucille," in *The Present Is a Dangerous Place to Live* (Chicago: Third World Press, 1974), p. 31.

32 Kgositsile, "Time," in *My Name Is Afrika* (Garden City, N.Y.: Doubleday, 1971), p. 46.

33 Kgositsile, "Epitaph," in ibid., p. 60.

34 Kgositsile, "The Awakening," in LeRoi Jones and Larry Neal, *Black Fire* (New York: Morrow, 1968), pp. 226–7.

35 Lebert Bethune, "Harlem Freeze Frame," in *A Juju of My Own* (n.p.: Afro-American Productions, 1965), p. 13.

36 Ibid., p. 11.

Chapter 12. Mumbo Jumbo

1 Bernard W. Bell, *The Afro-American Novel and Its Tradition* (Amherst: University of Massachusetts Press, 1987), p. 246.

2 Ronald Walcott, S.V. "Barry Beckham," *Afro-American Writers after 1955: Dictionary of American Biography*, vol. 33, p. 20.

3 George Cain, *Blueschild Baby* (New York: McGraw-Hill, 1971).

4 Louise Meriwether, *Daddy Was a Number Runner* (1970; rpt., New York: Pyramid Books, 1971).

5 Shane Stevens, *Go Down Dead* (1966; rpt., New York: Pocket Books, 1968).

6 All quotations are from Henry Dumas, *Rope of Wind and Other Stories* (New York: Random House, 1978). Page numbers are given in parentheses in the text.

7 Chester Himes, *A Rage in Harlem* (1957; rpt., London: Allison & Busby, 1985).

8 Charles Wright, *The Wig* (1966: rpt., New York: Ballantine, 1968).

9 Ishmael Reed, *Mumbo Jumbo* (New York: Doubleday, 1972).

Epilogue: Black Harlem and the Literary Imagination

1 It is intriguing to note that few, if any, British poets or novelists have been drawn to the motif, although one British painter is renowned for his striking visual interpretations of black Harlem. See *Edward Burra* (London: Arts Council of Great Britain, 1985).

2 Gaston Bachelard, *The Poetics of Space,* trans. Maria Jolas (Boston: Beacon, 1969).

3 "Migration by Blacks from the South Turns Around," *New York Times,* June 11, 1989, p. 36.

4 John H. Johnston, *The Poet and the City: A Study of Urban Perspective* (Athens: University of Georgia Press, 1984), p. 12.

5 Gail K. Paster, *The Idea of the City in the Age of Shakespeare* (Athens: University of Georgia Press, 1985), pp. 220–1.

6 Henry Louis Gates, Jr., *The Signifying Monkey: A Theory of Afro-American Literary Criticism* (New York: Oxford University Press, 1988).

7 Houston A. Baker, Jr., *Blues, Ideology, and Afro-American Literature: A Vernacular Theory* (Chicago: University of Chicago, 1984), p. 2.

Index